LITERACY
and
AUGMENTATIVE
and
ALTERNATIVE
COMMUNICATION

A VOLUME IN THE AUGMENTATIVE AND ALTERNATIVE
COMMUNICATION PERSPECTIVES SERIES

LITERACY

and

AUGMENTATIVE

and

ALTERNATIVE

COMMUNICATION

A VOLUME IN THE AUGMENTATIVE AND ALTERNATIVE
COMMUNICATION PERSPECTIVES SERIES

Martine Smith

School of Clinical Speech & Language Studies
Trinity College
Dublin, Ireland

ELSEVIER
ACADEMIC
PRESS

AMSTERDAM • BOSTON • HEIDELBERG • LONDON
NEW YORK • OXFORD • PARIS • SAN DIEGO
SAN FRANCISCO • SINGAPORE • SYDNEY • TOKYO

Academic Press is an imprint of Elsevier

Elsevier Academic Press
200 Wheeler Road, Burlington, MA 01803, USA
525 B Street, Suite 1900, San Diego, CA 92101-4495, USA
84 Theobald's Road, London WC1X 8RR, UK

This book is printed on acid-free paper.

Library of Congress: Application submitted

British Library Cataloguing in Publication Data
A catalogue record for this book is available from the British Library.

ISBN: 0-12-650359-1

For all information on all Academic Press publications
visit our Web site at www.books.elsevier.com

Printed in the United States of America
04   05   06   07   08   09   8   7   6   5   4   3   2   1

SERIES FOREWORD

The *Augmentative and Alternative Communication (AAC) Perspectives Series* is a series of extensively-referenced books based on the three cornerstones of evidence-based practice (EBP): research, clinical and/or educational expertise, and stakeholder perspectives. The first two books in the series focus on emerging areas of AAC that have relevant literature but no significant books. The inaugural book, *The Efficacy of Augmentative and Alternative Communication: Toward Evidence-Based Practice* (Schlosser, 2003), addresses the critical aspects of efficacy and EBP in the delivery of services to individuals with communication needs in general, and individuals with severe disabilities and little or no functional speech in particular. This book, *Literacy and Augmentative and Alternative Communication*, focuses on AAC users and the many aspects involved in the acquisition of literacy.

Other books in the series will focus on topics that have been discussed in journals and books but show a need for different perspectives on AAC, such as, for example, the topic of assistive technology (Quist & Lloyd, forthcoming 2005). A dictionary designed to promote terminologic and taxonomic consistency within the field along with short chapters that provide basic information on selected AAC topics will be the subject matter of another book in the series (Lloyd, Arvidson, & Fuller, forthcoming). Some of the books in the series will emphasize research and basic information. Others will emphasize clinical and educational practice. All of the books will relate to aspects of the broad communication model originally proposed by Lloyd, Quist, and Windsor (1990) and subsequently discussed in other sources (e.g., Fuller & Lloyd, 1997).

We are extremely fortunate to have Martine Smith author the first book on literacy that has an AAC focus as a part of the series. Smith has emerged as a leader in AAC with expertise in speech-language pathology personnel preparation, clinical service delivery, and research. She is the head of the School of Clinical Speech and Language Studies and senior lecturer at Trinity College in Dublin, Ireland. Her primary teaching responsibilities include courses in developmental disorders of speech and language and AAC. Smith's clinical work has focused on spoken and written language intervention with adolescents who have specific language impairment (SLI) and on literacy development with adults who use AAC. Smith is completing a major research project on enhancing communicative effectiveness for adults who use aided communication funded by the Health Research Board of Ireland. She is also a principal researcher in a major study of cross-linguistic literacy skills in children with severe speech and physical impairments (SSPI) with partners in Estonia, Spain, and Sweden, funded through Ireland's Central Remedial Clinic.

Smith is a founding member of the International Society for Augmentative and Alternative Communication (ISAAC)—Ireland. She served as co-chair of ISAAC'S biennial meeting in Dublin in 1998 and chair of the scientific program. Smith is currently president-elect of ISAAC and will assume the office of president in January 2005. Smith received the Editor's Award for her article in *Augmentative and Alternative Communication* titled "Reading Abilities of Non-speaking Students: Two Case Studies" (Smith, 1992). She has published articles in a number of professional journals including *Augmentative and Alternative Communication*; *European Journal of Disorders of Communication*; *International Journal of Disability, Development, and Education*; and *Journal of Clinical Speech and Language Studies*, as well as the chapter on literacy in *Augmentative and Alternative Communication: A Handbook of Principles and Practices* (Smith & Blischak, 1997). Smith is a former editor of the *Journal of Clinical Speech & Language Studies* and a reviewer for *Augmentative and Alternative Communication* and the *International Journal of Language and Communication Disorders*.

Literacy and Augmentative and Alternative Communication addresses general models of literacy, literacy acquisition, principles of literacy assessment and intervention, and the use of specific approaches and technologies as they relate to AAC users. The book is designed to (1) increase the understanding of literacy and its importance and impact on the education of individuals who use AAC, (2) provide fundamental information based on clinical practice and research that can help clinicians/educators plan and implement appropriate assessment and intervention, (3) serve as a resource that can help clinicians/educators guide stakeholders (including AAC users, family members, administrators, policy makers, and other professionals) in making informed and effective decisions that allow AAC users to participate more fully in the activities and opportunities in the world around them. We anticipate that this AAC perspective of literacy will add to the knowledge base in the field of literacy as well as provide a valuable resource in the field of AAC.

Lyle L. Lloyd, Ph.D., FAAMR, ASHA, CCC-A&SLP
Professor of Special Education, and Professor of Audiology & Speech Sciences
Purdue University
Helen H. Arvidson, Ph.D.
Porter County Education Interlocal

REFERENCES

Fuller, D. R., & Lloyd, L. L. (1997). AAC model and taxonomy. In L. L. Lloyd, D. R. Fuller, & H. H. Arvidson (Eds.), *Augmentative and Alternative Communication: A Handbook of Principles and Practices* (pp. 25–37). Boston: Allyn and Bacon.

Lloyd, L. L., Arvidson, H. H., & Fuller, D. R. (forthcoming). *AAC from A to Z.* San Diego, CA: Elsevier Academic Press.

Lloyd, L. L., Quist, R. W., & Windsor, J. (1990). A proposed augmentative and alternative communication model. *Augmentative and Alternative Communication, 6,* 172–183.

Quist, R. W., & Lloyd, L. L. (forthcoming 2005). *Assistive Technology: Principles and Applications for Communication Disorders and Special Education.* San Diego, CA: Elsevier Academic Press.

Schlosser, R. W. (2003). *The Efficacy of Augmentative and Alternative Communication.* San Diego, CA: Academic Press.

Smith, M. M. (1992). Reading abilities of nonspeaking students: Two case studies. *Augmentative and Alternative Communication, 8,* 57–66.

Smith, M. M., & Blischak, D. M. (1997). *Literacy.* In L. L. Lloyd, D. R. Fuller, & H. H. Arvidson (Eds.), *Augmentative and Alternative Communication: A Handbook of Principles and Practices* (pp. 414–444). Boston: Allyn and Bacon.

ACKNOWLEDGMENTS

Many people have supported this project—one that extended far beyond its anticipated time-scale. Dr. de Montfort Supple nurtured my interest in the complex area of written language, and started me on a path of enquiry that has led me to this point today. My colleagues in the School of Clinical Speech and Language Studies have provided unwavering support, coffee, and wise counsel in times of crisis. Many colleagues in the ISAAC community have enriched my understanding, opened my eyes, and pushed me on. In particular, I would like to mention Doreen Blischak, Lyle Lloyd, Annika Dahlgren-Sandberg, and Karen Erickson for the many stimulating discussions we have had on this topic, and their generosity with their time and ideas. While they contributed in no small way to my own journey of understanding, the shortcomings contained within this book are the sole responsibility of the author. Helen Arvidson was extraordinarily supportive and endlessly patient in the face of missed deadlines, hopeless formatting, and minor crises with technology. My children kept me focused, and reminded me of why I began this journey, as they themselves traveled the journey towards reading and writing. Particular thanks to Orla for her interest, her art, and her inspiration. None of it would have been possible without Hugh.

Finally, I would like to dedicate this book to Ian, Michael, Neil, and Siobhain who have worked with me over the last five years, as we explored the paths to literacy for adults who use AAC. I only hope you have learned as much as I have. Thank you.

Martine Smith

CONTENTS

CHAPTER 7 **Principles of Intervention**

CHAPTER 8 Some Practicalities: SCRAWLing a Path to Literacy

CHAPTER 9 The Role of Technology

CHAPTER 10 Planning the Way Forward

CHAPTER 1

Introduction

I. Why Aim for Literacy?
II. Literacy and Severe Speech Impairment
III. Organization of this Book

I. WHY AIM FOR LITERACY?

Many individuals with severe speech and physical impairments experience great difficulty in learning to read and write functionally. Because of the potential benefits of cracking the literacy code, difficulties in these areas are particularly significant. Effective literacy skills can open doors to flexible and potentially unconstrained communication systems. New vocational opportunities emerge, which are particularly significant given the very low levels of employment typically represented by individuals with little or no functional speech (McNaughton, Light, & Gulla, 2004), and possibilities for access to new recreational opportunities are opened. Although this has always been the case, the emergence of new communication media, especially the Internet, has vastly increased the opportunities and demands for written language skills (e.g., Cheng, 2001; Leu, 2000; Snow, Burns, & Griffin, 1998). As Kallen (1998) pointed out, the advent of extraordinary new technology creates a vast repertoire of new possibilities and new powers for individuals able to access the technologies, but, by implication, causes further disadvantages for individuals without the necessary skills or access. It has been suggested that current difficulties in reading "largely originate from rising demands for literacy, not from declining absolute levels of literacy" (Snow *et al.*, 1998). For those struggling to meet the demands for higher literacy skills, the consequences of falling short are increasingly significant. Information is often depicted as the new global currency, and any "skill gap" that affects access to information may have negative social and economic implications (Rassool, 1999).

The new demands of this "computer and technology age" have focused international attention on literacy levels, literacy development, and literacy disorders. Governments have launched programs to reduce literacy difficulties and support functional literacy for all—with questionable success (Rassool, 1999). The

United Nations Educational, Scientific, and Cultural Organization (UNESCO) has estimated that at the start of the new millennium, there were about 860 million adults in the world who were illiterate, with 70% of these living in three regions: Sub-Saharan Africa, South and West Asia, and the Arab States and North Africa. The General Assembly of the United Nations proclaimed the United Nations Literacy Decade for the period 2003 through 2012 (United Nations, 2002), with the aim of Literacy for All, and promoting the concept of "literacy as freedom" (UNESCO, 2003). Resolution 56/116 further proposed that "literacy is crucial to the acquisition, by every child, youth and adult, of essential life skills that enable them to address the challenges they can face in life, and represents an essential step in basic education, which is an indispensable means for effective participation in the societies and economies of the twenty-first century" (p. 2).

II. LITERACY AND SEVERE SPEECH IMPAIRMENT

Within the context of global literacy challenges, the needs of individuals with severe speech and physical impairments may seem relatively small and even unimportant. However, for this group of individuals in particular, unlocking the literacy code opens up tremendous opportunities, minimizing the disabling effects of underlying speech and motor impairments and supporting participation in society. Ironically, however, for a group for whom literacy is such an important achievement, our information to date suggests that achieving functional literacy skills is particularly challenging. From an early stage in documenting literacy skills, evidence suggests that individuals with severe congenital speech impairments are at risk for limited development of literacy skills (Dahlgren-Sandberg, 2001; Dahlgren-Sandberg & Hjelmquist, 1996a, 1996b, 1997, 2002; Koppenhaver & Yoder, 1992; McNaughton, 1998; Sturm & Clendon, 2004; Vandervelden & Siegel, 1999, 2001). Reading difficulties often seem disproportionate when language and other aspects of intellectual functioning are considered (Berninger & Gans, 1986; Smith, 1989). However, some individuals using augmentative and alternative communication do develop effective literacy skills (Bishop & Robson, 1989; Erickson, Koppenhaver, & Yoder, 2002; Foley & Pollatsek, 1999; Smith, 1992), so clearly a severe speech impairment does not necessarily limit reading and writing development. The acronym AAC is used for the term *augmentative and alternative communication*, that is, nonspeech communication that replaces or complements natural speech and/or writing for an individual (Lloyd, Fuller, & Arvidson, 1997). In general, AAC techniques can be divided into two broad categories—aided and unaided. Aided communication involves use of some external device or equipment, ranging from simple picture boards to complex computer-based devices that produce synthesized speech output. Unaided communication can be achieved without any additional pieces of equipment, relying instead on the individual's own body. The majority of individuals with congenital speech and physical impairments require the use of aided communication components, at least some of the time. Although the acronym AAC is widely used now, it is important to recognize that the terms *augmentative* and *alternative* are not synonymous and may reflect very different language and communication processes and experiences (Smith & Grove, 2003). However, there may be more similarities than differences in the written language experiences of individuals using aided AAC. A key similarity may lie in the common experience of difficulty learning to master the processes of reading and writing.

In 1996, David Yoder, Karen Erickson, and David Koppenhaver, working at the Center for Literacy and Disability Studies at the University of North Carolina in Chapel Hill, co-authored "A Literacy Bill of Rights" (Erickson *et al.*, 2002; Yoder, 1997), setting out the essential rights in relation to literacy that should be assured for all persons, including those who use AAC. These rights are set out in Figure 1.1.

The rights outlined by Erickson and her colleagues serve as a backdrop for much of the discussion within this book, not only acknowledging the importance of literacy acquisition but also stating explicitly that the right to intervention to support literacy development is a right that extends across the lifespan, for *all* individuals who use AAC.

Individuals with severe speech and physical impairments are unique in many ways—in their experiences of life, communication, and negotiation of roles in society. As a group, however, they are also far from homogeneous, representing as many diverse and varied life stories as any other arbitrarily chosen group of individuals. The superficial ways in which they may differ from individuals without speech impairments should not overshadow the far deeper and more important ways in which they are the same as other members of society. To read, individuals with severe speech impairments must access a set of written symbols and decode them to abstract meaning just as anyone else must do. They must convert underlying messages into an alternative external symbol format to write. To become expert in both of these activities, they must learn at least a certain core of knowledge about how symbols and messages relate to each other. Just as there are many ways to skin a chicken (or so I am told), there may be many ways to achieve mastery of reading and writing. Although the essence of the task may remain the same for individuals with congenital speech impairments, they may process the task or develop task mastery in ways that are quite different from those of speaking children who have no physical impairments.

It would certainly be easier to explore this possibility if there were consensus about either the process of reading and writing or the developmental path by which typically developing children achieve mastery in these areas. These big questions are far from resolved and remain a source of considerable controversy.

All persons, regardless of the extent or severity of their disabilities, have a basic right to use print. Beyond this general right, there are certain literacy rights that should be assured for all persons. These basic rights are the following:

1. The right to an opportunity to learn to read and write. Opportunity involves engagement in active participation in tasks performed with high success.

2. The right to have accessible, clear, meaningful, culturally and linguistically appropriate texts at all times. Texts, broadly defined, range from picture books to newspapers to novels, cereal boxes, and electronic documents.

3. The right to interact with others while reading, writing, or listening to a text. Interaction involves questions, comments, discussions, and other communications about or related to the text.

4. The right to life choices made available through reading and writing competencies. Life choices include, but are not limited to, employment and employment changes, independence, community participation, and self-advocacy.

5. The right to lifelong educational opportunities incorporating literacy instruction and use. Literacy educational opportunities, regardless of when they are provided, have potential to provide power that cannot be taken away.

6. The right to have teachers and other service providers who are knowledgeable about literacy instruction methods and principles. Methods include, but are not limited to, instruction, assessment, and the technologies required to make literacy accessible to individuals with disabilities. Principles include, but are not limited to, the beliefs that literacy is learned across places and time, and no person is too disabled to benefit from literacy learning opportunities.

7. The right to live and learn in environments that provide varied models of print use. Models are demonstrations of purposeful print use such as reading a recipe, paying bills, sharing a joke, or writing a letter.

Figure 1.1. A Literacy Bill of Rights. (From Erickson, K., Koppenhaver, D., & Yoder, D. E. (2002). *Waves of words: Augmented communicators read and write* (p. iii). Toronto, Ontario, Canada: ISAAC Press.)

Nonetheless, the position adopted in this book is that it is important to attempt to frame the reading and writing challenge for individuals with congenital speech impairments in the context of our understanding of the broader picture—the process for individuals who are developing typically.

An expert may approach a task in a very different way than an apprentice. Yet somewhere along the way to mastery, the apprentice must engage in the same kind of ways of doing things as the master; otherwise the state of mastery could never be achieved. Thus, the process at any point along the way to mastery may look slightly different, but the seeds of mastery must germinate through each and every repetition of the task.

III. ORGANIZATION OF THIS BOOK

This volume is presented in three major sections. In the first section, we look at mastery-level processes in reading and writing (Chapter 2) and explore some of what is currently understood about the developmental progression toward mastery of these skills (Chapter 3). Chapter 4 focuses on our current understanding of how severe speech and physical impairments affect the experience of learning to read and write and the unique learning environment faced by individuals who use aided communication as they address this task. The second section of the book addresses the complex issue of assessment, with a discussion of general principles in Chapter 5 and some practical suggestions outlined in Chapter 6. The focus in the third section is on intervention—the general principles that guide good intervention practice (Chapter 7), illustrations of practical suggestions (Chapter 8), and a discussion of the potential impact of technology on the intervention process (Chapter 9). The text concludes with a look back over the journey already traveled within the book and also a view to the future, outlining where we have come from and where we might aim to go.

This book focuses on individuals with combined physical and communication difficulties, who rely at least some of the time on aided communication. It is important to note that not all individuals who are nonspeech communicators rely on or utilize aided communication. Those with a primary learning or social-emotional difficulty may rely far more on unaided systems such as gesture and sign. The focus here reflects the author's clinical, educational, and research experience, but it is by no means clear that the process or challenges implicit in learning to read and write are any different for individuals who rely primarily on unaided communication. It is hoped that, within this volume, there will be food for thought for readers from many different backgrounds, sparking discussion and critical reflection on our knowledge base and our practice.

REFERENCES

Berninger, V., & Gans, B. (1986). Language profiles in nonspeaking individuals of normal intelligence with severe cerebral palsy. *Augmentative and Alternative Communication, 2,* 45–50.

Bishop, D. V. M., & Robson, J. (1989). Unimpaired short-term memory and rhyme judgement in congenitally speechless individuals: Implications for the notion of "Articulatory Coding." *The Quarterly Journal of Experimental Psychology, 41A*(1), 123–140.

Cheng, L.-R. L. (2001). The multilingual/multicultural millennium generation. *Journal of Clinical Speech & Language Studies, 11,* 1–8.

Dahlgren-Sandberg, A. (2001). Reading and spelling, phonological awareness and short-term memory in children with severe speech production impairments—A longitudinal study. *Augmentative and Alternative Communication, 17,* 11–26.

Dahlgren-Sandberg, A., & Hjelmquist, E. (1996a). A comparative, descriptive study of reading and writing skills among non-speaking children: A preliminary study. *European Journal of Disorders of Communication, 31,* 289–308.

Dahlgren-Sandberg, A., & Hjelmquist, E. (1996b). Phonologic awareness and literacy abilities in non-speaking preschool children with cerebral palsy. *Augmentative and Alternative Communication, 12*(3), 138–154.

Dahlgren-Sandberg, A., & Hjelmquist, E. (1997). Language and literacy in nonvocal children with cerebral palsy. *Reading and Writing: An Interdisciplinary Journal, 9,* 107–133.

Dahlgren-Sandberg, A., & Hjelmquist, E. (2002). Phonological recoding problems in children with severe congenital speech impairments—The importance of productive speech. In E. Witruk, A. Friederici, & L. T. (Eds.), *Basic mechanisms of language and language disorder.* Dordrecht, The Netherlands: Kluwer Academic.

Erickson, K., Koppenhaver, D., & Yoder, D. E. (2002). *Waves of words: Augmented communicators read and write.* Toronto, Ontario, Canada: ISAAC Press.

Foley, B. E., & Pollatsek, A. (1999). Phonological processing and reading abilities in adolescents and adults with severe congenital speech impairments. *Augmentative and Alternative Communication, 15,* 156–173.

Kallen, J. (1998, August 24–27). *Micro-chip or micro-culture: Does technology help or hinder communication?* Paper presented at the Biennial Conference of the International Society for Augmentative and Alternative Communication, Dublin, Ireland.

Koppenhaver, D., & Yoder, D. E. (1992). Literacy issues in persons with severe speech and physical impairments. In R. Gaylord-Ross (Ed.), *Issues and research in special education* (Vol. 2., pp. 156–201). New York, NY: Columbia University Teachers College.

Leu, D. (2000). Literacy and technology: Deictic consequences for literacy education in an information age. In M. Kamil, P. Mosenthal, D. Pearson, & R. Barr (Eds.), *Handbook of reading research* (Vol. 3, pp. 743–770). London: Erlbaum.

Lloyd, L. L., Fuller, D., & Arvidson, H. (1997). Introduction and overview. In L. L. Lloyd, D. Fuller, & H. Arvidson (Eds.), *Augmentative and alternative communication: A handbook of principles and practices* (pp. 1–17). Boston: Allyn & Bacon.

McNaughton, D., Light, J., & Gulla, S. (2004). Opening up a 'whole new world': Employer and co-worker perspectives on working with individuals who use augmentative and alternative communication. *Augmentative and Alternative Communication, 19,* 235–253.

McNaughton, S. (1998). *Reading acquisition of adults with severe congenital speech and physical impairments: theoretical infrastructure, empirical investigation, education implication.* Unpublished doctoral dissertation, University of Toronto, Toronto, Ontario, Canada.

Rassool, N. (1999). *Literacy for sustainable development in the age of information.* Toronto, Ontario, Canada: Multilingual Matters.

Smith, M. (1989). Reading without speech: A study of children with cerebral palsy. *Irish Journal of Psychology, 10,* 601–614.

Smith, M. (1992). Reading abilities of nonspeaking students: Two case studies. *Augmentative and Alternative Communication, 8,* 57–66.

Smith, M., & Grove, N. (2003). Asymmetry in input and output for individuals who use AAC. In J. Light, D. R. Beukelman, & J. Reichle (Eds.), *Communicative competence for individuals who use AAC: From research to effective practice* (pp. 163–195). Baltimore: Paul H. Brookes.

Snow, C., Burns, M. S., & Griffin, P. E. (1998). *Preventing reading difficulties in young children.* Washington, DC: National Academy Press.

Sturm, J., & Clendon, S. (2004). Augmentative and alternative communication, language and literacy. *Topics in Language Disorders, 24*(1), 76–91.

UNESCO. (2003). *United Nations literacy decade.* Retrieved May 19, 2003, from http://portal.unesco.org/education/ev.php.

United Nations. (2002). *United Nations literacy decade: education for all.* United Nations General Assembly. From http://portal.unesco.org/education/en/ev.php-URL_ID=11559&URL_DO=DO_TOPIC&URL_SECTION=201.html.

Vandervelden, M., & Siegel, L. (1999). Phonological processing and literacy in AAC users and students with motor speech impairments. *Augmentative and Alternative Communication, 15,* 191–211.

Vandervelden, M., & Siegel, L. (2001). Phonological processing in written word learning: Assessment for children who use augmentative and alternative communication. *Augmentative and Alternative Communication, 17*(1), 11–26.

Yoder, D. E. (1997). "Having my say." *Augmentative and Alternative Communication, 17,* 7.

CHAPTER 2

The Process of Reading and Writing

I. INTRODUCTION

The history of written language is relatively recent, at least in relation to that of spoken language. Adams (1990) outlined the roughly 5,000-year history of written language systems, compared with the million or so years of history when humans communicated through speech. Given that such a long period of time lapsed before writing systems evolved, the relationship between spoken and written language systems is understandably complex.

There is a range of ways in which writing systems can encode spoken language, along a continuum from logographic to phonemic. Regardless of the nature of the orthography, the typical process of constructing meaning from written text involves the visual processing of the symbols presented, the decoding of symbols into a spoken language format, and the construction of meaning. Visual processing, language processing, and conceptual processing must all be engaged at some level. The relative importance of each, however, is far from resolved and may, in fact, be so fluid and dynamic across contexts as to be, to a large extent, irresolvable. In this chapter, the focus is on two models of reading and writing that serve to illustrate the complex processes involved in decoding and encoding text. Attention is then turned to the complex relationships that exist between spoken and written language and the bidirectional influence they exert on each other.

II. MODELS OF READING AND WRITING

Relationships between spoken and written language are, without doubt, complex and, to some degree, controversial. Nonetheless, it is generally agreed that at least four systems work synergistically in fluent reading: (1) the visual system receives visual patterns or orthographic information; (2) the phonological processing system converts perceived patterns into corresponding sound units; (3) the linguistic system maps language forms and meanings onto the decoded sound units; and (4) and the conceptual system integrates linguistic information into a general system of knowledge and beliefs (Adams, 1990).

Two models that provide a framework for understanding both the process and the development of reading and writing skills are discussed briefly in this chapter and throughout this book. The first comes from the work of Pumfrey and Reason (1991). It is not intended as a model of the real-time processes of reading and writing, but rather sets out the "Ingredients of Literacy" inherent in every act of reading and writing. The second model draws on Adams' (1990) interpretation of the work of Seidenberg and McClelland (1989). In contrast to Pumfrey and Reason's Ingredients of Literacy model, Seidenberg and McClelland's model does attempt to capture the real-time processes involved in reading and writing.

Regardless of the model proposed, however, what must be considered is the relationship between the reader–writer and the encountered or created text. The process of reading and writing must always be viewed as a dynamic, created by the engagement of a reader–writer with a particular text for a particular purpose. Such fluid relationships are extremely difficult to capture in static models.

A. Ingredients of Literacy

Pumfrey and Reason (1991) suggested that three main contexts cooperatively influence reading (Figure 2.1). These are the contexts of learning, language, and print.

1. The Learning Context

Meaningful reading and writing necessarily involve cognitive engagement. We read for a particular purpose, to achieve a predetermined goal, even if the

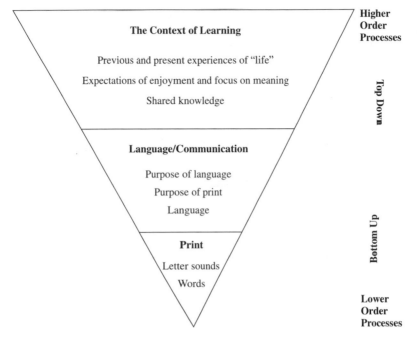

Figure 2.1. A model of reading: ingredients of literacy. (Adapted from Pumfrey, P. D., & Reason, R. (1991). *Specific learning difficulties: Challenges and responses.* Berks, UK: NFER-Nelson.)

goal is only loosely defined, such as to pass the time. Our expectations of text influence how we approach it—with pleasant anticipation, curiosity, dread, apprehension, or excitement. We read a story to a young child very differently from the way we read a question on an examination paper. If the writer is describing something with which we are familiar, we "test" the text to determine how much we agree with it. We may, on the other hand, scan the text on a shopping list as we mentally compare what we have picked up and what we still need to get. The nature of the cognitive activity differs according to the purpose of the task in which we are engaged. The learning context, therefore, encompasses our cognitive set and purpose, our expectations of a text, and the knowledge we bring to the encounter.

2. The Language Context

The context of language incorporates the language skills we bring to the encounter with text and the language demands of the text itself. Competent language users draw on their spoken language skills to support text comprehension by predicting likely clause and phrase boundaries, segmenting text to match language structures, and enhancing integration across a stretch of text by retaining material already read. A text may place considerable demands on linguistic skills. Vocabulary may be unfamiliar, such as that seen in a specialized text or in texts in which the content domain is unfamiliar. The text itself may be linguistically dense or in Butler and Wallach's (1995) terms "inconsiderate," requiring considerable untangling by the reader. A "considerate" text, in contrast, clearly outlines the structure and purpose of the text, uses accessible language, and respects the knowledge available to, and required by, the reader.

3. The Print Context

Engaging with written language, whether to decode or create a text, of necessity requires engagement with print—a system for representing spoken language in an arbitrary symbol form. In alphabetic scripts such as English, one pays particular attention to the sound units of the language, specifically phonemes. In logographic scripts such as Chinese, attention focuses on other larger units such as morphemes. The print context includes the written symbol forms used, their relationship to the spoken language, information about conventional orthographic patterns, and understanding about the conventions of print: spacing, punctuation, orientation, and so on.

All three contexts reflect different processes, and all three are relevant for readers and writers, although the relative proportion of the work carried may differ according to text demands and levels of expertise. Expert readers may be most aware of the learning context, because they focus on the meaning of text. Nonetheless, the only access to the "meaning" of text is through the decoding of print information and the mapping of the print information onto language. For expert readers, decoding operates so rapidly that it is largely unconscious. However, if a text has become compromised in some way, for example, by poor photocopying that results in the margins of the text no longer being visible, expert readers may more consciously draw on linguistic and print knowledge to predict likely text possibilities to fill in the gaps. Poor readers, on the other hand, may find themselves diverting most of their cognitive energy to the print context most of the time. Pumfrey and Reason (1991) suggested that, for these readers, the triangle of literacy ingredients has, in a sense, become inverted. The wide end of the triangle is given over to lower level processes. If access to the written word is conceived of as a gateway and Pumfrey and Reason's triangle as an arrowhead to fit that gateway, then inverting the arrowhead drastically reduces the effectiveness of the arrow's function. The diversion of cognitive energy to deciphering the print leaves little cognitive energy over for the construction of meaning.

B. Processes of Fluent Reading

Adams (1990) drew on the work of Seidenberg and McClelland (1989), proposing four processors involved in reading: (1) The orthographic processor, (2) the phonological processor, (3) the meaning processor, and (4) the context processor (Figure 2.2). The processors are presumed to interface with each other in complex relationships. Loosely speaking, the orthographic and phonological processors relate to the print context, as proposed by Pumfrey and Reason (1991), whereas the meaning and the context processors are broadly comparable, respectively, to the language and learning contexts discussed previously.

The orthographic processor receives information from the printed page. It connects directly with the phonological processor as well as with the meaning

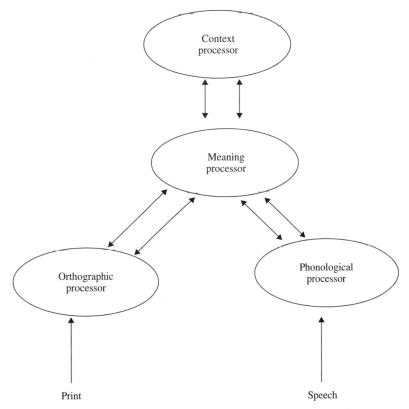

Figure 2.2. Four processors in reading. (From Seidenberg, M., & McClelland, J. L. (1989). A distributed, developmental model of word recognition and naming. *Psychological Review, 96*, 523–568.)

processor. The phonological processor normally receives speech as input, but, for the purposes of reading and writing, interfaces with both the orthographic and meaning processors. Phonological processing is activated on initiation of orthographic processing. A direct connection between the orthographic processor and the meaning processor may also be possible. This direct route may be particularly important in fluent reading (Barker, Torgesen, & Wagner, 1992). This raises another point—reading must not only be accurate, but it must also be fast, particularly if (1) meaning is to be retained and (2) connections across texts are to be integrated (Adams, 1990). Once again, it may be that master strategies for reading and writing differ in important ways from apprentice strategies.

1. The Orthographic Processor

Visual processing provides the gateway for orthographic processing. The role of visual processing, however, has been somewhat neglected over the last several decades, perhaps partly because of its fall from grace as an explanation for reading difficulties. Since the convincing demonstration by Vellutino (1979) that reading difficulties are almost overwhelmingly reflective of language-based difficulties and that visuomotor patterns differ primarily as a reflection rather than a cause of reading difficulties (Rayner, 1999), the contribution of visual processing within reading has been largely ignored. Nonetheless, it is important to consider that print (apart from Braille) is accessible only through the visual modality. Any difficulty with the reception or processing of visual information is likely to significantly affect the data available for orthographic, phonological, meaning, and context processing.

Fluent readers seem to process words as wholes, rather than decode them letter-by-letter. This perception spawned many teaching controversies focusing on the question of whether children learning to read should be introduced to word shapes rather than individual letters. Two points are worth considering in relation to this debate. First, it would be impossible to anticipate and hence teach every new sight word a reader might encounter in a text (see Share, 1995, for discussion). Exclusive reliance on whole-word recognition rather than on decoding strategies makes it extremely difficult for a reader to decode unfamiliar words. The ability to decode letter-by-letter would seem to be an important back-up system for such a situation.

Second, although it seems true that fluent readers recognize orthographic patterns, rather than attending to letters in isolation, patterns themselves are made up of letter sequences. Orthographic processing requires a reader to process not only individual letters within words, but also their exact order. The impressive ease and speed with which fluent readers of English accomplish this task derives from their vast experience with likely letter sequences or, in connectionist terms, strengths of associations across letters cumulatively built up through experience with print (Adams, 1990; Share, 1995). Adams (1990) summarized: "through experience, the network of associations . . . comes to capture the ordered sequences of letters that represent whole familiar words. And eventually . . . it becomes responsive to frequent spelling patterns independent of the particular word presented" (p. 109). However, the facilitation and excitation effect across letters still depends on readers processing each letter of a string. "Only by virtue of being viewed, can any letter of a word productively send or receive excitation to others. Readers can get the system to work for them only by visually processing the individual letters of the words they read" (Adams, 1990, p. 111).

It is possible that vowels and consonants behave differently in this respect, because constraints on consonantal sequences are far more stringent than those on vowels. Adams demonstrated elegantly that vowels could be omitted from text, without excessively compromising text legibility, as long as a consistent marker indicates vowel positions: #v#n w#rds th#t #cc#r #nfr#q##ntly #r h#v# #rr#g#l#r sp#ll#ng p#tt#rns c#n b# r#tr##v#d fr#m # t#xt w#th##t t## m#ch d#ff#c#lty, #s l#ng #s v#w#l p#s#t##ns #r# sp#c#f##d, w#th##t f#rth#r #d#nt#f#c#t##n #f th# v#w#l.[1] (Similar evidence of letter deletion is, of course, also available in the rapidly advancing use of text messages in mobile or cell phones, where each letter must pay its way. Most abbreviations of words are achieved by deleting vowels, and frequent text users rapidly become expert at decoding messages, despite the absence of many of the letters conventionally used.) In contrast, random deletion of consonants devastates comprehension of text, even if the text is composed of frequently occurring and regularly spelled words (Adams, 1990). For example, the sequence #a## #a# a #i#t#e #am# is difficult to recognize as "Mary had a little lamb" despite the familiarity of the words and the sequence, whereas m#ry h#d # l#ttl# l#mb is far more recognizable. The evidence, to date, suggests that fluent readers probably abstract orthographic patterns based largely around syllable structure (Ventura, Kolinsky, Brito-Mendes, & Morais, 2001). The abstraction of patterns, however, requires attention to individual letters and their sequence. Even a "whole-word" strategy requires that the whole word be read accurately.

2. The Phonological Processor

There is little dispute that, at least within alphabetic scripts, phonological processing skills play a crucial role (Adams, 1990; Blachman, 1991, 2000; Goswami, 2000a, 2000b; Goswami & East, 1999, 2000; Share, 1995; Stanovich,

---

[1]Even words that occur infrequently or have irregular spelling patterns can be retrieved from a text without too much difficulty, as long as vowel positions are specified without further identification of the vowel. This demonstration technique is borrowed from Adams (1990) to illustrate the contrasting role of vowel and consonant information in text processing and associations.

West, Cunningham, Cipielewski, & Siddiqui, 1996). Adrián, Alegria, and Morais (1995) distinguished between phonological sensitivity, phonological awareness, and phonemic awareness. Phonological sensitivity refers to the natural capacity that "allows one to deal with the phonological properties of speech in a functional way" (Adrián *et al.*, 1995, p. 311). It includes skills such as auditory discrimination. In contrast, phonological awareness is the capacity to consciously represent and reflect on phonological properties, that is, to think about the sound properties rather than the meaning of spoken stimuli. Phonological awareness covers a range of abilities and skills. Phonemic awareness, the explicit awareness of phonemes as units of sound, is a skill within the general domain of phonological awareness. Phonemic awareness is intimately linked with alphabetic literacy (Perfetti, Beck, Bell, & Hughes, 1987).

The operation of the phonological processor is crucial in reading, at least within alphabetic scripts. Even with highly familiar visual orthographic patterns for which one might anticipate direct orthographic processing, there is evidence to suggest that phonological processing is automatic (Adams, 1990; Van Orden, Pennington, & Stone, 1990). Spinks, Lin, Perfetti, and Tan (2002) went so far as to suggest that phonological processing occurs automatically, even with a logographic orthography such as Chinese.

Adams (1990) proposed two roles for the phonological processor. First, it provides an alphabetic back-up system "a redundant processing route—that is critical for maintaining the speed as well as the accuracy of word recognition necessary for productive reading" (p. 159). Second, it supports text comprehension by providing on-line memory for individual words. It is important also to note, however, that the relationship between phonological processing and reading and writing is bidirectional. The orthographic and phonological processors are interconnected. Phonological processing affects orthographic processing, but orthographic experience can also influence phonological processing, a point for further discussion later in this chapter.

3. The Meaning Processor

Functional use of print requires the processing of meaning. In reading, individual decoded words must be understood and interpreted in light of their role within a particular linguistic structure in a text. Similarly, in writing, communicative intent must be encoded, the starting point being the linguistic units, rather than the print form. Often, this engagement of meaning processing is termed *top-down* processing. Some have argued (Smith, 1971) that use of linguistic context is primary in efficient reading, with *bottom-up*, print-related processing serving only to confirm linguistic predictions. A more widely agreed upon position is that efficient reading requires the smooth operation of complementary bottom–up and top–down processes, the relative proportion of work carried by print or language processing varying according to task demands and supports (Snow, Burns, & Griffin, 1998). Rapid, efficient reading of text involves setting up predictions while simultaneously processing print information in a smoothly coordinated flow, with language and print processing working synergistically.

There is no doubt that individuals who have difficulties with spoken language are likely to have difficulties with written language. Weak syntax skills make it difficult to interpret and comprehend text (Nation & Snowling, 2000). Limitations in vocabulary are also linked to difficulties with reading and, not surprisingly, with text comprehension. As with the complex relationship between phonological processing and reading–writing skills, vocabulary skills are both predictive of and supported by literacy skills (Nagy & Anderson, 1984; Nagy & Herman, 1987; Nagy & Scott, 2000; Stanovich, 1986). As learners progress beyond early school years, the primary context for acquisition of new vocabulary is in written material (Nippold, Allen, & Kirsch, 2001). To deduce the meaning of novel words encountered in a text, a reader must be able to logically explore the context and reason through likely candidate meanings for target words. Understanding the meaning of a text requires more than simply understanding the individual words or even the sentential relations. It demands higher-level language skills, such as the understanding of abstract and figurative language and the comprehension of ambiguity (Nippold *et al.*, 2001). As with vocabulary, exposure to such uses of language most typically occurs in written texts.

4. The Context Processor

If reading is to be informative, then the mere meaning of a text is only a bridge to the intent of the writer. Productive reading requires on-line integration of decoded meanings with a system of knowledge. To learn from reading, we must map what has been read onto a frame of reference. When there is considerable overlap between the knowledge base of the reader and the writer, this integration may be achieved easily. When there is little shared knowledge, the reader must struggle more consciously and laboriously to integrate new information in a meaningful way. The *point* of reading derives from the context processor. Fluent readers are most likely to be aware of the context processing rather than the language or print demands.

5. Complex Interrelationships

Although orthographic, phonological, meaning, and context processing have been discussed individually earlier, under different headings, the essence of efficient reading and writing is a seamless integration of all levels and directions of processing, with cognitive energy distributed across all domains. In degraded print situations, a reader must often struggle to decipher individual letters or words. In unusual language forms such as Shakespearian English, for example, the reader's attention is drawn to the language demands. When struggling with text about quantam physics, the reader's energy may focus more on *making sense* of what is being read. Strategies available do not necessarily speak to the strategy chosen. Strategy selection is probably influenced by both reader–writer characteristics and text demands that vary according to mastery level, text familiarity, and text features (isolated words or connected text; sentences versus connected sections of text). It is quite possible, if not probable, that different strategies are applied, should the reader have to cope with degraded reading materials, novel orthographic strings, familiar content in simple texts, or familiar/unfamiliar content in complex, dense texts. The point of mastery is reached when all the necessary strategies are available and the appropriate strategy can be effectively and efficiently chosen.

III. WHAT DOES IT MEAN TO BE A COMPETENT READER–WRITER?

Learning to read and write influences how we perceive spoken language; the impact of becoming literate, however, may extend far beyond phonological processing abilities, to a whole range of meta-skills. Scribner (1997) proposed that "literacy . . . is a pivotal mechanism in cognitive growth" (p. 163). She went on to argue that the act of writing requires a writer to focus on language as an object in its own right. Having written, the writer can reflect on the language produced, so that "every act of writing in any writing system with the use of any implements gives language a corporeal form, objectifies it . . . the writer, looking upon what he has written, reviews his own thought . . . conceptual thought embodied in written language may well be the necessary condition for the analysis of thought itself" (p. 166). By this argument, the acquisition of literacy has profound significance, not only in a collective, historical sense, but also at an individual level in the here and now.

Written language is often considered to be dependent upon spoken language. Although it is undeniable that interpretation or construction of written language draws greatly on spoken language skills, the relationship is not simply one of spoken-to-written language. One of the areas in which this is most clearly evident is phonological processing. There is a wealth of evidence to support the view that levels of phonological awareness at an early age are uniquely predictive of subsequent literacy achievement (Goswami, 2000b; Goswami & Bryant, 1990). Being able to read and write enables us to perceive and process spoken language differently. However, the nature of the orthographic code with which readers and writers engage may also influence the processing of spoken language.

In other words phonological awareness undoubtedly affects literacy acquisition, but learning to read and write may also exert an influence on the units of sound consciously available for manipulation, and the characteristics of the target orthography may also be important. This bidirectional influence is discussed further later in this chapter.

A. THE IMPACT OF PHONOLOGICAL AWARENESS ON LITERACY

Phonological awareness comprises a wide range of skills, varying in complexity in terms of the size of the unit under consideration to the nature of the required manipulation of the unit. Bradley and Bryant (1983) proposed three levels of awareness: (1) the syllabic level; (2) the intrasyllabic level, for which the focus is on subunits of the syllable, typically the onset and rime; and (3) the phonemic level. In English, the number of syllables within a word can vary, but rarely exceeds six syllables. For example, "cat" has one syllable, "catfish" has two, "caterpillar" has three, "catastrophic" has four, and so on. Awareness at the syllable level involves awareness of the number of syllables within a word, and the boundaries of those syllables (Goswami & Bryant, 1990). The intrasyllabic level is a level below that of the syllable. Awareness at this level focuses on divisions of syllables into those consonants that precede the first vowel (the *onset*) and the vowel and consonants that occur within the remainder of the syllable (the *rime*). In the word "string," the onset is "str," and the rime is "-ing"; in "cat" the onset is "c" and the rime is "-at." Awareness at the phonemic level involves awareness of the individual phonemes within words and syllables, for example, the three phonemes in "cat" or the five phonemes of "string." Developmentally, as age and exposure to text increase, children progress from implicit awareness of relatively large units of speech (e.g., syllables) to explicit awareness of smaller units such as phonemes (Goswami & East, 2000; Stackhouse & Wells, 1997), although this view is not completely without controversy (Duncan, Seymour, & Hill, 1997; Seymour & Duncan, 1997). Children who can easily and efficiently manipulate sublexical units of spoken language as, for example, in rhyme detection and production or syllable segmentation tasks, are likely to progress more quickly in development of both reading and writing skills (Blachman, 2000; Bradley & Bryant, 1983; Bryant, Maclean, Bradley, & Crossland, 1990; Chaney, 1992, 1994; Goswami & Bryant, 1990), at least in an orthographically irregular language such as English (Harris & Beech, 1998). Individuals with phonological processing difficulties have a high risk for difficulties with written language (Dodd *et al.*, 1995). Specific training in phonological awareness, however, can influence success in reading and writing (Ball & Blachman, 1991; Blachman, 2000; Bradley & Bryant, 1983; Lundberg, Frost, & Petersen, 1988; Wagner & Torgesen, 1987).

B. The Impact of Literacy on Phonological Processing

With an alphabetic script, cracking the code requires the insight to recognize that individual letters or groups of letters represent phonemes. Mere exposure to spoken language does not seem sufficient to trigger attention to phonemes as units of language (Blachman, 2000). In a series of studies, Morais and colleagues (Morais, Bertelson, Cary, & Alegria, 1986; Morais, Cary, Alegria, & Bertelson, 1979) explored phonological awareness skills in Portuguese adults who had not had the opportunity to become literate. Their findings suggest that attention to the syllabic structure of a language is a fairly robust and universal skill (Morais, Content, Cary, & Mehler, 1989). Indeed, research with deaf children (Sterne & Goswami, 2000) supports the notion that awareness of syllables is a primary skill and is not literacy dependent. Individuals who have not acquired literacy, however, find it far more difficult to segment out smaller units of spoken language, such as the phoneme (Adrián et al., 1995; Morais et al., 1989; Scliar-Cabral, Morais, Nepomuceno, & Kolinsky, 1997).

Conversely, once awareness of letters and sound-letter correspondences has developed, it becomes difficult to switch it off, opening the possibility that orthographic information will *contaminate* phonological representations. Evidence for this cross-back effect comes from a number of sources. Seidenberg and Tanenhaus (1979), for example, reported that literate students take longer to decide that two spoken words rhyme when their spellings are dissimilar (e.g., "toast" and "ghost") than when they are not (e.g., "toast" and "roast"). The opposite effect holds true for negative decisions; that is, students could decide that words with dissimilar spellings (e.g., "leaf" and "ref") did not rhyme more quickly than they could decide that words with similar spellings (e.g., "leaf" and "deaf") did not rhyme. Spelling patterns may mislead students into counting additional phonemes. Students may, for example, count an additional phoneme in "pitch" compared with "rich" (Ehri & Wilce, 1979).

In a similar vein, Ventura et al. (2001) proposed that internal representations of syllable structure are vulnerable to contamination from orthographic experience. They asked Portuguese students to blend two spoken syllables into a new syllable, a task thought to offer a window into internal representations of syllable structure. Previous research with English (Treiman, 1983, 1986) had consistently found a preference for intrasyllabic divisions that respect onset-rime boundaries (e.g., "shout-yell" > "shell") compared to segmentation that cuts across such boundaries (e.g., "bit-ten" > "bin"), suggesting that onset-rime divisions represent the major syllable constituents in English.

In Portuguese, some closed syllables are spelled with a final mute "e" (Ventura et al., 2001), whereas others are not. Thus, "pele" (/pɛl/, meaning skin) was described by Ventura and colleagues as orthographically bisyllabic, whereas "mel" (/mɛl/, meaning honey) is orthographically monosyllabic, even though phonologically, both words represent a monosyllabic consonant-vowel-consonant (CVC) structure and share a rime (/ɛl/). In blending syllables, students were significantly influenced by underlying orthographic information, showing a clear preference for C/VC divisions for orthographically monosyllabic words, but CV/C divisions for orthographically bisyllabic words. Ventura *et al.* (2001) interpreted their findings as suggesting that the "mental representation of the syllable's constituents, which the participants used in the blending task, reflects an underlying phonological structure contaminated by the orthographic representation" (p. 414).

C. The Influence of Orthography Type on Phonological Processing

Evidence of the importance of orthography type on phonological processing skills also comes from comparing the performance of individuals who are alphabetic-literate and logographic-literate on tasks involving phonological processing. Although alphabetic orthographies focus attention on the phoneme, logographic systems such as Chinese typically represent morphemic elements. Individuals who have learned an alphabetic script (e.g., English) have been found to retrieve different phonemic information from spoken language, compared with individuals whose writing system focuses on elements other than phonemes (Nakamura, Kolinsky, Spagnoletti, & Morais, 1998). Holm and Dodd (1996) explored the phonological processing abilities of university students from Australia, China, Hong Kong, and Vietnam. All the students were at universities in Australia, and all had a high degree of fluency in spoken English. The first language (spoken and written) for the students from China and Hong Kong was Chinese. In China, children are introduced to *pinyin*, a phonemic representation of the language, as a transitional alphabet for learning literacy of the Chinese logographic system. In contrast, in Hong Kong, written language instruction focuses on a *look-and-say* visual strategy, both for Chinese and English (Holm & Dodd, 1996). Holm and Dodd assessed the students on a range of measures of phonological awareness, including phoneme segmentation and manipulation tasks, real and nonword reading and spelling, and verbal and visual rhyming tasks. Performance of students from Hong Kong was consistently and significantly less accurate than that of the other students with comparable spoken language proficiency across the range of phonological processing tasks, despite having had more written English instruction (mean of 15 years compared with means of 10.4 years for Chinese students and 4.9 years for Vietnamese students). Given that the Hong Kong and Chinese students differed only in the focus of their literacy instruction, Holm and Dodd (1996) interpreted their findings as indicating that "the ability to detect, isolate and manipulate single phonemes that are co-articulated in speech does not develop spontaneously. . . . Learning to read an alphabetic orthography provides the opportunity to develop phonemic awareness" (p. 137).

Similar evidence comes from research with Braille. In Guide I Braille, each letter of the alphabet is represented by a pattern that is formed by a combination of one to six dots, in various spatial configurations. As children's learning of Braille progresses, they are introduced to Guide II Braille that contains contracted forms of symbols, where several letters are represented by a single tactile symbol (Dodd & Conn, 2000). Such contractions may represent phonemes that are represented through digraphs in English (e.g., "sh," "ch") or, alternatively, commonly occurring orthographic sequences (e.g., "-ed," "-ing," "-in," "-tion."). Contractions may cut across phonological boundaries, so that, for example, the contraction for "the" is used for the words "*the*ir," " *the*m," "fur*the*r," and "ca*the*dral" (Dodd & Conn, 2000).

Dodd and Conn (2000) compared blind children and sighted children on their ability to segment spoken words, when half the word sets contained contractions in the Braille orthography. They found that words with Braille contractions were less well segmented by the blind children, with most of the errors representing an underestimate of the number of sounds in a word. The sighted children did not perform any more poorly on the items containing Braille contractions. The results of this study provide further support for the hypothesis that the nature of the orthography with which a reader–writer engages influences phonological processing.

Even within alphabetic orthographies, there are differences in the consistency with which orthographies represent the phonology of a spoken language. In some languages, such as Serbo-Croatian, the link between sounds and letters is consistent and transparent (Lukatela, Carello, Shankweiler, & Liberman, 1995), whereas in other languages, such as English, individual letters do not consistently represent the same phoneme. Other etymological and morphological factors may influence orthographic representations. Lukatela et al. argued that the penetrability of the orthographic-phonological links is an important factor to consider in exploring the extent to which alphabetic experience affects the development of segmentation skills. In their study of adult illiterate Serbo-Croatian women, Lukatela et al. repeated many of the tasks used by Morais and colleagues (Morais, Bertelson, Cary, & Alegria, 1986; Morais, Content, Bertelson, & Cary, 1988; Morais & Kolinsky, 1994; Morais et al., 1979, 1989) with very similar findings. Segmentation tasks involving manipulation of syllables were significantly easier than phonemic segmentation tasks, and alphabetic familiarity significantly affected phonemic segmentation skills. All of the women involved in the study with Lukatela et al. had received minimal literacy instruction, ranging from a number of days to a maximum of a month at least 40 years before the initiation of the study in question. Despite this, 7 of the 23 participating women were able to identify all the letters of the alphabet. In addition, all of these women demonstrated both reading and writing skills, often at an impressive level. Lukatela *et al.* (1995) described Serbo-Croatian as *orthographically shallow* and highly *phonologically penetrable*. They argued that although the insight that letters correspond to sounds and that speech can be segmented into relevant units is a prerequisite for literacy in an alphabetic script, this alphabetic insight is easier in orthographically-shallow languages and buys more rapid and greater progress than in less penetrable languages. In other words, although alphabetic knowledge and phonemic segmentation skills are important to all alphabetic scripts, the nature of the script itself may not be neutral. A continuum of orthography depth may exist across different language contexts and may have an impact on how far and how quickly one can progress in literacy with little instruction (Harris & Beech, 1998).

IV. SUMMARY

Throughout this chapter, the primary focus has been on fluent readers and writers and the impact of the acquisition of literacy on other aspects of spoken language and meta-linguistic skills. The complex interrelationships between orthographic, phonological, meaning, and context processing have been explored, and it has been argued that within all of this processing, the target orthography may not be neutral. Rather, the impact of developing phonological awareness may differ considerably, depending on the transparency or consistency of the target orthography. Like development of spoken language, becoming an expert reader–writer takes time, and it is likely that the strategies an apprentice reader–writer adopts differ in many ways from those of the expert. Unlike spoken language, in all but a few exceptional cases, becoming an expert reader–writer involves direct instruction. The next chapter focuses on describing some of the changes that may occur as individuals progress on the developmental path of learning to read and write and on exploring the role of instruction in this process.

REFERENCES

Adams, M. J. (1990). *Beginning to read: Thinking and learning about print*. Cambridge, MA: MIT Press, A Bradford Book.

Adrián, J., Alegria, J., & Morais, J. (1995). Metaphonological abilities of Spanish illiterate adults. *International Journal of Psychology, 30*(3), 329–353.

Ball, E. W., & Blachman, B. A. (1991). Does phoneme awareness training in kindergarten make a difference in early word recognition and developmental spelling? *Reading Research Quarterly, 26,* 49–66.

Barker, T., Torgesen, J. K., & Wagner, R. K. (1992). The role of orthographic processing skills on five different reading tasks. *Reading Research Quarterly, 27,* 335–345.

Blachman, B. A. (1991). Early intervention for children's reading problems: Clinical applications of the research in phonological awareness. *Topics in Language Disorders, 12*(1), 51–65.

Blachman, B. A. (2000). Phonological awareness. In M. Kamil, P. Mosenthal, P. D. Pearson, & R. Barr (Eds.), *Handbook of reading research* (Vol. 3, pp. 483–502). London: Erlbaum.

Bradley, L., & Bryant, P. E. (1983). Categorising sounds and learning to read: A causal connection. *Nature, 310,* 419–421.

Bryant, P. E., Maclean, M., Bradley, L., & Crossland, J. (1990). Rhyme, alliteration, phoneme detection, and learning to read. *Developmental Psychology, 26,* 429–438.

Butler, K., & Wallach, G. P. (1995). Language learning disabilities: Moving in from the edge. *Topics in Language Disorders, 16*(1), 1–26.

Chaney, C. (1992). Language development, metalinguistic skills and print awareness in 3-year-old children. *Applied Psycholinguistics, 13,* 485–514.

Chaney, C. (1994). Language development, metalinguistic awareness and emergent literacy skills of 3-year-old children in relation to social class. *Applied Psycholinguistics, 15,* 371–394.

Dodd, B., & Conn, A. (2000). The effect of Braille orthography on blind children's phonological awareness. *Journal of Research in Reading, 23,* 1–11.

Dodd, B., Gillon, G., Oerlemans, M., Russell, T., Syrmis, M., & Wilson, H. (1995). Phonological disorder and the acquisition of literacy. In B. Dodd (Ed.), *Differential diagnosis and treatment of children with speech disorder.* London: Whurr.

Duncan, L. G., Seymour, P. K. H., & Hill, S. (1997). How important are rhyme and analogy in beginning reading? *Cognition, 63,* 171–208.

Ehri, L. C., & Wilce, L. S. (1979). The mnemonic value of orthography among beginning readers. *Journal of Educational Psychology, 71,* 26–40.

Goswami, U. (2000a). Phonological and lexical processes. In M. Kamil, P. Mosenthal, P. D. Pearson, & R. Barr (Eds.), *Handbook of reading research* (pp. 251–268). London: Erlbaum.

Goswami, U. (2000b, July). *Phonological awareness and reading acquisition in different orthographies.* Paper presented at the 27th International Congress of Psychology, Stockholm, Sweden.

Goswami, U., & Bryant, P. E. (1990). *Phonological skills and learning to read.* Hillsdale, NJ: Erlbaum.

Goswami, U., & East, M. (1999). Integrating orthographic and phonological knowledge as reading develops: Onsets, rimes and analogies in children's reading. In R. Klein & P. McMullen (Eds.), *Converging methods for understanding reading and dyslexia* (pp. 57–75). London: MIT Press.

Goswami, U., & East, M. (2000). Rhyme and analogy in beginning reading: Conceptual and methodological issues. *Applied Psycholinguistics, 21,* 63–93.

Harris, M., & Beech, J. R. (1998). Implicit phonological awareness and early reading development in prelingually deaf children. *Journal of Deaf Studies and Deaf Education, 3*(3), 205–216.

Holm, A., & Dodd, B. (1996). The effect of first written language on the acquisition of English literacy. *Cognition, 59,* 119–147.

Lukatela, K., Carello, C., Shankweiler, D., & Liberman, I. (1995). Phonological awareness in illiterates: Observations from Serbo-Croatia. *Applied Psycholinguistics, 16,* 463–487.

Lundberg, I., Frost, J., & Petersen, O. (1988). Effects of an extensive program for stimulating phonological awareness in preschool children. *Reading Research Quarterly, 23,* 263–284.

Morais, J., Bertelson, P., Cary, L., & Alegria, J. (1986). Literacy training and speech segmentation. *Cognition, 24,* 45–64.

Morais, J., Cary, L., Alegria, J., & Bertelson, P. (1979). Does awareness of speech as a sequence of phones arise spontaneously? *Cognition, 17,* 323–331.

Morais, J., Content, A., Bertelson, P., & Cary, L. (1988). Is there a critical period for the acquisition of segmental analysis? *Cognitive Neuropsychology, 5*(3), 347–352.

Morais, J., Content, A., Cary, L., & Mehler, J. (1989). Syllabic segmentation and literacy. *Language and Cognitive Processes, 4*(1), 57–67.

Morais, J., & Kolinsky, R. (1994). Perception and awareness in phonological awareness: The case of the phoneme. *Cognition, 50*(3), 287–297.

Nagy, W. E., & Anderson, R. C. (1984). How many words are there in printed school English? *Reading Research Quarterly, 19*, 304–330.

Nagy, W. E., & Herman, P. A. (1987). Breadth and depth of vocabulary knowledge: implications for acquisition and instruction. In M. McKeown & M. Curtis (Eds.), *The nature of vocabulary acquisition* (pp. 19–35). Hillsdale, NJ: Erlbaum.

Nagy, W. E., & Scott, J. (2000). Vocabulary processes. In M. Kamil, P. Mosenthal, P.D. Pearson, & R. Barr (Eds.), *Handbook of reading research* (Vol. 3, pp. 269–284). London: Erlbaum.

Nakamura, M., Kolinsky, R., Spagnoletti, C., & Morais, J. (1998). Phonemic awareness in alphabetically literate Japanese adults: The influence of the first acquired writing system. *Current Psychology of Cognition, 17*(2), 417–450.

Nation, K., & Snowling, M. (2000). Factors influencing syntactic awareness skills in normal readers and poor comprehenders. *Applied Psycholinguistics, 21*, 229–241.

Nippold, M., Allen, M., & Kirsch, D. (2001). Proverb comprehension as a function of reading proficiency in preadolescents. *Language Speech and Hearing Services in Schools, 32*, 90–100.

Perfetti, C. A., Beck, I., Bell, L., & Hughes, C. (1987). Phonemic knowledge and learning to read are reciprocal: A longitudinal study of first grade children. *Merrill-Palmer Quarterly, 33*, 283–319.

Pumfrey, P. D., & Reason, R. (1991). *Specific learning difficulties: Challenges and responses.* Berks, UK: NFER-Nelson.

Rayner, K. (1999). What have we learned about eye movements during reading? In R. Klein & P. McMullen (Eds.), *Converging methods for understanding reading and dyslexia* (pp. 23–56). London: MIT Press.

Scliar-Cabral, L., Morais, J., Nepomuceno, L., & Kolinsky, R. (1997). The awareness of phonemes: So close—So far away. *International Journal of Psycholinguistics, 13*(3), 211–240.

Scribner, S. (1997). *Mind and social practice: Selected writings of Sylvia Scribner.* Cambridge, UK: Cambridge University Press.

Seidenberg, M., & McClelland, J. L. (1989). A distributed, developmental model of word recognition and naming. *Psychological Review, 96*, 523–568.

Seidenberg, M., & Tanenhaus, K. K. (1979). Orthographic effects on rhyme monitoring. *Journal of Experimental Psychology: Human Learning and Memory, 5*, 546–554.

Seymour, P. K. H., & Duncan, L. G. (1997). Small vs. large unit theories of reading acquisition. *Dyslexia, 3*, 125–134.

Share, D. L. (1995). Phonological recoding and self-teaching: *Sine qua non* of reading acquisition. *Cognition, 55*, 151–218.

Smith, F. (1971). *Understanding reading.* New York: Holt, Rinehart & Winston.

Snow, C., Burns, M. S., & Griffin, P. E. (1998). *Preventing reading difficulties in young children.* Washington, DC: National Academy Press.

Spinks, J., Lin, Y., Perfetti, C. A., & Tan, L. (2002). Reading Chinese characters for meaning: The role of phonological information. *Cognition, 76*, B1–B11.

Stackhouse, J., & Wells, B. (1997). *Children's speech and literacy difficulties: A psycholinguistic framework.* London: Whurr.

Stanovich, K. (1986). Matthew effects in reading: Some consequences of individual differences in the acquisition of literacy. *Reading Research Quarterly, 21*, 360–407.

Stanovich, K., West, R. F., Cunningham, A. E., Cipielewski, J., & Siddiqui, S. (1996). The role of inadequate print exposure as a determinant of reading comprehension problems. In C. Cornoldi & J. Oakhill (Eds.), *Reading comprehension disabilities* (pp. 15–32). Hillsdale, NJ: Erlbaum.

Sterne, A., & Goswami, U. (2000). Phonological awareness of syllables, rhymes and phonemes in deaf children. *Journal of Child Psychology and Psychiatry and Allied Disciplines, 41*(5), 609–625.

Treiman, R. (1983). The structure of spoken syllables: Evidence from novel word games. *Cognition, 15*, 49–74.

Treiman, R. (1986). The division between onsets and rimes in English. *Journal of Memory and Language, 25*, 476–491.

Van Orden, G. C., Pennington, B. F., & Stone, G. O. (1990). Word identification in reading and the promise of subsymbolic psycholinguistics. *Psychological Review, 97,* 488–522.

Vellutino, F. R. (1979). *Dyslexia: Theory and research.* Cambridge, MA: MIT Press.

Ventura, P., Kolinsky, R., Brito-Mendes, C., & Morais, J. (2001). Mental representations of the syllable internal structure are influenced by orthography. *Language and Cognitive Processes, 37,* 126–141.

Wagner, R. K., & Torgesen, J. K. (1987). The nature of phonological processing and its causal role in the acquisition of reading skills. *Psychological Bulletin, 1011,* 192–212.

CHAPTER 3

Literacy Learning

I. INTRODUCTION

Two puzzles present in exploring the development of reading and writing: How do good readers learn so much so quickly? Why is the same task so difficult for poor readers? Clearly there is something about reading and writing that draws on existing skills. Once a certain mix is present, the scene seems set for takeoff. At the same time, lack of the critical skill mix makes the transition to fluent reading and writing extremely difficult. In this chapter we provide a brief overview of what is commonly understood about the development of literacy in children and the stages that may be observed in the developmental process. Attention then turns to changes that underpin development.

II. STAGE THEORIES OF LITERACY DEVELOPMENT

What do children learn to be able to read and write?

A. DEVELOPMENTAL STAGES IN READING

Stage models of literacy development describe the observable changes in children's behavior as they progress in reading and writing. One such model comes from the work of Ehri (1991, 2000). Drawing on the work of Chall (1983), Ehri suggested four stages of reading development in an alphabetic orthography. With minor modifications, the suggested sequence is as follows.

1. Pre-Alphabetic Stage

At Stage 1, the pre-alphabetic or emergent stage, "background literacy skills" are developed. Children learn key ideas about reading: print carries the message; books and print have a certain orientation and must be read in a particular order—front to back, word by word, left to right, or top to bottom; readers use print and pictures differently; particular vocabulary is used to talk about reading and print (e.g., "page" and "word"); and the language of books differs sometimes from spoken language (Clay, 1985; Galda, Cullinan, & Strickland, 1993). At this stage, sight word reading is logographic based on salient visual cues, the classic example being the golden arches behind McDonald's (Ehri, 1991). Thus, whole words are the main focus of attention, usually from a restricted set, including names of significant people.

2. Decoding or Alphabetic Stage

At Stage 2, the decoding stage, the link between specific grapheme and phoneme elements is established. Sight word reading begins to take account of letters rather than other visual cues, signaling the beginning of the alphabetic or phonemic cue stage of word decoding (Adams, 1990). Initially, only a few letter cues are used in word identification. Letter names may have primacy over phoneme-grapheme information (Ehri, 2000), so that, for example, the word "ran" may be read as orange. Gradually apprentice readers become able to read words "by storing in memory complete associations between specific spellings and their pronunciations" (Ehri, 1991, p. 73).

3. Fluency Stage

During Stage 3, the fluency stage, skills are consolidated and expanded. Attention again turns to larger units, as sight words are processed as single units. Patterns within words, perhaps based on syllable (Adams, 1990) or morphological divisions (Royer, Colé, Breton-Marec, & Gombert, 2000; Stackhouse & Wells, 1997), are the basis for word identification in this "orthographic phase" of reading. Superficially, the orthographic stage may appear to be similar to the early logographic stage of reading when attention is focused on large units or whole words. However, the nature of the orthographic information drawn on to support word identification is very different in the two stages. Successful progress into the orthographic stage allows children to read by analogy, using shared spelling patterns within words as the basis for identification of unfamiliar words (Adams, 1990; Bruck & Treiman, 1992; Goswami & Bryant, 1990; Goswami & East, 2000; Share, 1995). Alphabetic skills continue to be necessary for decoding some unfamiliar words.

4. "Reading to Learn" Stage

By Stage 4, the reading to learn stage, skills of the previous stages have become automatic and rapid, and so the process of reading is subordinate to the goals of reading. Although reading skills continue to develop, potentially across the lifespan, there is little conscious awareness of this development, because the focus is on learning of content accessed through reading.

B. DEVELOPMENTAL STAGES IN SPELLING

A similar and probably overlapping developmental sequence can be identified in spelling skills (Ehri, 2000; Kamhi & Hinton, 2000; Templeton & Morris, 2000), although it is likely that spelling creates greater demands on the child's developing written language abilities (Ehri, 2000). Initially, background principles are established: that print is different from pictures and that print proceeds in a particular orientation, represents a consistent message, and can be created by the writer. In addition, the motor and perceptual skills necessary for pen control must be acquired. Children start to differentiate their picture drawings and letter attempts (Treiman & Bourassa, 2000b) and begin to respect the conventions of both modalities. Figure 3.1 shows an example of a labeled drawing created by a child aged 2 years and 6 months. Already at this early stage, it is evident that although drawing and writing occur within the same space, letters are treated differently from an illustration in terms of size, linkages, and orientation.

Children in the early stages of reading and writing may regard the two activities as being quite separate. Orla at age 4 years and 6 months had just started formal schooling and was making her first tentative steps in reading words and recognizing letters. She was also able to write most of the letters of the alphabet and enjoyed "writing" messages and letters that she delivered personally. When asked one day to read out a note, she explained, "No, I can only write them, I can't read them yet."

Spelling skills change as children's insights into the relationship between spoken and written language evolve, in much the same way as their reading skills

Figure 3.1. Labeled drawing by Orla, aged 2 years and 6 months. Copyright © Martine Smith.

change. Indeed, many authors have suggested that the processes of reading and writing are far more intimately linked than has been traditionally recognized (Kamhi & Hinton, 2000; Templeton & Morris, 2000; Treiman & Bourassa, 2000b). Parallels can be traced between the development of skills in spelling and the skills in reading previously outlined.

1. Pre-Alphabetic and Semi-Alphabetic Spelling

The earliest spellings may bear no relationship to the sounds in a target word—sometimes termed the pre-communicative or pre-alphabetic stage. Children may write apparently random sequences of letters or a mix of letters and other letter-like patterns. With the development of alphabetic insight, initial spelling attempts rely heavily on letter names and incomplete alphabetic information. Single letters may be used to represent whole words, in what is termed the early semi-phonetic phase. Templeton and Morris (2000) used the example of "truck" spelt as h-r-k.

2. Alphabetic Spelling

In the alphabetic stage, increasing alphabetic information is included, with the noticeable inclusion of vowels, so that spellings are often plausible and phonetically accurate, even if not conventionally correct (e.g., Orla aged 5 years and 5 months spelled "tyrannosaurus" as c-h-r-a-n-u-s-r-i-s). In a purely or transparently alphabetic orthography, reaching this stage of spelling heralds a major milestone, with little additional spelling learning to follow (Goswami & East, 1999b). However, English spelling has developed in such a way that word meaning has a crucial influence on spelling. Far from being the "illogical" or "inefficient" system still deplored by many, logical relations across word meanings determine shared spelling patterns, so that "define" and "definition" share the common spelling d-e-f-i-n, despite differences in the pronunciation of those common letters. As Templeton (2002) pointed out, the word meaning links are crucial to understanding the logic of the English spelling system, a logic that later can support vocabulary as well as spelling development.

3. Orthographic/Semiconventional Spelling

As children's general print skills advance, orthographic within-word patterns appear in their spellings, so that "rain" may be spelled as r-a-n-e. To produce spellings of this kind, children must abstract and store orthographic patterns extending beyond mere phonetic information, recognizing that certain orthographic units can be "silent." The importance of the orthographic information is further highlighted by the fact that, even at this stage, children's written spelling attempts are more accurate than their oral attempts (Treiman & Bourassa, 2000a).

4. Derivational Relations Spelling

Over time, apprentice spellers come to recognize that spelling patterns can also derive from the morphological make-up of a word. As the influence of morphological information over spelling attempts increases, what Templeton and Morris (2000) referred to as derivational constancy emerges—morphological roots are respected as key determinants of spelling. Mastery is finally achieved as conventional and exceptional spellings are incorporated into the knowledge system.

C. Writing Development

In addition to increasing their sophistication in linking sounds to print at the level of the single word, children learning to write also generate increasingly sophisticated texts. Singer (1995) summarized several models of the development of written language, drawing particularly on the work of Kroll (1981), to outline four main phases.

1. Preparation Phase

In the preparation phase, spoken and written language remain autonomous of each other. For example, as stated earlier, Orla felt able to write but not to read her notes. Specific skills such as recognizing letter names, writing an alphabet, and decoding are mastered as tasks separate from spoken language skills, although there may be some interlinking.

2. Consolidation Phase

The consolidation phase occurs typically around age 6 to 7 years. In this phase children write as they would speak. The separate conventional forms of written language have not yet been mastered, but increasing automaticity is developed in lower level skills such as the decoding and technical aspects of writing.

3. Differentiation Phase

As children approach the age of approximately 10 years, they gradually differentiate the forms of spoken and written language. Traditionally, spoken and written language forms have been contrasted on formal-informal dimensions. However, with the advent of email and text messaging, such contrasts are rapidly changing. Many different types of language forms are now required for both spoken and written language.

4. Systematic Integration Phase

In this last phase of development, toward the end of primary school years, children integrate both spoken and written language, and become able to flexibly apply rules and styles from either mode.

Thus, speaking, reading, and writing develop as complementary processes, undergoing a gradual process of differentiation and integration, linked intimately with the context, materials, and purpose of any given literacy activity. The modality differences between oral and written language become more important and the unique conceptual, linguistic, and mechanical constraints posed by written language are accommodated with increasing sophistication.

III. ARE STAGE THEORIES HELPFUL?

Not all authors agree with the delineation of stages in reading and writing. Ellis (1993), for instance, argued that the stages reported reflect teaching approaches in vogue at the time of study, rather than universally based developmental stages. Further criticisms point to the fact that "stages" of reading and writing competence depend intimately on the task in hand. Text demands may elicit different reading styles and strategies, so that the "competence" (or more accurately, the performance) observed may vary across different text contexts. Reading words in isolation or decoding nonwords or unfamiliar words may necessitate the use of alphabetic strategies, whereas reading connected text may allow a reader to demonstrate orthographically based strategies (Barker, Torgesen, & Wagner, 1992).

A further limitation of stage models of reading is that they may predispose a view of the stages as discrete and mutually exclusive. Even if readers appear to be reading and spelling primarily through processing larger units such as morphemes, they can only access the morphemic information through their alphabetic skills. As Adams (1990) pointed out, identifying common orthographic patterns can only be accomplished by processing all the individual letters in the pattern and their sequence. Similarly, children may be able to use analogy from an early stage to support both reading and spelling, yet not necessarily avail themselves of this strategy (Treiman & Bourassa, 2000a). Although able to recognize the similarities between "pat" and "sat," they may still read or spell both words on the basis of individual letter-sound relationships, rather than on a shared pattern of "-at." Particularly for early readers, any single text is likely to throw up many different demands, so that considerable overlap between apparently discrete stages is likely. Likewise in spelling, children typically demonstrate many different kinds of knowledge within any one piece of writing, as illustrated in Figure 3.2. Development may be better characterized as increasing sophistication in strategies and their application, rather than as distinct stages.

However, despite the above limitations, there is no doubt that learning to read and write takes time, and the repertoire of reading and writing behaviors available change over the course of the learning period. Furthermore, needs may differ across the various stages (e.g., Harris & Beech, 1998). Thus, although it is widely recognized that providing print-rich environments for young children gives them a considerable advantage when they start formal reading instruction, most children still require specific instruction to make a breakthrough to

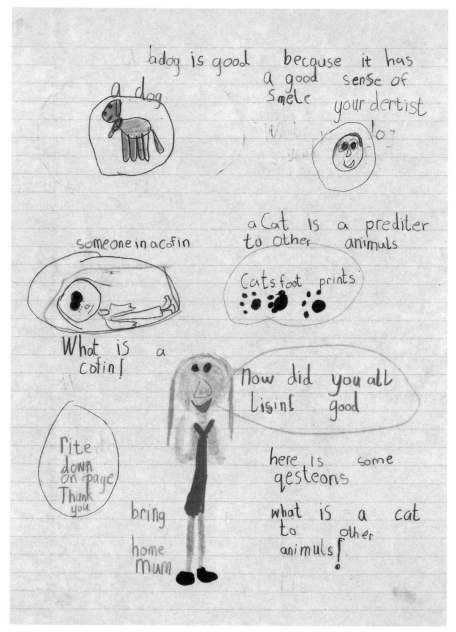

Figure 3.2. A sample of writing with alphabetic and conventional spelling patterns. Copyright ©
Martine Smith.

alphabetic competence. Developing fluency in reading depends on having sufficient opportunities to practice with texts at an appropriate level. Getting to the stage of being able to read to learn requires development across a range of cognitive and linguistic domains. Although stage theories present difficulties if interpreted rigidly and as representing discrete phases of development, they are useful in highlighting for us that certain ingredients only become relevant in the mix at certain points.

IV. HOW DO CHILDREN LEARN TO READ AND WRITE?

The simple answer to this question is "they are taught." It is, of course, true that instruction plays in important role in literacy acquisition. Although there is anecdotal evidence of individuals who have learned to read and write before ever starting formal schooling, on the whole, explicit instruction is necessary to unravel the code of written language.[1] Instruction is clearly important; the question is whether it is enough.

Share (1995) suggested that instruction alone cannot account for the rapid progress in reading observed through the early school years, primarily because of the vastness of the task and the sheer volume of words learned. One estimate is that fifth grade students encounter approximately 10,000 new words during the school year (Nagy & Herman, 1987), and Share (1995) cited studies by Firth (1972) and Rodenborn and Washburn (1974) suggesting a comparable volume of novel vocabulary encounters in the beginning school years. Share (1995) concluded, "in the face of this orthographic avalanche, direct instruction is unlikely to offer a feasible acquisition strategy" (p. 153). There simply are not enough hours in the day, let alone in the school day, to teach on a word-by-word basis all or even most of the words likely to be encountered. Furthermore, if children learn to read and write simply by virtue of what they are taught, how then do we explain the range of reading abilities observed in any classroom? Why do some children make rapid progress, whereas others, given exactly the same instruction, struggle throughout their school careers?

If children do not learn to read and write simply by being taught, then how do they learn? Although there has been considerable research activity directed toward explicating this process and many detailed descriptions of component relationships have been proposed, the exact causal mechanisms underlying literacy learning are not fully understood.

Learning to read and write represents a complex synthesis and coordination of many different skills, a complex partnership of endogenous and exogenous

---

[1]Exceptions here may be individuals who present with hyperlexia, a condition in which decoding skills are extremely well developed, but there is little comprehension.

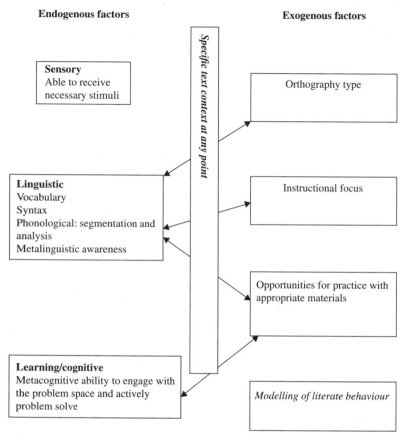

Figure 3.3. Factors underlying literacy development. Copyright © Martine Smith.

factors. Apprentice reader–writers have certain resources at their disposal, and they encounter certain phenomena in their literacy learning contexts. These influences are considered below as exogenous and endogenous factors, and are illustrated in Figure 3.3.

A. Partnership of Factors

1. Exogenous Factors

On the exogenous, or external context side of things, a number of factors may exert an important influence on how easily and effectively an individual learns to read and write.

a. Context

The socio-cultural context of literacy within the apprentice reader–writer's experience may fundamentally affect his or her context of learning. Within this broad context, considerations such as whether or not literacy is a highly valued achievement, and the functions ascribed to literacy may have an impact on an individual's self-perception as a reader–writer, as well as motivation to become an expert reader–writer (Clay, 1985; Scribner, 1997; Teale & Sulzby, 1987, 1989).

b. Instruction

The literacy instruction provided is also a potential key influence. The focus (whole-word or analysis of within-word components), intensity, and duration (Adams, 1990; McBride-Chang & Suk-Han Ho, 2000) of instruction may all affect progress toward mastery of reading and writing, as well as the strategies employed in reading and writing.

c. Opportunities

Learning to read and write takes time and practice. The opportunities available to participate in literacy activities (Share, 1995) may be crucial in determining ultimate success.

d. Nature of Orthography

The nature of the orthography encountered and its relationship to the target spoken language (Dodd & Conn, 2000; Holm & Dodd, 1996; McBride-Chang & Suk-Han Ho, 2000) may also have an impact on the learning process.

2. Endogenous Factors

On the endogenous side, the resources brought to bear by a child can be grouped under three main headings.

a. Sensory, Perceptual, and Motor Skills

Reading and writing draw on visual, auditory, and moto-kinesthetic skills. Stimuli must be perceived before they can be decoded for reading; symbols must be encoded through some form of motor activity.

b. Cognitive Skills

Learning to read and write requires the application of meta-cognitive resources to the problem space, the active engagement with the task by the reader–writer.

c. Linguistic Skills

Reading and writing require the mapping of spoken (or signed) language into an alternative modality. Spoken language therefore provides an important platform for the development of written language skills. Many aspects of children's spoken language skills have been studied and implicated in written language performance, including syntax, vocabulary, phonological skills, and metalinguistic skills.

B. LANGUAGE SKILLS AND READING

1. Syntax and Reading

Fluent reading requires the integration of the meaning of single words at both sentence and text levels and ongoing monitoring of comprehension. It seems reasonable therefore to suggest that syntactic and semantic skills serve as important bootstrapping resources for literacy development (Nation & Snowling, 2000). Deficiencies in semantic processing (Denckla & Rundel, 1976; Ellis, 1981; Silva, Williams, & McGee, 1987) and syntactic processing (Catts & Kamhi, 1986; Shankweiler & Crain, 1986) have been found to correlate with difficulties in reading and writing. Traditionally, syntactic processing has been presumed to contribute primarily to reading comprehension rather than to word recognition.

Nation and Snowling (2000) matched 15 children identified as "poor reading comprehenders" with 15 children with no literacy difficulties for age, nonverbal ability, and, importantly, for decoding skill. The children who were experiencing difficulties understanding what they read also performed less successfully than their matched peers on tasks requiring them to correct word order errors in sentences presented orally. Their difficulties were exacerbated by factors such as semantic ambiguity and sentence length in the stimuli sets. These findings point to a general underlying difficulty with syntactic processing for these children, rather than a specific reading-based problem. However, there is also evidence to suggest that children with poor decoding skills may draw disproportionately on syntactic information to inform decoding attempts (Tunmer & Hoover, 1992), leading Nation and Snowling (2000) to conclude the following:

> . . . such language weaknesses impact upon reading development in at least two ways. In addition to facilitating text integration and comprehension monitoring, processes that are integral to successful comprehension, syntactic awareness may also constrain the development of skilled word recognition, by influencing the ease with which children learn to read words they could not read via simple decoding mechanisms. (p. 237)

2. Vocabulary and Reading

The relationship between vocabulary and reading and writing is complex and bidirectional. There are two important ways in which vocabulary can be linked to reading and writing skills. First, decoding words within a text involves matching orthographic information to lexical representations. Efficient hypothesizing about likely candidate word matches, based on contextual information, can speed up the process of word identification. In other words, having a rich semantic and syntactic field of information combined with some decoding information, a reader should be able to identify a word relatively quickly. In contrast, an impoverished lexical set means that proportionately more unknown words will be encountered within a text, so that for any given word in the text contextual support is also proportionately reduced, magnifying the difficulty of word identification. The fewer words in your receptive vocabulary, the harder it is to guess what any novel, unfamiliar word in a text might mean and how it might be pronounced.

Second, lexical development also benefits directly from literacy. As children progress through school, much of their lexical development occurs through reading (Nagy & Scott, 2000; Nippold, Allen, & Kirsch, 2001). Vocabulary size is uniquely predictive of reading ability (Stanovich, 1986), but is also dependent on literacy skills. Thus, a bootstrapping relationship between vocabulary development and reading emerges and continues throughout adolescence and potentially adulthood.

Vocabulary development may play a third important role in relation to reading and writing development. Children in the early stage of spoken language acquisition initially have to cope with only a small set of words. However, lexical growth over the first few years of life is extraordinarily rapid (Ingram, 1989; Locke, 1995). One hypothesized outcome of this rapid expansion in vocabulary is that the organization of lexical representations undergoes radical revision and respecification. With a small vocabulary, holistic, relatively undifferentiated representational forms may be quite adequate. However, as vocabulary size grows, the sheer volume of items to be represented renders such holistic representations impractical. Within this hypothesis, global representations are gradually restructured, so that smaller segments, such as syllables, onsets, rimes, and ultimately phonemes are represented (Fowler, 1991; Fowler & Lieberman, 1995; Goswami, 2000a). This restructuring occurs on an item-by-item basis, so that the level of specification may differ across items at any given time (Goswami & East, 2000). Representational specificity is also likely to be highest for words in dense neighborhoods, in which there are many similar representations (Goswami, 2000b; Metsala & Walley, 1998), because the need for careful detail is greater in such contexts. For example, "bin" may contrast with "pin," "fin," "bun," "ban," "ben," "bit," "bill," etc., so that fine and detailed phonetic information is required to distinguish it from other potential foils. "Bin" serves as a minimal pair with many other targets. By contrast, "voice" presents with fewer minimal pair neighbors— "vice" or "void." Less detailed phonetic information is required to identify "voice." As new words are learned, they must be contrasted with existing lexical items. The more words that are processed through the lexicon, the greater the number of potential minimal pairs represented. Vocabulary development may thus be an important trigger, kick-starting representational segmentation and specification. These two processes have themselves been hypothesized as critical component skills in learning to read.

3. Phonological Processing and Reading

As mentioned earlier, phonological processing is an umbrella term, covering a range of different skills, including phonological awareness, verbal memory, and naming. At its most simple, it refers to the ability to perceive and analyze speech stimuli, whether internal or externally presented. Processing can occur at many different levels and with many different kinds of stimuli—speech versus nonspeech, sound or nonword stimuli, or word-based tasks (Stackhouse & Wells, 1997). Phonological processing is a stable set of skills: Children identified as being "good" processors retain this advantage at least through fourth grade (Wagner et al., 1997). However, that is not to say that what can be processed does not change over the developmental period. Two aspects of phonological processing are discussed here: segmentation and phonological awareness.

a. Segmentation

One view of development is that children gradually shift their processing focus from segmentation of large units to segmentation of smaller units (e.g., Bruck & Treiman, 1992; Goswami, 2000a; Goswami & Bryant, 1990; Goswami & East, 1999b). Initially words or short phrases (e.g., "wanna go") are the primary processing units. However, as discussed earlier, when children are challenged by significant increases in vocabulary, alternative within-word units, such as morphemes (dogs), syllables, or subsyllabic units may form the basis for representation. Young, preliterate children and illiterate adults are able to segment words into syllables, before they can attempt phoneme-level tasks (e.g., Blachman, 1983, 1984; Morais, Bertelson, Cary, & Alegria, 1986; Morais, Cary, Alegria, & Bertelson, 1979; Morais, Content, Bertelson, & Cary, 1988; Morais, Content, Cary, & Mehler, 1989; Morais & Kolinsky, 1994). Onset and rimes represent an intermediate stage between syllables and phonemes (in the syllable string, "str" represents the onset, whereas "ing" is the rime). After the landmark study of Bradley and Bryant, (1983) many other studies have reported on children's ability to segment onset–rime distinctions before phoneme-level segmentation, even though in many instances an onset may represent a single phoneme (Goswami, 2000a). In other words, children may be able to select the mismatched word in a list such as "fun," "fish," "shop★" or "cat," "rat," "man★" but not in "flat," "flop," "fig★," for which detection of "fig" requires the segmentation of the onset "fl" into its constituent phonemes.

Simultaneous with the progression from large-to-small unit processing, awareness of processing outcomes or products progresses along a continuum from implicit to explicit (Stackhouse & Wells, 1997), as children gradually become more consciously aware of the sound system of their spoken languages. Karmiloff-Smith (1992) used the term *representational redescription* for the process by which children cyclically reanalyze and reorganize their mental representations to accommodate new knowledge and experiences. Drawing on this work, Gombert (1992) proposed several phases in the development of conscious access to linguistic representations, from epilinguistic knowledge to metalinguistic control. He used the term *epilinguistic knowledge* to refer to linguistic knowledge that is used to inform linguistic behavior, but that is not accessible to conscious inspection. Epilinguistic knowledge is implicit and is not available at a level of purposeful awareness. For example, children may demonstrate awareness of fine phonetic distinctions in their own speech (e.g., the increased aspiration of /p/ in word–initial position), but this awareness is not available for conscious introspection. Metalinguistic control emerges as conscious awareness of the structure of mental representations develops, usually in response to an external pressure (e.g., being taught to read). In the final phase, automation of the metaprocess, aspects of meta-functioning become more automatic, reducing the cognitive load (Gombert, 1992).

Two issues are worthy of note here. One is that restructuring of spoken language representations is presumed to occur for all individuals, even if they never encounter written language. Rerepresenting of lexical items requires segmentation and analysis of existing representations, even though this process may be implicit rather than explicit. Second, conscious access to representations (i.e., metalinguistic awareness) occurs in response to an environmental trigger. For example, in encountering print, children are forced to pay conscious attention to their representations. How they encounter print and the nature of the print they encounter will probably have an impact on the kinds of units they become aware of. If children are faced with an alphabetic script, considerable attention will focus on phoneme-level correspondences, so that their early metalinguistic awareness may be phonemic. If the script represents alternative units (e.g., morphemes), then their meta-awareness may also reflect this different focus, as the findings by Holm and Dodd (1996) suggested. Difficulties may thus emerge with either type of competence. Representations may be poorly specified; that is, segmentation may be based only on relatively large units. Alternatively, children may have difficulty either developing conscious awareness of their representations or developing automation of access, so that the metademands may remain very high.

b. Phonological Awareness

Of the two aspects of representational competence described, there is no doubt that over the last decade the range of skills coming under the heading of phonological awareness has received unprecedented research attention. There is now a large body of research to support the view that phonological awareness, even measured in very young preschool children, remains a robust predictor of early reading achievement (e.g., Bradley & Bryant, 1983; Bryant, Maclean, Bradley, & Crossland, 1990; Maclean, Bryant, & Bradley, 1987; Scarborough, 1998). Enhancing phonological awareness through direct intervention programs facilitates early acquisition of reading and spelling skill (Ball & Blachman, 1991; Blachman, Ball, Black, & Tangel, 1994; Bradley & Bryant, 1983; Lundberg, Frost, & Petersen, 1988), and problems with phonological awareness persist for poor readers through the teenage years (Fawcett & Nicolson, 1995). Two dimensions of phonological awareness have attracted particular attention. The first and developmentally earlier skill represents intrasyllabic awareness, that is, awareness of onset–rime boundaries, explored through rhyme–related tasks. Bradley and Bryant (1983) showed that rhyme awareness measured in preschool children was a significant predictor of later progress in reading and spelling in English. The early availability of rhyme as a phonological structure and its links with reading have received support from a wide range of studies (Bryant et al., 1990; Chaney, 1992; Goswami & East, 2000; Webster & Plante, 1995) although the relationship appears more robust in nontransparent alphabetic orthographies such as English and Swedish, rather than highly regular alphabetic orthographies such as Norwegian or Italian (Goswami & East, 1999b).

The second dimension of phonological awareness is phonemic awareness—awareness of phonemes as units of sound. Phonemic awareness is particularly relevant in alphabetic scripts and may be uniquely predictive of reading and spelling skill (Lundberg, Olofsson, & Wall, 1980; Perfetti, Beck, Bell, & Hughes, 1987), but develops in a reciprocal relationship with written language skills (Alexander, Anderson, Heilman, Voeller, & Torgesen, 1991; Perfetti et al., 1987; Vandervelden & Siegel, 1995). Introduction to an alphabetic script forces attention on phonemes as processing units; introduction to graphemes provides a hook on which to hang phonemic information. Although programs to increase phonological awareness offer positive benefits to reading and writing development, these programs are even more effective if instruction in the alphabet is included (Adams, 1990; Alexander et al., 1991; Lundberg et al., 1988).

Tasks measuring phonological awareness differ also in their metademands (Vandervelden & Siegel, 1995). Identification tasks (find the odd one out: "pin," "tin," "ball★"; "bun," "bus," "car★") are easier than synthesis or segmentation tasks (e.g., say stop without the "t"). Phoneme manipulation tasks, such as those involved in spoonerism tasks ("shoe-top" > "two-shop"), are the most difficult of all (Catts & Kamhi, 1986; Dodd *et al.*, 1995; Stackhouse & Wells, 1997).

The question "How do children learn to read and write?" is still far from answered here. Goswami and East (2000; p. 65) summarized three causal connections presumed to underpin reading development:

1. A connection between preschool awareness of rhyme and alliteration and later progress in reading and spelling;

2. A connection between instruction at the level of the phoneme and the development of phonemic awareness; and

3. A connection between progress in spelling and progress in reading (and vice versa).

These causal connections are represented in Figure 3.4.

In the view represented here, children come to the task of learning to read and write with preexisting epilinguistic phonological awareness skills and specifically with the ability to segment lexical representations at a subsyllabic level. They receive instruction in an alphabetic script, drawing their attention to the phonemic level of analysis and encouraging metalinguistic development. Children draw on this phonemic awareness in their early attempts to spell and decode and in so doing provide practice for themselves in phonemic segmentation, thus further supporting developments in the second strand in a reciprocal relationship. Underpinning both the first and second strands must be a general phonological segmentation ability, that is, a capacity to segment phonological data at whatever level is required within a specific context. This model thus respects both the endogenous and the exogenous factors outlined earlier.

V. DEVELOPING THE INGREDIENTS

In the Pumfrey and Reason (1991) model outlined in Chapter 2, three domains of development were considered—the learning context, the language context, and the print context. Long before children encounter formal instruction in reading and writing, they are acquiring knowledge and skills related to the learning and language contexts and in the emergent literacy paradigm are also acquiring critical print knowledge. As they receive instruction in an alphabetic orthography, they are faced with specific sound-print matching demands. The causal connections proposed by Goswami and Bryant (1990) and Goswami and East (2000) certainly provide a mechanism for progressing to the alphabetic stage of reading and a semiphonetic or phonetic stage of spelling. However, if reading and writing skills remain at this stage, two crucial difficulties emerge.

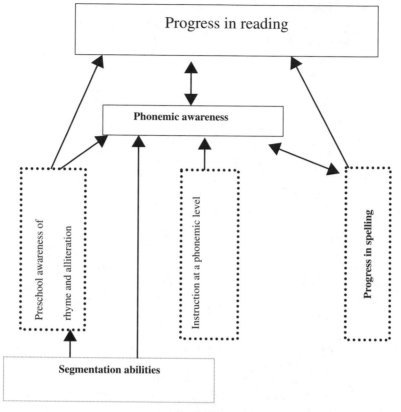

Figure 3.4. Strands of development. Copyright © Martine Smith.

One is that many words encountered will be impossible to decode, because they do not conform to strictly phonetic spelling (e.g., "beak" and "break"; "though," "thought," and "through"). The second is that reading and writing will be extremely slow and effortful. How then can a reader–writer progress to a more fluent, automatic level of competence?

Share (1995) offered one solution, which put simply means that children teach themselves to read and write. The self-teaching hypothesis depends on three factors being present:

1. Letter-sound knowledge so that children can convert graphemic information into phonemic information

2. A basic level of phonological awareness defined by Share as "the ability to recognize identity between learned letter names or sounds and sublexical phonological segments in spoken words" (p. 161)

3. The ability to use contextual information to determine exact pronunciations of partially decoded words

Given this skill mix, Share suggested that children are well positioned to use phonological recoding as a key strategy for dealing with unfamiliar words. As they re-encounter previously decoded words, associations across letter sequences are strengthened, and word-specific print-to-meaning connections are reinforced. Phonological recoding thus functions as a self-teaching mechanism "enabling the learner to acquire the detailed orthographic representations necessary for rapid, autonomous, visual word recognition" (Share, 1995, p. 152). The impact of recoding success is presumed to be item based, rather than stage based. The frequency with which a child has encountered a particular word will influence word recognition, as will the success of previous recoding attempts. Share argued that as connections across letter sequences are strengthened, orthographic patterns can be abstracted, creating the potential for rapid visual word recognition. At the same time, abstracted orthographic patterns become available for further representational restructuring, to incorporate regularities of spelling patterns (e.g., "-ight"), context sensitivity, and positional and morphemic constraints (e.g., "-ed" represents a past-tense morpheme and pronunciation varies across lexical items). The self-teaching mechanism therefore starts with phonological recoding but rapidly incorporates orthographic processes also.

The self-teaching hypothesis has much to recommend it. It fits neatly with Goswami and Bryant's causal connections—phonological awareness, instruction in the alphabet, and reading and spelling experience. Goswami's suggestion that children can use their rhyming abilities to support reading and spelling by analogy (e.g., Goswami & East, 1999a, 1999b; Goswami & East, 2000) is entirely consistent with the self-teaching hypothesis. The hypothesis also implies that frequency of print encounters is critical—the more reading and writing engaged in, the stronger the connections across letter sequences, the greater the number of orthographic patterns that can be abstracted, and the greater the speed of reading. Self-teaching may provide the critical link from a primary reliance on decoding to fluent reading.

Stanovich (1986) coined the phrase "Matthew effects" to describe a cumulative cycle of advantage for good readers, after the Gospel according to Matthew: "Unto every one that hath shall be given, and he shall have abundance; but from him that hath not shall be taken away even that which he hath" (Mt. 25:29). Good readers tend to read a lot. By reading they practice the skills required in reading and so improve their reading. In contrast, poor readers tend to avoid print as much as possible, depriving themselves of the very experience they need to develop skills in reading, into a downward spiral of reading and writing difficulty. If much reading and writing learning derives from self-teaching, then clearly the sheer quantity of opportunities exploited by readers should have a direct effect on their rate of progress and the extent to which they become expert.

VI. SUMMARY

Learning to read and write draws on a complex web of exogenous factors, such as sociocultural expectations, instruction, opportunities, and endogenous resources, including motor, sensory, cognitive, and linguistic skills. From their encounters with literate adults and from their own explorations with print resources, children develop insights into the purpose and characteristics of written language. From their earliest interactions with spoken language, they begin to develop the skills that will serve as a foundation for their reading and writing. Primary among these skills is the ability to consciously attend to the sound properties of language and to perform segmentation and synthesis operations on phonological information. The type of phonological information required depends on the orthographic demands of the target language and on the instructional approach adopted (Holm & Dodd, 1996). Experience with writing and spelling supports explicit awareness of phoneme information. Once a critical mass of skill and instruction has been achieved, children may be in a position to take over, as it were, their own instruction. Phonological recoding skills can provide them with a strategy for decoding unfamiliar words. Sufficient practice in this task with materials that are at a suitable level of difficulty (i.e., are easily comprehended and not overly difficult) provides children with the opportunity to automatize word recognition and to abstract orthographic information (e.g., frequently occurring letter sequences) to support further word identification through morphology- and analogy-based strategies. Opportunities to practice reading and writing, with appropriate materials, are therefore also critical to this process. Finally, underpinning the process are other language skills, such as vocabulary and syntactic abilities.

What started out as largely dissimilar processes—spoken and written language—over time become intimately and reciprocally linked. Written language gradually emerges as a primary source of learning of vocabulary, complex syntax structures, and figurative language. Increased linguistic insights support further reading and writing development. When the process halts or fails to progress, individuals are therefore disadvantaged linguistically, academically, and potentially socially.

REFERENCES

Adams, M. J. (1990). *Beginning to read: Thinking and learning about print.* Cambridge, MA: MIT Press, A Bradford Book.

Alexander, A. W., Anderson, H. G., Heilman, P. C., Voeller, K. K., & Torgesen, J. K. (1991). Phonological awareness training and remediation of analytic decoding deficits in a group of severe dyslexics. *Annals of Dyslexia, 41*, 193–206.

Ball, E. W., & Blachman, B. A. (1991). Does phoneme awareness training in kindergarten make a difference in early word recognition and developmental spelling? *Reading Research Quarterly, 26*, 49–66.

Barker, T., Torgesen, J. K., & Wagner, R. K. (1992). The role of orthographic processing skills on five different reading tasks. *Reading Research Quarterly, 27*, 335–345.

Blachman, B. A. (1983). Are we assessing the linguistic factors critical in early reading? *Annals of Dyslexia, 33*, 91–109.

Blachman, B. A. (1984). Relationship of rapid naming ability and language analysis skill to kindergarten and first grade reading achievement. *Journal of Educational Psychology, 76*, 610–622.

Blachman, B. A., Ball, E. W., Black, R., & Tangel, D. (1994). Kindergarten teachers develop phoneme awareness in low-income, inner-city classrooms: Does it make a difference? *Reading and Writing: An Interdisciplinary Journal, 6*, 1–17.

Bradley, L., & Bryant, P. E. (1983). Categorising sounds and learning to read: A causal connection. *Nature, 310*, 419–421.

Bruck, M., & Treiman, R. (1992). Learning to pronounce words: The limitations of analogies. *Reading Research Quarterly, 27*, 375–388.

Bryant, P. E., Maclean, M., Bradley, L., & Crossland, J. (1990). Rhyme, alliteration, phoneme detection, and learning to read. *Developmental Psychology, 26*, 429–438.

Catts, H., & Kamhi, A. (1986). The linguistic bases of reading disorders: Implications for the speech-language pathologist. *Language, Speech, and Hearing Services in Schools, 17*, 329–341.

Chall, J. (1983). *Stages of reading development.* New York: McGraw-Hill.

Chaney, C. (1992). Language development, metalinguistic skills and print awareness in 3-year-old children. *Applied Psycholinguistics, 13*, 485–514.

Clay, M. M. (1985). *The early detection of reading difficulties.* Portsmouth, NH: Heinemann.

Denckla, M., & Rundel, R. (1976). Naming of object-drawings by dyslexic and other learning disabled children. *Brain and Language, 3*, 1–15.

Dodd, B., & Conn, A. (2000). The effect of Braille orthography on blind children's phonological awareness. *Journal of Research in Reading, 23*, 1–11.

Dodd, B., Gillon, G., Oerlemans, M., Russell, T., Syrmis, M., & Wilson, H. (1995). Phonological disorder and the acquisition of literacy. In B. Dodd (Ed.), *Differential diagnosis and treatment of children with speech disorder.* London: Whurr.

Ehri, L. C. (1991). The development of reading and spelling in children: An overview. In M. Snowling & M. Thomson (Eds.), *Dyslexia: Integrating theory and practice* (pp. 63–79). London: Whurr.

Ehri, L. C. (2000). Learning to read and learning to spell: two sides of a coin. *Topics in Language Disorders, 20*(3), 19–36.

Ellis, N. (1981). Visual and name coding in dyslexic children. *Psychological Research, 43*, 201–219.

Ellis, N. (1993). *Reading, writing and dyslexia: A cognitive analysis* (2nd. ed). Hove, UK: Erlbaum.

Fawcett, A. J., & Nicolson, R. I. (1995). Persistence of phonological awareness deficits in older children with dyslexia. *Reading and Writing: An Interdisciplinary Journal, 7*, 361–376.

Firth, I. (1972). *Components of reading disability.* Unpublished doctoral dissertation, University of New South Wales, Sydney, Australia.

Fowler, A. E. (1991). How early phonological development might set the stage for phoneme awareness. In D. Shankweiler (Ed.), *Phonological processes in literacy* (pp. 97–117). Hillsdale, NJ: Erlbaum.

Fowler, A. E., & Lieberman, I. Y. (1995). The role of phonology and orthography in morphological awareness. In L. B. Feldman (Ed.), *Morphological aspects of language processing* (pp. 189–209). Hillsdale, NJ: Erlbaum.

Galda, L., Cullinan, B., & Strickland, D. (1993). *Language, literacy and the child*. London: Harcourt Brace Jovanovich College.

Gombert, J. E. (1992). *Metalinguistic development*. Hemel Hempstead, Herts. UK: Harvester Wheatsheaf.

Goswami, U. (2000a). Phonological and lexical processes. In M. Kamil, P. Mosenthal, P. D. Pearson, & R. Barr (Eds.), *Handbook of reading research* (pp. 251–268). London: Lawrence Erlbaum Associates.

Goswami, U. (2000b, July). Phonological awareness and reading acquisition in different orthographies. Paper presented at the 27th International Congress of Psychology, Stockholm, Sweden.

Goswami, U., & Bryant, P. E. (1990). *Phonological skills and learning to read*. Hillsdale, NJ: Erlbaum.

Goswami, U., & East, M. (1999a). Integrating orthographic and phonological knowledge as reading develops: Onsets, rimes and analogies in children's reading. In R. Klein & P. McMullen (Eds.), *Converging methods for understanding reading and dyslexia* (pp. 57–75). London: MIT Press.

Goswami, U., & East, M. (1999b). The relationship between phonological awareness and orthographic representation in different orthographies. In M. Harris & A. Hatano (Ed.), *Learning to read and write: A cross-linguistic perspective*. Cambridge, UK: Cambridge University Press.

Goswami, U., & East, M. (2000). Rhyme and analogy in beginning reading: Conceptual and methodological issues. *Applied Psycholinguistics, 21*, 63–93.

Harris, M., & Beech, J. R. (1998). Implicit phonological awareness and early reading development in prelingually deaf children. *Journal of Deaf Studies and Deaf Education, 3*(3), 205–216.

Holm, A., & Dodd, B. (1996). The effect of first written language on the acquisition of English literacy. *Cognition, 59*, 119–147.

Ingram, D. (1989). *First language acquisition*. Cambridge, UK: Cambridge University Press.

Kamhi, A., & Hinton, L. N. (2000). Explaining individual differences in spelling ability. *Topics in Language Disorders, 20*(3), 37–49.

Karmiloff-Smith, A. (1992). *Beyond modularity: A developmental perspective on cognitive science*. Cambridge, MA: MIT Press, A Bradford Book.

Kroll, B. (1981). Developmental relationships between speaking and writing. In B. Kroll & R. Vann (Eds.), *Exploring speaking-writing relationships: Connections and contrasts*. (pp. 32–54). Champaign, IL: National Council of Teachers of English.

Locke, J. L. (1995). *The child's path to spoken language*. Cambridge, MA: Harvard University Press.

Lundberg, I., Frost, J., & Petersen, O. (1988). Effects of an extensive program for stimulating phonological awareness in preschool children. *Reading Research Quarterly, 23*, 263–284.

Lundberg, I., Olofsson, A., & Wall, S. (1980). Reading and spelling in the first school years predicted from phonemic awareness skills in kindergarten. *Scandinavian Journal of Psychology, 21*, 159–173.

Maclean, M., Bryant, P. E., & Bradley, L. (1987). Rhymes, nursery rhymes and reading in early childhood. *Merrill-Palmer Quarterly, 33*, 255–282.

McBride-Chang, C., & Suk-Han Ho, C. (2000, July). Predicting beginning reading in Chinese and English: A two-year longitudinal study of Chinese kindergartners. Paper presented at the 27th International Congress of Psychology, Stockholm, Sweden.

Metsala, J. L., & Walley, A. C. (1998). Spoken vocabulary growth and the segmental restructuring of lexical representations: Precursors to phonemic awareness and early reading ability. In J. L. Metsala & L. C. Ehri (Eds.), *Word recognition in beginning literacy* (pp. 89–120). Hillsdale, NJ: Erlbaum.

Morais, J., Bertelson, P., Cary, L., & Alegria, J. (1986). Literacy training and speech segmentation. *Cognition, 24*, 45–64.

Morais, J., Cary, L., Alegria, J., & Bertelson, P. (1979). Does awareness of speech as a sequence of phonemes arise spontaneously? *Cognition, 17*, 323–331.

Morais, J., Content, A., Bertelson, P., & Cary, L. (1988). Is there a critical period for the acquisition of segmental analysis? *Cognitive Neuropsychology, 5*(3), 347–352.

Morais, J., Content, A., Cary, L., & Mehler, J. (1989). Syllabic segmentation and literacy. *Language and Cognitive Processes, 4*(1), 57–67.

Morais, J., & Kolinsky, R. (1994). Perception and awareness in phonological awareness: the case of the phoneme. *Cognition, 50*(3), 287–297.

Nagy, W. E., & Herman, P. A. (1987). Breadth and depth of vocabulary knowledge: implications for acquisition and instruction. In M. McKeown & M. Curtis (Eds.), *The nature of vocabulary acquisition* (pp. 19–35). Hillsdale, NJ: Erlbaum.

Nagy, W. E., & Scott, J. (2000). Vocabulary processes. In M. Kamil, P. Mosenthal, P. D. Pearson, & R. Barr (Eds.), *Handbook of reading research* (Vol. 3, pp. 269–284). London: Erlbaum.

Nation, K., & Snowling, M. (2000). Factors influencing syntactic awareness skills in normal readers and poor comprehenders. *Applied Psycholinguistics, 21*, 229–241.

Nippold, M., Allen, M., & Kirsch, D. (2001). Proverb comprehension as a function of reading proficiency in preadolescents. *Language Speech and Hearing Services in Schools, 32*, 90–100.

Perfetti, C. A., Beck, I., Bell, L., & Hughes, C. (1987). Phonemic knowledge and learning to read are reciprocal: A longitudinal study of first grade children. *Merrill-Palmer Quarterly, 33*, 283–319.

Pumfrey, P. D., & Reason, R. (1991). *Specific learning difficulties: Challenges and responses.* Berks, UK: NFER-Nelson.

Rodenborn, L. V., & Washburn, E. (1974). Some implications of new basal readers. *Elementary English, 51*, 885–888.

Scarborough, H. S. (1998). Early identification of children at risk for reading disabilities: Phonological awareness and some other promising predictors. In P. Accardo, A. Capute, & B. Shapiro (Eds.), *Specific reading disability: A review of the spectrum* (pp. 75–119). Timonium, MD: York Press.

Scribner, S. (1997). *Mind and social practice: Selected writings of Sylvia Scribner.* Cambridge, UK: Cambridge University Press.

Shankweiler, D., & Crain, S. (1986). *Language mechanisms and reading disorder: A modular approach.* New Haven, CT: Status Report on Speech Research, Haskins Laboratories.

Share, D. L. (1995). Phonological recoding and self-teaching: *Sine qua non* of reading acquisition. *Cognition, 55*, 151–218.

Silva, P., Williams, S., & McGee, R. (1987). A longitudinal study of children with developmental language delay at age 3: Later intelligence, reading and behaviour problems. *Developmental Medicine and Child Neurology, 29*, 630–640.

Singer, B. (1995). Written language development and disorders: Selected principles, patterns and intervention possibilities. *Topics in Language Disorders, 16*(1), 83–98.

Stackhouse, J., & Wells, B. (1997). *Children's speech and literacy difficulties: A psycholinguistic framework.* London: Whurr.

Stanovich, K. (1986). Matthew effects in reading: Some consequences of individual differences in the acquisition of literacy. *Reading Research Quarterly, 21*, 360–407.

Teale, W., & Sulzby, E. (1987). Literacy acquisition in early childhood: The roles of access and mediation in storybook telling. In D. A. Wagner (Ed.), *The future of literacy in a changing world* (pp. 111–130). New York: Pergamon Press.

Teale, W., & Sulzby, E. (1989). Emergent literacy: New perspectives on young children's reading and writing. In D. Strickland & L. M. Morrow (Eds.), *Emerging literacy: Young children learn to read and write* (pp. 1–15). Newark, DE: International Reading Association.

Templeton, S. (2002, Feb 19). Spelling: Logical, learnable—and critical. *The ASHA Leader*, pp. 4–5.

Templeton, S., & Morris, D. (2000). Spelling. In M. Kamil, P. Mosenthal, P. D. Pearson, & R. Barr (Eds.), *Handbook of reading research* (Vol. 3, pp. 525–543). Mahwah, NJ: Erlbaum.

Treiman, R., & Bourassa, D. (2000a). Children's written and oral spelling. *Applied Psycholinguistics, 21*, 183–204.

Treiman, R., & Bourassa, D. (2000b). The development of spelling skill. *Topics in Language Disorders, 20*(3), 1–18.

Tunmer, W. E., & Hoover, W. A. (1992). Cognitive and linguistic factors in learning to read. In P. Gough, L. C. Ehri, & R. Treiman (Eds.), *Reading acquisition* (Vol. X, pp. 175–214). Hillsdale, NJ: Erlbaum.

Vandervelden, M., & Siegel, L. (1995). Phonological encoding and phoneme awareness in early literacy: A developmental approach. *Reading Research Quarterly, 30,* 854–875.

Wagner, R. K., Torgesen, J. K., Rashotte, C. A., Hecht, S. S., Barker, T. A., Burgess, S. R., Donahue, J., *et al.* (1997). Changing relations between phonological processing abilities and word-level reading as children develop from beginning to skilled readers: A 5-year longitudinal study. *Developmental Psychology, 33,* 468–479.

Webster, P. E., & Plante, A. S. (1995). Productive phonology and phonological awareness in preschool children. *Applied Psycholinguistics, 16,* 43–57.

CHAPTER 4

Literacy and Augmentative and Alternative Communication

I. INTRODUCTION

One of the issues about which there is virtually complete agreement is that there is no "typical" user of augmentative and alternative communication (AAC). Even among individuals with apparently similar levels of physical abilities, individual and unique profiles of perceptual, cognitive, linguistic, and sociocommunicative abilities, not to mention attention preferences, motivation, and personal interests combine to thwart attempts to make generalizations. Furthermore, the number of individuals with severe congenital speech impairments is relatively small, so that much of what we have learned about the challenges and successes of the literacy experiences of such individuals is based on the study of small numbers of individuals or individual case studies. Study findings often conflict, further muddying the waters. In this chapter, we review some of what is currently understood about the potential influences on literacy learning for individuals using AAC. These influences may be both intrinsic to individuals who use AAC and extrinsic, in their home and learning environments. Many of the experiences of young users of AAC are different from those of their naturally speaking peers. However, it is important to dispel the myth that severe speech difficulties preclude the development of literacy skills and, equally, the myth that severe speech difficulties do not affect the literacy learning process. Clearly, it is impossible to predict the typical path followed by an AAC user learning to read and write, although we do know some common pitfalls along the way, pitfalls that in general are much the same as those awaiting typically developing children. Consider, for example, the following two adults, who both have severe congenital speech impairments.

II. CASE EXAMPLES

Angela is 43 years old. She has severe *dysarthria*, with reported speech production abilities that seem to be variably available to her, but typically only when she is completely relaxed, lying on her bed. Most of the time, Angela produces almost no vocalization at all. Based on assessment of her letter knowledge, her ability to spell many words, and her self-reports of good literacy skills, Angela was provided with a laptop computer with word prediction software accessed via a head switch to augment her expressive communication. Angela clearly enjoys her laptop, but her use of it is extremely limited. Within a group of individuals with similar communication difficulties, she does not spontaneously contribute to any discussions and requires considerable prompting to respond to group questions. When Angela fails to respond to a conversational initiative, it is often difficult to determine why. It could be that she simply cannot think of a conversational contribution. Perhaps she has something she wishes to say but is unable to spell the message. Alternatively, she may be experiencing difficulty in seeing the screen or in accessing her switch. She may be fatigued, or her switch may have moved out of optimal position. It may be the software that is causing the problem, or she may be having difficulty understanding the scanning process. It may be that she simply does not like the voice output from the laptop and so chooses not to use it for expressive communication. Perhaps by the time she has the message planned, and has initiated the motor access process, she simply has forgotten what she intended to say. Angela presents something of a puzzle then, apparently confident about her literacy skills, but very limited in her ability to use those skills for functional communication.

Stephen is younger than Angela, and he also has severe dysarthria/anarthria. He uses a device that uses Minspeak™ for expressive communication, accessed by a head-switch. He is extremely familiar with his device, having used it for more than 10 years. However, despite knowing most of the codes of his Minspeak™ program, he typically relies on spelling for expressive communication—even when use of Minspeak™ would be quicker, more efficient, less physically tiring, and equally transparent, from the point of view of communication. In other words, Stephen relies on use of his literacy skills for communication, even though this strategy has a negative effect on his rate of communication and therefore potentially limits his opportunities to communicate. However, he uses his literacy skills only for expressive communication. He describes himself as a poor reader, but has indicated that he does not wish to develop his reading skills further. He cannot recall how he started to develop spelling skills (although he does not attribute much credit to his school education experiences), and in this respect he is unable to point us in a direction that might support intervention with other individuals who have similar difficulties.

Angela and Stephen present contrasting profiles with Angela apparently underutilizing her spelling skills for communication and Stephen over-relying on his abilities in this area, although both share an emphasis on the encoding rather than decoding aspects of written language. In one respect, Angela and Stephen are somewhat exceptional—they have achieved a level of literacy that is potentially adequate to support expressive communication. For many individuals who use AAC, such levels of competence remain elusive. Despite the heterogeneity of individuals involved, it is possible to speculate on possible factors common to the experiences of many individuals using AAC that may conspire to make the process of learning to read and write more difficult than the process for their naturally speaking peers. Smith and Blischak (1997) referred to the intrinsic and extrinsic factors that must be taken into consideration.

III. INTRINSIC FACTORS TO CONSIDER

Intrinsic factors can be broadly divided into four areas of potential difficulty: physical, sensory/perceptual, linguistic, and cognitive. Here, it is important to bear in mind the fact that many AAC users have multiple impairments. In many instances, severe speech impairments are associated with underlying brain damage. Probably the largest group of individuals using aided communication are individuals with congenital physical impairments, arising from cerebral palsy (von Tetzchner & Martinsen, 2000). Neurological damage is rarely selective. Several aspects of functioning may be impaired, each aspect of which alone, or in combination with other impairments, may hamper literacy development.

A. Physical Impairment

Cerebral palsy refers to a group of motor disorders arising from damage to the central nervous system before, at, or shortly after birth (McDonald, 1987).

The level of physical impairment varies greatly, from a general clumsiness to extremely limited physical motor control, perhaps of only eye or head movements. The range of additional impairments associated with cerebral palsy is also very varied, and for many individuals the motor impairment is but one of a range of challenges they face in their daily lives.

Rutter (1987) noted that children with cerebral palsy show a high rate of reading problems. Schonell (1956) reported a clear and negative correlation between extent of physical impairment and reading achievement. Although it is clear that simply having adequate motor control is not sufficient to guarantee literacy learning, physical exploration of the world is an important avenue of learning for young children (Piaget, 1977). From an early age, children with physical impairments are constrained by limited opportunities to interact with the environment, severely restricting their sensorimotor experiences (Carlson, 1987). They are often unable to independently seek out books, turn pages, scribble with pencils and crayons, and interact directly with early literacy experiences. Thus, the physical impairment may constitute a first link in a chain of second-order effects, including reduced opportunities for stimulation and interaction, restricted experiences, and changed expectations for educational placement and achievement. These constraints, along with the increased time demand for activities of daily living, often result in decreased emphasis on literacy experiences and development for children with physical impairments (Light & Kelford-Smith, 1993).

B. Sensory/Perceptual Impairment

1. Visual Impairment

The printed word must initially be accessed through visual processing. It is clear that visual acuity difficulties will have a major effect on the print information available to a beginning reader. There is additional evidence that children with severe visual impairments may experience restricted opportunities for sensorimotor interactions. They may also encounter differences in linguistic experiences that are important in the development of literacy (Locke, 1997). Many individuals who use AAC have atypical visual abilities. Individuals with cerebral palsy are particularly vulnerable to visual impairments. Erhardt (1990) suggested that the incidence of visual impairments may be as high as 60%, with a range of visuomotor and visuoperceptual impairments. Other reports proposed estimates ranging from 15% to 92% (Duckman, 1987). Marozas and May (1985) compared the visuomotor and visuoperceptual performance of 24 children with cerebral palsy to that of typically developing, age-matched peers and found that the typically developing children outperformed the children with cerebral palsy on all aspects assessed. They further found that reversing the color of black and white figure and ground materials significantly enhanced the performance of the children with cerebral palsy but not that of their peers. Dorman (1985) likewise referred to specific perceptual and visuomotor difficulties in a case study.

Vision must also be considered as a function of the integration of eye function, physical positioning, and cognitive interpretation. In other words, vision is itself a complex activity. Intact ocular function does not automatically yield effective vision. Poor positioning or limited head control may significantly and negatively affect the visual field available to individuals with additional motor impairments, and assessment may yield inconclusive results. Access to orthography relies on effective and intact visual abilities, hence the importance of being aware of potential impairments in this area.

The relationship between visual processing and reading is complex. Whereas vision acts as the gateway to orthography, the process of reading also influences visuomotor patterns (Rayner, 1999). When both reading and visual processing difficulties are present, uncovering the direction of causality is difficult. For example, in an early study involving adults with cerebral palsy, disordered eye movements were found to impair reading rate but not text comprehension (Jones *et al.*, 1966). Abnormal eye movements, coupled with difficulty maintaining postural control of the head and neck in children with cerebral palsy, may increase visual perceptual difficulties as well (Katayama & Tamas, 1987). However, it is important to remember that eye movement patterns are at least as likely to *reflect* difficulties processing text (i.e., be a consequence of reading difficulty) rather than actually causing reading disruption (Rayner, 1999).

2. Hearing Impairment

Like visual impairment, the effects of hearing impairment on literacy development are well documented (Grushkin, 1998; Harris & Beech, 1998). The typical congenitally or postnatally deafened (before age 2) child achieves reading skills at or around the third to fourth grade level and demonstrates dramatic differences in producing written language, compared with his or her hearing peers (Harris & Beech, 1998). Experience with auditory language lies at the very heart of reading development and, as such, is very reduced or unavailable for deaf children. Hearing children internalize spoken language, gaining real-world knowledge that provides a base for top-down reading. Deaf children do not have access to auditory language and its associated experiential, cognitive, and linguistic skills. Thus, for deaf children, learning to read serves also to build experience "and to support cognitive development and language learning" (King & Quigley, 1985, p. xi).

Deaf individuals are also expected to have difficulty with bottom–up reading processes that depend upon knowledge of the sound structure of the spoken language. Recent evidence has shown, however, that some individuals with prelingual, profound deafness can demonstrate skill in phonological awareness (Hanson, 1991; Hanson & Fowler, 1987; Sterne & Goswami, 2000), although there is no clear evidence that they make use of these skills in learning to read in a way comparable to that of their hearing peers (Grushkin, 1998). Many individuals using AAC have hearing impairments. Siegenthaler (1987) reviewed a number of studies of the incidence of hearing difficulties in individuals with cerebral palsy and reported estimates varying from 25% to 41%, compared with an incidence of 2.5% to 3% in the general population. Severity of hearing loss may vary greatly, as may the type of loss present. However, the high incidence suggests that individuals using AAC are vulnerable to reduced access to phonological information and hence may lack critical information for reading and writing development.

C. COMMUNICATION DIFFICULTIES

1. Language Difficulties

The vast majority of children with specific reading difficulties also have difficulty processing and producing spoken language (Goldsworthy, 1996; Nation & Snowling, 2000; Stackhouse, 2000). Many aspects of language are vulnerable—semantic, syntactic, phonologic, and metalinguistic (Catts & Kamhi, 1986; Flax, Realpe, Hirsch, Nawyn, & Tallal, 2001; Gallagher, Frith, & Snowling, 2000; Snowling, 2000). Individuals with cerebral palsy and many other individuals who use AAC are also vulnerable to language difficulties, especially vocabulary and/or morphological deficits, which is a recurring theme across a range of studies (Berninger & Gans, 1986; Bishop, Byers-Brown, & Robson, 1990; Blockberger, 1997; Smith, 2001; Sutton, Soto, & Blockberger, 2002). As discussed in the last chapter, such impairments create further challenges in learning to read and write.

2. Speech Impairment

Severe speech impairment has long been a focus of interest as a potential causative factor in the failure to achieve appropriate literacy levels, with particular interest in the investigation of a link between severe speech impairment and phonological awareness skills (Bishop, 1985; Bishop et al., 1990; Bishop & Robson, 1989; Dahlgren Sandberg, 2001; Dahlgren-Sandberg & Hjelmquist, 1996a, 1996b, 1997, 2002; Foley, 1989, 1993; Foley & Pollatsek, 1999; Vandervelden & Siegel, 1997, 1999, 2001). Although some individuals with severe speech impairments demonstrate skill in phonological awareness, results from the various studies remain inconclusive. The majority of studies report disproportionate difficulties with phonological processing, particularly among individuals with congenital speech impairments. However, phonological working memory seems to be emerging as being especially vulnerable to constraints arising from lack of availability of subvocal rehearsal. It only takes one Christopher Nolan (Nolan, 1987) to dispel any notion that reading and writing difficulties are an inevitable consequence of a severe speech impairment. The fact that there are a number of individuals who have significant speech difficulties and nonetheless achieve literacy skills that are impressive by any standards indicates that speech production is not itself essential to learning to read and write. In fact, what has traditionally probably been the most popular explanation for the prevalence of literacy difficulties in this group turns out to be the least likely candidate. Before leaving the question of speech and language impairments, it is worthwhile exploring the potential overlap between these two domains of functioning.

Across the range of studies of the language abilities of individuals with severe congenital speech impairments, two domains of functioning have perhaps stood out—performance on phonological awareness tasks and measures of vocabulary. Although by no means do all individuals using AAC have vocabulary difficulties, nonetheless many studies (Berninger & Gans, 1986; Bishop *et al.*, 1990; Bishop & Robson, 1989; Dahlgren-Sandberg & Hjelmquist, 1997; Smith, 1989, 2001) have reported unexpectedly low vocabulary scores, particularly for individuals with congenital speech impairments. Stackhouse and Wells (1997) proposed that an intact speech processing system is fundamental to the development of both spoken and written language and also to the development of phonological awareness, as illustrated in Figure 4.1 below. Difficulties within the speech processing system therefore will have an impact not only on the development of phonological awareness but also on the analysis, segmentation, and

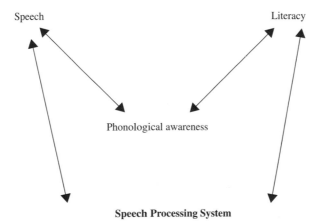

Figure 4.1. Speech processing. (Adapted from Stackhouse, J., & Wells, B. (1997). *Children's speech and literacy difficulties: A psycholinguistic framework* (p. 58). London: Whurr.)

representation of the phonological structure of the incoming speech stream. Difficulties in segmentation and analysis may make it difficult to identify, analyze, represent, or retain novel phonological information the processes recruited in learning new vocabulary. The same processing difficulties may emerge on tasks tapping phonological awareness. A common underlying deficit in speech processing may therefore manifest in superficially different domains of development. In Stackhouse and Wells's (1997) model, the relationship between speech processing and speech and literacy development is unidirectional. It seems plausible that the relationship may also be bidirectional (Figure 4.1). The potential for subvocal rehearsal may support the functioning of the speech processing system. Certain aspects of speech processing may benefit from such rehearsal, particularly if phonological memory demands are implicated in the tasks. Vocabulary and phonological awareness difficulties reported for individuals with severe congenital speech impairments may share a common link arising from the speech processing system. This hypothesis will be explored further when assessment approaches are considered.

D. COGNITIVE IMPAIRMENT

The presence of a cognitive impairment may create pervasive developmental delays, affecting physical, sensory/perceptual, and/or linguistic abilities and may also coexist with other impairments. Studies have reported that approximately 60% to 70% of children with cerebral palsy, for example, demonstrate some degree of cognitive impairment (Koppenhaver & Yoder, 1992a). Impairments of specific cognitive abilities, such as attention and memory (McDonald, 1987) have also been reported (Parker, 1987). Learning to read and write requires cognitive application. Learning difficulties, whether general and pervasive or specific, will significantly affect the ease with which individuals negotiate the road to literacy and will probably influence, at least to some extent, the distance they travel along that road. However, it is important to note that assessing cognitive functioning of individuals with significant communication and physical impairments is extremely difficult, and analysis of findings must always be tempered with caution. In addition, the relationship between "intelligence" and reading is still open to question (Stanovich, 1991) and is unlikely to be linear and unidirectional.

From these various explorations, the evidence suggests that many AAC users are at risk for the influence of a range of intrinsic factors that may interact in complex ways to impede literacy development. However, there may be further interactions with factors extrinsic to the individual (such as reduced language input to a child with little or no functional speech), creating a complex web of first- and second-order effects. In the previous chapter, it was pointed out that very few individuals, if any, "acquire" the ability to read and write without explicit modeling and instruction and opportunities to practice. We now examine research that has shifted the focus to extrinsic factors that might be contributing to the reported deficits in literacy.

IV. EXTRINSIC FACTORS TO CONSIDER

A. HOME ENVIRONMENT

From emergent literacy research we know that children learn to read and write through active participation in meaningful, functional literacy activities, such as storytelling and nursery rhyme games (Clay, 1991; Teale & Sulzby, 1987, 1989). Adults and children commonly engage in prolonged discussions about what has been read, an activity that, although involving repetition, goes far beyond a mere repetitious exercise. Children internalize these dialogues and engage in *protoreading*, a constructive process of orally recreating the story, facilitating progression ultimately to conventional literacy. Typically, AAC users have less time available for participation in these types of activities (Light & Kelford-Smith, 1993) and when they do, their experiences may be very different from those of peers. It is extraordinarily difficult to maintain an interactive dialogue while one is simultaneously positioning a child who has high physical dependency needs and managing reading materials. Similar practical difficulties are encountered in trying to get the child to engage in writing activities, which require an even greater degree of motor skill. Coordinating physical positioning and writing materials and encouraging independent writing activities at the same time stretch the abilities of even the most skilled facilitators.

Further, parental priorities for children who use AAC may emphasize other aspects of development over literacy. In Light and Kelford-Smith's study (1993), parents of typically developing preschool children considered learning to read and write to be second in importance only to making friends and learning to communicate effectively. Parents of preschool AAC users from similar family groups placed learning to communicate effectively as the most important priority. Independent mobility, feeding, and toilet-training came next on the list. The lowest priority was given to reading and writing. Very similar patterns were reported by Light and McNaughton (1993) in a study of older AAC users (older than 9 years of age). Only 9 of 59 students (15%) were able to read the newspaper or more complex texts and almost a quarter (24%) of the parents indicated that they did not expect any improvement in their children's current level of literacy by age 25. This extension of different priorities beyond the preschool years suggests a life-span effect of differing expectations and priorities. Coleman (1992) referred to the cumulative effects of reduced opportunities for active participation, lower expectations, and different priorities as an equation summing to "literacy lost." However, Dahlgren-Sandberg (1998) explored the home and school literacy experiences and expectations of 35 children using AAC and reported no differences in the home literacy experiences or values and priority given to literacy achievement for children using AAC, compared with either matched typically developing peers or children with intellectual impairments. As with many studies of individuals using AAC, homogeneity of the early literacy experience seems to be the pattern least likely to emerge.

B. School Environment

For most students, school is the primary context for formal literacy instruction. Although much can be done in preparation at home, much can also be compensated for in a school environment, which provides a knowledgeable and enthusiastic teacher to guide, an environment that encourages social interaction around books, a structure that allows students to make choices about what they will do with books, and the time and materials to allow students to read and respond to what they read (Galda, Cullinan, & Strickland, 1993; Smith & Blischak, 1997). Practice in reading is one of the best predictors of reading ability (Anderson, Wilson, & Fielding, 1988; Galda et al., 1993). Instruction may be particularly crucial in developing alphabetic insight, whereas opportunities to practice reading and writing independently provide the launch pad for the transition to the fluency stage of reading, particularly within the paradigm of the self-teaching hypothesis (Share, 1995) discussed in Chapter 3.

AAC users may require extra practice in learning to read, simply to survive educationally. Furthermore, given the many challenges AAC users face, it is likely that explicit instruction on the specific skills involved in reading and writing is essential. In reality, they sometimes receive even less instructional time than their peers. Koppenhaver and Yoder (1992b, 1993) reviewed a number of studies of classroom literacy instruction time available to students with speech impairments and concluded that substantial proportions of instructional time may be lost to noninstructional activities, such as transportation within and between rooms, feeding, toileting, and therapies. Koppenhaver (1991) reported that students spent more time on nonliteracy activities (up to 38%) than on any single literacy activity during their literacy instruction time. Much of the time lost in such situations resulted from equipment breakdown or set-up time. Additional time may be spent also in trying to resolve communication problems and/or breakdowns.

In the same study, Koppenhaver (1991) reported that the instructional focus during the period of observation was primarily geared toward words and sentences in isolation, fill-in-the-blank exercises, and spelling practice and seldom included writing more than sentence-length passages or reading more than paragraphs. As Koppenhaver and Yoder (1992a) pointed out, research with naturally speaking children has shown these to be the least effective strategies for improving literacy. Far more effective strategies involve building background knowledge, setting purposes for reading (generic, specific, and student-generated), and using easy materials and tasks. There is now also a substantial body of research indicating the value of including explicit instruction in phonemic awareness as part of literacy programs (Adams, 1990; Goswami, 2000).

Comparable issues arise in relation to generation of written output. As outlined in Chapter 3, evidence to date suggests that, for most children, writing provides an important learning context to support the development of insights into the nature of the orthographic code and its relationship to the sound structure of language. For individuals with severe motor impairments, providing opportunities for independent writing experiences is challenging. Often, technology must be recruited, with each type requiring time to set up, try, evaluate, and maintain. Even when effective technologies have been identified, it is extremely difficult to replicate the rate of composition achieved by individuals with no motor impairments. Whereas a fluent writer may generate 40 to 60 words per minute (DeCoste, 1997), far slower rates of composition are typical for most aided communicators. For example, Kelford-Smith, Thurston, Light, Parnes, & O'Keefe (1989) reported that on average the six adults with whom they worked produced 0.7 to 3.3 words per minute. Although techniques such as word prediction can speed writing rates and reduce physical effort, such techniques also impose cognitive demands and require a certain level of literacy attainment before they can become useful. The sheer effort involved in generating written output makes it very difficult for individuals with severe motor impairments to produce anything like the amount of text available to their physically able peers, thus further constraining their literacy learning opportunities.

Therefore, for individuals using AAC, many factors seem to conspire to make the task of achieving literacy skills difficult. On the other hand, it also seems clear that the task is not insurmountable. The need to use an AAC system does not *explain* difficulties in reading and writing.

V. INGREDIENTS OF LITERACY FOR AAC USERS

Pumfrey and Reason (1991) proposed that three contexts provide the crucial ingredients for learning to read: the learning context, the language context, and the print context. Factors both intrinsic and extrinsic to AAC users may combine to alter the ingredient mix available to them, as they attempt to learn to read and write.

A. The Learning Context

The learning context encompasses our cognitive set and purpose, our expectations of a text, and the knowledge we bring to an encounter with text (Pumfrey & Reason, 1991). It encompasses the sociocultural context of literacy learning, the potential roles assigned to written language, and the value placed on the written word within that context. Written language plays the same roles for individuals using AAC that it does for their typically developing peers within their social environment. However, in addition to these traditional roles (such as education and recreation), learning to read and write opens up new possibilities for communication for AAC users, providing access to an open-ended system, with infinite possibilities. Being literate yields new leisure opportunities for individuals who otherwise may have very limited options available to them. Access to employment for individuals with disabilities is more difficult than for their peers. Without literacy skills, many individuals using AAC face an insurmountable challenge. For individuals with acquired communication difficulties, written language skills may be the main way of demonstrating their competence and establishing or maintaining continuity with their former social roles. Taking all these factors into account, it is clear that the motivation and conscious expectations of learning to read and write may be even more salient for individuals using AAC than for natural speakers.

The home, school, and community experiences of individuals using AAC may differ in important ways from the experiences of typically developing peers. The research outlined earlier in this chapter is summarized here:

1. AAC users may have less time available for participation in early literacy experiences (Light & Kelford-Smith, 1993).

2. Lower priority may be attached to reading for children with severe speech and physical impairments compared with that for their typically developing peers (Dahlgren-Sandberg, 1998; Light & Kelford-Smith, 1993).

3. Young AAC users are less able to directly access literacy activities and participate actively (Coleman, 1992; Light & Kelford-Smith, 1993).

4. Students may spend more time in nonliteracy activities than in any single literacy activity during their literacy instruction time (Koppenhaver, 1991; Mike, 1995).

5. Substantial proportions of literacy instruction time may be lost to non-instructional activities (Koppenhaver & Yoder, 1992b).

6. Discussions with AAC users suggested that at least some individuals are more interested in learning to write than in learning to read and may engage primarily with encoding rather than decoding tasks (Smith, 2003).

B. The Language Context

Pumfrey and Reason (1991) suggested that, as reading involves the construction of meaning from print, language and communication skills are fundamental to the connection between the author and the reader. They suggested also that not only facility with the structure of language but also facility with the purposes of language could be used to provide a scaffold for the construction of meaning. The language and communication experiences of individuals using AAC are clearly different from those of their naturally speaking peers. Performance constraints limit the extent to which we can make inferences about underlying competencies of AAC users, but a range of performance characteristics suggests that many individuals may experience difficulty either developing or demonstrating competence in language and communication skills considered crucial to literacy development.

1. Communication/Interaction

Several differences in communication/interaction between aided communicators and their naturally speaking peers emerge:

1. Aided communicators tend to interact less than their naturally speaking peers (Kraat, 1987; Smith, 1998), so that their overall communication opportunities are often reduced, relative to those of their peers.

2. Aided communicators are generally less successful than naturally speaking partners at taking the initiative in conversation (Basil, 1992; Buzolich & Wiemann, 1988; Light, Collier, & Parnes, 1985b; Udwin & Yule, 1991).

Naturally speaking partners tend to dominate interactions (Björck-Åkesson, 1990; Harris, 1982; von Tetzchner & Martinsen, 1996), so that AAC users may have limited opportunities to develop skills in conversation strategies and general discourse conventions and management. These skills provide a foundation for extended dialogue, both spoken and written. In addition, aided communicators may have few opportunities to make extended contributions within a dialogue and hence have little opportunity to develop "spoken" narrative skills. Such spoken narrative skills may provide an important base for later written language development.

2. Language Purposes/Communicative Functions

Many aided communicators use formal communication systems that differ substantially from the usual communication systems within their environment (typically spoken language). In this scenario, an aided communication system may play a fundamentally different role than spoken language in conversation, being used primarily to suggest a topic that is subsequently expanded through a series of question-answer sequences with a naturally speaking partner (von Tetzchner & Martinsen, 1996). Unaided modalities, such as gesture, facial expression, or vocalization, may be dominant in most interactions. Several generalizations regarding the purposes/functions of language emerge:

1. The purposes for which AAC users use linguistic production may differ greatly from the purposes typically assumed for spoken language (Smith, 1991, 1998).

2. A restricted range of communicative functions may be fulfilled linguistically (Light, 1988; Light, Collier, & Parnes, 1985a).

3. External vocabulary constraints may interact in complex ways to limit potential experiences of a wide range of language purposes (Smith, 1998).

3. Language Structures

In both top-down and interactive models of reading, considerable importance is placed on a reader's ability to use knowledge of language structure to support predictions within texts, to resolve ambiguities, and to support comprehension. Inferring competence in syntax and morphology for individuals who cannot speak is extremely difficult, because of the complexity of the communication demands imposed by rate constraints, vocabulary restrictions and an atypical communication mode, often lacking in morphological markers in the first place. The output of many aided communicators is characterized by the following:

1. A reliance on single word utterances (Basil, 1992; Iacono, Mirenda, & Beukelman, 1993; Kraat, 1991; Spiegel, Benjamin, & Spiegel, 1993; Udwin & Yule, 1990; von Tetzchner & Martinsen, 1996).

2. A developmentally slow transition to multiterm utterances, with an apparent lack of development of internal structure (Blockberger & Sutton, 2003; Smith, 1998; Udwin & Yule, 1990; van Balkom & Donker-Gimbrére, 1996; von Tetzchner & Martinsen, 1996).

3. Atypical word-order output, compared with spoken language expectations, reflecting a possible topic-comment organization (Hjelmquist & Dahlgren-Sandberg, 1996; Light et al., 1985a; von Tetzchner & Martinsen, 1996).

However, whether the apparent structural differences in output reflect underlying differences in organization of linguistic structure or occur in response to other interaction constraints cannot yet be resolved and may differ among individual AAC users. Regardless of whether these differences reflect primarily competence or performance constraints, lack of expressive experience with a range of linguistic structures may have implications for the development of skills in the domain of language structure and hence have relevance for the development of written language competence.

C. The Print Context

In Pumfrey and Reason's (1991) terms, the print context represents the written symbol forms used, their relationship to the target spoken language, information about conventional orthographic patterns, and understanding about the conventions of print—spacing, punctuation, orientation, and so on. In a nontransparent alphabetic script, such as English, print knowledge includes knowledge about how graphemes represent sound, knowledge about how words are represented, and knowledge about how these two dimensions relate to each other (e.g., that "-ed" is used to represent past tense, regardless of the phonetic production of the target word).

As with the learning and the language/communication contexts discussed above, the print context ingredients may have a slightly different flavor for individuals using AAC, compared with their naturally speaking peers. However, these different flavors may serve as an advantage to AAC users more in the print context than in the other contexts discussed. Individuals with congenital speech impairments who use aided communication may, from a very early age, interface relatively intensively with print forms for communication purposes. Learning to read and write an alphabetic script presupposes conscious attention to the form and the content of a message. Use of graphic symbols for communication externalizes the content-form distinction, making symbols available for inspection right from the start. Nonspeech symbol formats may foster a precocious meta-awareness of aspects of linguistic organization, for example, metalinguistic awareness at the word level (Rankin, Harwood, & Mirenda, 1994).

Early communication boards are often composed primarily of symbols for important content words, most typically comprising graphic symbols and associated written labels. Communication board users or those using graphic symbols on speech generating devices are therefore consistently exposed to pairings of symbols and words. Preliminary evidence from children receiving articulation training that incorporated printed words below target stimulus pictures (Stewart, Gonzalez, & Page, 1997) suggests that incidental learning of sight vocabulary is possible with very little exposure (two to four 45-minute sessions). It seems reasonable to suggest that comparable incidental learning opportunities are potentially available to individuals exposed to symbols paired with written labels, provided the written label is perceivable.

There may also be aspects of symbol use that foster the development of metacognitive strategies that can later bootstrap the acquisition of reading and writing abilities. McNaughton and Lindsay (1995) proposed that a distinction should be made between two types of structure in graphic symbols or in their terms, graphic representational systems:

- In *Type One* symbols, each symbol's representation relates to the *visual appearance* of its referent. It is a *picture* (that) matches its referent's salient visual features.
- *Type Two* symbols relate to domains other than visual appearance (phonological or semantic) and portray meaning by the sequencing of their component parts and the logic or rules by which the component parts are ordered, both intrasymbols (components or letters) and intersymbols (within phrases and sentences). (p. 219)

Many commonly used, highly iconic picture sets, such as Picture Communication Symbols (Mayer Johnson, 1981, 1985), come under the category of Type One symbols. The *pictures* in these symbol sets are designed to represent a visual gestalt and cannot be divided into component parts. In contrast, Blissymbols (Bliss, 1965, 1978) can be composed of multiple elements, each of which conveys meaning. Formational constraints govern the development of new symbols, and the relation of components to each other must be interpreted to access the meaning of a symbol.

McNaughton and Lindsay (1995) contrasted the holistic versus analytic processing demands across both symbol types. They speculated whether or not extensive experience with Type Two symbols (such as Blissymbols) might yield benefits in terms of fostering speed and accuracy of visual analysis, a skill that in turn may support subsequent phonological decoding in word recognition. The metacognitive strategies used in constructing and interpreting messages encoded through Type Two symbols may also yield important carryover benefits when individuals are faced with decoding and/or encoding of meaningless elements (letters) to generate meaningful texts. Hjelmquist, Dahlgren-Sandberg, and Hedelin (1994) explored the metalinguistic abilities of adolescents who use Blissymbols as a primary communication system and reported evidence of metalinguistic awareness at both word and discourse levels for the individuals they studied.

Early experience with graphic symbols may foster awareness of print and of content-form distinctions for individuals who use AAC and provide important scaffolds for early experiences with written language instruction. Learning to read and write an alphabetic script also requires explicit awareness of the sound structure of language, as discussed previously. As mentioned earlier, the impact of a severe speech impairment on the development of such awareness is still unresolved, although evidence suggests it does not preclude the development of such awareness (Foley & Pollatsek, 1999).

Children learning to read and write gain much of their insights into phonemic structure through their attempts to write, as they consciously analyze the sound structure of words to capture them on a page. Individuals with severe physical impairments have a considerable disadvantage in this regard. Independent access to writing attempts may take a long time to develop, as motor capabilities and potential adaptations are explored. Hence, an important avenue of learning may have many barriers or even be closed off.

An alternative route to such awareness may be available through the use of voice-output technology. Many speech-generating devices incorporate text-to-speech technology, so that individuals can experiment with generation of novel phonetic strings accessed through orthography. In one study, only two of the six participants with dysarthria demonstrated anticipated levels of phonological awareness (Foley & Pollatsek, 1999). These two individuals were unusual within the group, having had extensive experience manipulating the synthetic speech output of their communication devices, using text-to-speech facilities. Dahlgren-Sandberg and Hjelmquist (1997) also reported positive benefits deriving from voice output as a support for literacy learning. However, Smith (2001) found that although most of the participants in her study had many years of experience using voice output, only one of the participants (the most proficient at spelling) used the text-to-speech feature. It is likely that a reciprocal relationship exists between use of text-to-speech synthesis and literacy development. A certain level of skill may be needed before any useful outcome can be anticipated from use of text-to-speech. Increased use of the facility provides crucial feedback about phoneme-grapheme correspondences and builds the literacy skills that support more efficient use of text-to-speech in a bootstrapping relationship. Self-teaching becomes possible, yielding the "Matthew effects" proposed by Stanovich (1986) whereby good readers read frequently, further strengthening their reading abilities. Poor readers avoid reading at all costs and so deprive themselves of the learning opportunities they need to develop higher skill levels.

For individuals using AAC, therefore, the print context is similar to that of their naturally speaking peers in many ways. Knowledge about the sound structure of language and how it is represented in orthographic form must be acquired. Aided communicators bring unique experience with graphic symbols forms to the print context, but also face unique challenges in relation to the sound aspect of language, because of their speech impairments. The following conclusions seem warranted.

1. Letter Sounds and Phonological Awareness

1. Severe speech impairment does not preclude the development of phonological awareness (Bishop, 1985; Bishop et al., 1990; Bishop & Robson, 1989; Dahlgren-Sandberg & Hjelmquist, 1996a, 1996b; Foley, 1993; Foley & Pollatsek, 1999).
2. Severe speech impairment is most likely to interfere with phonological coding (Foley, 1993; Foley & Pollatsek, 1999; Smith, 2001).

3. Graphic symbols probably have a limited effect on developing phonological/phonemic awareness skills (Bishop, Rankin, & Mirenda, 1994).

4. Access to text-to-speech synthesis may provide a crucial link for those learning alphabetic scripts and support self-teaching (Foley & Pollatsek, 1999), but may not be availed of unless a critical level of skill has already been achieved (Smith, 2001).

2. Words

1. Graphic symbol systems may support metalinguistic awareness (Hjelmquist *et al.*, 1994), particularly at the word level (Rankin *et al.*, 1994).

2. There may be important differences related to the nature of the graphic symbol itself (McNaughton, 1998; McNaughton & Lindsay, 1995).

VI. MYTHS REVISITED

Learning to read and write represents a complex integration of many different skills. It seems only reasonable therefore that simplistic statements regarding learning to read and write should be questioned. Complexity should be the order of the day in discussing the development of reading and writing in individuals with complex communication impairments. Two related statements are addressed here as myths.

A. MYTH 1

A severe speech impairment causes reading and writing difficulties.

The existence of even one individual with a severe speech impairment who nonetheless has learned effective literacy skills is sufficient to condemn this myth to the myth cemetery. In fact, there are numerous examples of individuals with severe congenital speech impairments who go on to pursue college educations, work in contexts dependent on written language skills, and produce extraordinary examples of creative writing (e.g., Chapple, 2000; Rush, 2000). The notion that literacy is an unachievable goal for individuals using AAC or that "dyslexia" is a necessary outcome of a severe speech impairment places the literacy difficulty firmly within the individual. Such a position ignores the fact that by and large children and adults only learn to read and write when they are offered formal instruction and are given opportunities to practice.

The need to use AAC rarely arises from a "simple" speech impairment. Therefore, literacy development should not be considered as being influenced simply by speech production abilities. There are many barriers intrinsic to individual AAC users that challenge their attempts to read and write. However, equally as many barriers are imposed extrinsically in terms of the learning opportunities made available to them and learning supports required. Beukelman and Mirenda (1992, 1998) advocated a model of communication assessment that focuses on the opportunities, needs, and barriers to communication that exist for an individual, considering both the intra- and interindividual contexts in which they operate. A comparable focus on intrinsic and extrinsic factors operating to influence the written language opportunities, needs, and barriers may yield a more realistic view of the nature of written language difficulties faced by AAC users.

B. MYTH 2

A severe speech impairment has no effect on written language development.

To ignore the presence of a severe speech impairment may be to do as great a disservice to individuals using AAC as to attribute all their learning difficulties to the speech impairment. There may be aspects of phonological processing that are made considerably more difficult if speech production is not possible. Although we are not suggesting that a speech impairment *necessarily* causes a phonological processing difficulty, it seems clear that the presence of a severe speech impairment may mask additional phonological impairments, processing difficulties that themselves may have a significant impact on literacy learning.

VII. SUMMARY

This chapter has provided an overview of some of our current understanding of the complex factors affecting the acquisition of literacy by individuals who use AAC. There are a range of impairments that can affect an AAC user's ability to engage in learning to read and write, from visual difficulties to cognitive impairments. However, it is important to remember that reading and writing are learned and that the environment contributes in no small way to the ultimate success of an individual as a reader–writer. Educational experiences of AAC users are crucial. Information to date suggests that for many people who use AAC, educational opportunities to support the necessary skills involved in reading and writing are less than optimal. Communication experiences and opportunities are also crucial and again may differ in important ways from the experiences of naturally speaking peers. Understanding the complex web of factors that are relevant for any one individual requires careful assessment. In the next chapter, we turn our attention to the assessment process and consider principles that can guide our assessment toward useful intervention.

REFERENCES

Adams, M. J. (1990). *Beginning to read: Thinking and learning about print.* Cambridge, MA: MIT Press, A Bradford Book.

Anderson, R. C., Wilson, P., & Fielding, L. (1988). Growth in reading and how children spend their time outside of school. *Reading Research Quarterly, 23,* 285–303.

Basil, C. (1992). Social interaction and learned helplessness in severely disabled children. *Augmentative and Alternative Communication, 8,* 188–199.

Berninger, V., & Gans, B. (1986). Language profiles in nonspeaking individuals of normal intelligence with severe cerebral palsy. *Augmentative and Alternative Communication, 2,* 45–50.

Beukelman, D., & Mirenda, P. (1992). *Augmentative and alternative communication: Management of severe communication disorders in children and adults.* Baltimore, MD: Paul H. Brookes.

Beukelman, D., & Mirenda, P. (1998). *Augmentative and alternative communication: Management of severe communication disorders in children and adults.* (2nd ed). Baltimore, MD: Paul H. Brookes.

Bishop, D. V. M. (1985). Spelling ability in congenital dysarthria: Evidence against articulatory coding in translating between phonemes and graphemes. *Cognitive Neuropsychology, 2*(3), 229–251.

Bishop, D. V. M., Byers-Brown, B., & Robson, J. (1990). The relationship between phoneme discrimination, speech production, and language comprehension in cerebral-palsied individuals. *Journal of Speech & Hearing Research, 33,* 210–219.

Bishop, D. V. M., & Robson, J. (1989). Unimpaired short-term memory and rhyme judgement in congenitally speechless individuals: Implications for the notion of "articulatory coding." *The Quarterly Journal of Experimental Psychology, 41A*(1), 123–140.

Bishop, K., Rankin, J., & Mirenda, P. (1994). Impact of graphic symbol use on reading acquisition. *Augmentative and Alternative Communication, 10,* 113–125.

Björck-Åkesson, E. (1990, August 12–16). *Communicative interaction of young physically disabled nonspeaking children and their parents.* Paper presented at the Fifth Biennial Meeting of the International Society of Augmentative and Alternative Communication (ISAAC), Stockholm, Sweden.

Bliss, C. (1965, 1978). *Semantography (Blissymbolics).* Sydney: Semantography Publications.

Blockberger, S. (1997). *The acquisition of grammatical morphology by children who are unable to speak.* University of British Columbia, Vancouver, Canada.

Blockberger, S., & Sutton, A. (2003). Toward linguistic competence: Language experiences of children with extremely limited speech. In J. Light, D. Beukelman, & J. Reichel, *Communicative competence for individuals who use AAC: From research to effective practice.* Baltimore: Brooker, 63–106.

Buzolich, M., & Wiemann, J. (1988). Turn taking in atypical conversations: The case of the speaker/augmented communicator dyad. *Journal of Speech and Hearing Research, 31,* 3–18.

Carlson, F. (1987). Communication strategies for infants. In E. McDonald (Ed.), *Treating cerebral palsy* (pp. 191–207). Austin, TX: PRO-Ed.

Catts, H., & Kamhi, A. (1986). The linguistic bases of reading disorders: Implications for the speech-language pathologist. *Language, Speech, and Hearing Services in Schools, 17,* 329–341.

Chapple, D. (2000). Empowerment. In M. Fried-Oken & H. Bersani (Eds.), *Speaking up and spelling it out* (pp. 153–160). Baltimore, MD: Paul H. Brookes.

Clay, M. M. (1991). *Becoming literate.* Portsmouth, NH: Heinemann Education Books.

Coleman, P. P. (1992). *Literacy lost: A qualitative analysis of the early literacy experiences of preschool children with severe speech and physical impairments*, University of North Carolina, Chapel Hill.

Dahlgren Sandberg, A. (1998). Reading and spelling among nonvocal children with cerebral palsy: Influences of home and school literacy environment. *Reading and Writing: An Interdisciplinary Journal, 10*, 23–50.

Dahlgren-Sandberg, A., & Hjelmquist, E. (1996a). A comparative, descriptive study of reading and writing skills among non-speaking children: a preliminary study. *European Journal of Disorders of Communication, 31*, 289–308.

Dahlgren-Sandberg, A., & Hjelmquist, E. (1996b). Phonologic awareness and literacy abilities in non-speaking preschool children with cerebral palsy. *Augmentative and Alternative Communication, 12*(3), 138–154.

Dahlgren-Sandberg, A., & Hjelmquist, E. (1997). Language and literacy in nonvocal children with cerebral palsy. *Reading and Writing: An Interdisciplinary Journal, 9*, 107–133.

Dahlgren Sandberg, A., & Hjelmquist, E. (2002). Phonological recoding problems in children with severe congenital speech impairments—The importance of productive speech. In A. F. E. Witruk & T. Lachmann (Eds.), *Basic mechanisms of language and language disorders*. Dordrecht, The Netherlands: Kluwer Academic.

DeCoste, D. (1997). The role of literacy in augmentative and alternative communication. In S. Glennen & D. DeCoste (Eds.), *Handbook of Augmentative and Alternative Communication* (pp. 283–334). London: Singular Press.

Dorman, C. (1985). Classification of reading disability in a case of congenital brain damage. *Neuropsychologia, 23*, 393–402.

Duckman, R. (1987). Visual problems in cerebral palsy. In E. McDonald (Ed.), *Treating cerebral palsy* (pp. 105–132). Austin TX: PRO-Ed.

Erhardt, R. P. (1990). *Developmental visual dysfunction*. Tucson, AZ: Therapy Skill Builders.

Flax, J., Realpe, T., Hirsch, L., Nawyn, J., & Tallal, P. (2001, November 23). *Relationship of language subtypes and literacy skills in families with a history of SLI*. Paper presented at the Association for Speech, Language and Hearing Research Conference, Washington, DC.

Foley, B. E. (1989). *Phonological recoding and congenital dysarthria*. University of Massachusetts, Amherst.

Foley, B. E. (1993). The development of literacy in individuals with severe congenital speech and motor impairments. *Topics in Language Disorders, 13*, 16–32.

Foley, B. E., & Pollatsek, A. (1999). Phonological processing and reading abilities in adolescents and adults with severe congenital speech impairments. *Augmentative and Alternative Communication, 15*, 156–173.

Galda, L., Cullinan, B., & Strickland, D. (1993). *Language, literacy and the child*. London: Harcourt Brace Jovanovich College.

Gallagher, A., Frith, U., & Snowling, M. (2000). Precursors of literacy delay among children at genetic risk of dyslexia. *Journal of Memory and Language, 29*, 336–360.

Goldsworthy, C. (1996). *Developmental reading disabilities: a language based treatment approach*. London: Singular Press.

Goswami, U. (2000). Phonological and lexical processes. In M. Kamil, P. Mosenthal, P. D. Pearson, & R. Barr (Eds.), *Handbook of reading research* (pp. 251–268). London: Erlbaum.

Grushkin, D. A. (1998). Why shouldn't Sam read? Towards a new paradigm for literacy and the deaf. *Journal of Deaf Studies and Deaf Education, 3*(3), 179–203.

Hanson, V. L. (1991). Phonological processing without sound. In S. Brady & D. Shankweiler (Eds.), *Phonological processes in literacy* (pp. 153–161). Hillsdale, NJ: Erlbaum.

Hanson, V. L., & Fowler, C. A. (1987). Phonological coding in word reading: Evidence from hearing and deaf readers. *Memory and Cognition, 15*, 199–207.

Harris, D. (1982). Communicative interaction processes involving nonvocal physically handicapped children. *Topics in Language Disorders, 2*, 21–37.

Harris, M., & Beech, J. R. (1998). Implicit phonological awareness and early reading development in prelingually deaf children. *Journal of Deaf Studies and Deaf Education, 3*(3), 205–216.

Hjelmquist, E., & Dahlgren-Sandberg, A. (1996). Sounds and silence: Interaction in aided language use. In S. von Tetzchner & M. Jensen (Eds.), *Augmentative and alternative communication: European perspectives.* London: Whurr.

Hjelmquist, E., Dahlgren Sandberg, A., & Hedelin, L. (1994). Linguistics, AAC and metalinguistics in communicatively handicapped adolescents. *Augmentative and Alternative Communication, 10,* 169–183.

Iacono, T. A., Mirenda, P., & Beukelman, D. (1993). Comparison of unimodal and multimodal AAC techniques for children with intellectual disabilities. *Augmentative and Alternative Communication, 9,* 83–94.

Jones, M. H., Dayton, G. O., Bernstein, L., Strommen, E., Osborne, M., & Watanabe, K. (1966). Pilot study of reading problems in cerebral palsied adults. *Developmental Medicine and Child Neurology, 8,* 417–427.

Katayama, M., & Tamas, L. B. (1987). Saccadic eye-movements of children with cerebral palsy. *Developmental Medicine and Child Neurology, 29,* 36–39.

Kelford-Smith, A., Thurston, S., Light, J., Parnes, P., & O'Keefe, B. (1989). The form and use of written communication produced by physically disabled individuals using microcomputers. *Augmentative and Alternative Communication, 5,* 115–124.

King, C. M., & Quigley, S. P. (1985). *Reading and deafness.* San Diego, CA: College Hill Press.

Koppenhaver, D. (1991). *A descriptive analysis of classroom literacy instruction provided to children with severe speech and physical impairments,* University of North Carolina, Chapel Hill.

Koppenhaver, D., & Yoder, D. E. (1992a). Literacy issues in persons with severe speech and physical impairments. In R. Gaylord-Ross (Ed.), *Issues and research in special education* (Vol. 2, pp. 156–201). New York, NY: Columbia University Teachers College Press.

Koppenhaver, D., & Yoder, D. E. (1992b). Literacy learning of children with severe speech and physical impairments in school settings. *Seminars in Speech and Language, 12,* 4–15.

Koppenhaver, D., & Yoder, D. E. (1993). Classroom literacy instruction for children with severe speech and physical impairments (SSPI): What is and what might be. *Topics in Language Disorders, 13*(2), 1–15.

Kraat, A. (1987). *Communication interaction between aided and natural speakers: An IPCAS study report.* Madison: University of Wisconsin-Madison Trace Research and Development Centre.

Kraat, A. (1991). *Methodological issues in the study of language development among children using aided language; Reactant Paper 1.* Paper presented at the First ISAAC Research Symposium, August 16–17, Stockholm, Sweden.

Light, J. (1988). Interaction involving individuals using augmentative and alternative communication: State of the art and future directions. *Augmentative and Alternative Communication, 4,* 66–82.

Light, J., Collier, B., & Parnes, P. (1985a). Communicative interaction between young nonspeaking physically disabled children and their primary caregivers: Discourse patterns. *Augmentative and Alternative Communication, 1,* 74–83.

Light, J., Collier, B., & Parnes, P. (1985b). Communicative interaction between young nonspeaking physically disabled children and their primary caregivers: Modes of communication. *Augmentative and Alternative Communication, 1,* 125–133.

Light, J., & Kelford-Smith, A. (1993). The home literacy experiences of preschoolers who use augmentative communication systems and of their nondisabled peers. *Augmentative and Alternative Communication, 9,* 10–25.

Light, J., & McNaughton, D. (1993). Literacy and augmentative and alternative communication: The expectations and priorities of parents and teachers. *Topics in Language Disorders, 13*(2), 33–46.

Locke, J. L. (1997). *Blindness and psychological development in young children.* Leicester, UK: British Psychological Society.

Marozas, D., & May, D. (1985). Effects of figure-ground reversal on the visual perceptual and visuo-motor performances of cerebral palsied and normal children. *Perceptual and Motor Skills, 60*, 591–598.

Mayer Johnson, R. (1981). *Picture communication symbols*. Solana Beach, CA: Mayer Johnson.

Mayer Johnson, R. (1985). *Picture communication symbols* (Vol. 2). Solana Beach, CA: Mayer Johnson.

McDonald, E. (1987). *Treating cerebral palsy: For clinicians, by clinicians*. Austin, TX: PRO-Ed.

McNaughton, S. (1998). *Reading acquisition of adults with severe congenital speech and physical impairments: Theoretical infrastructure, empirical investigation, education implication.* Unpublished doctoral dissertation, University of Toronto, Toronto, Ontario, Canada.

McNaughton, S., & Lindsay, P. (1995). Approaching literacy with AAC graphics. *Augmentative and Alternative Communication, 11*, 212–228.

Mike, D. (1995). Literacy and cerebral palsy: Factors influencing literacy learning in a self-contained setting. *Journal of Reading Behavior, 27*(4), 627–642.

Nation, K., & Snowling, M. (2000). Factors influencing syntactic awareness skills in normal readers and poor comprehenders. *Applied Psycholinguistics, 21*, 229–241.

Nolan, C. (1987). *Under the eye of the clock: The life story of Christopher Nolan*. New York: St Martins' Press.

Parker, L. G. (1987). Educational programming. In E. McDonald (Ed.), *Treating cerebral palsy: For clinicians, by clinicians*. Austin, TX: PRO-Ed.

Piaget, J. (1977). *The origin of intelligence in children*. Harmondsworth, UK: Penguin.

Pumfrey, P. D., & Reason, R. (1991). *Specific learning difficulties: Challenges and responses*. Berks, UK: NFER-Nelson.

Rankin, J., Harwood, K., & Mirenda, P. (1994). Influence of graphic symbol use on reading comprehension. *Augmentative and Alternative Communication, 10*, 269–281.

Rayner, K. (1999). What have we learned about eye movements during reading? In R. Klein & P. McMullen (Eds.), *Converging methods for understanding reading and dyslexia* (pp. 23–56). London: MIT Press.

Rush, W. (2000). Liberating myself. In M. Fried-Oken & H. Bersani (Eds.), *Speaking up and spelling it out* (pp. 147–152). Baltimore, MD: Paul H. Brookes.

Rutter, M. (1987). Assessment of language disorders. In W. Yule & M. Rutter (Eds.), *Language development and disorders* (pp. 295–311). Oxford, UK: Blackwell Scientific.

Schonell, F. E. (1956). *Educating spastic children: The education and guidance of the cerebral palsied*. London: Oliver & Boyd.

Share, D. L. (1995). Phonological recoding and self-teaching: Sine qua non of reading acquisition. *Cognition, 55*, 151–218.

Siegenthaler, B. (1987). Auditory problems. In E. McDonald (Ed.), *Treating cerebral palsy* (pp. 85–104). Austin TX: PRO-Ed.

Smith, M. (1989). Reading without speech: A study of children with cerebral palsy. *Irish Journal of Psychology, 10*, 601–614.

Smith, M. (1991). Assessment of interaction patterns and AAC use—A case study. *Journal of Clinical Speech & Language Studies, 1*, 76–102.

Smith, M. (1998). *Pictures of language: The role of PCS in the language acquisition of children with severe congenital speech and physical impairments.* Unpublished doctoral dissertation, Trinity College, Dublin, Ireland.

Smith, M. (2001). Literacy challenges for individuals with severe congenital speech impairments. *International Journal of Disability, Development and Education, 48*, 331–353.

Smith, M. (2003). Perspectives on augmentative and alternative communication and literacy. In S. von Tetzchner & M. Jensen (Eds.), *Perspectives on Theory and Practice in Augmentative and Alternative Communication: Proceedings of the Seventh ISAAC Biennial Research Symposium, Odense, Denmark, August 2002.* Toronto, Ontario: ISAAC, 170–182.

Smith, M., & Blischak, D. (1997). Literacy. In L. Lloyd, D. Fuller, & H. Arvidson (Eds.), *Augmentative and alternative communication: Principles and practices* (pp. 414–444). London: Allyn & Bacon.

Snowling, M. (2000). Language and literacy skills: who is at risk and why? In D. V. M. Bishop & L. B. Leonard (Eds.), *Speech and language impairments in children* (pp. 245–260). Hove, East Sussex, UK: Psychology Press.

Spiegel, B., Benjamin, B. J., & Spiegel, S. (1993). One method to increase spontaneous use of an assistive communication device: A case study. *Augmentative and Alternative Communication, 9,* 111–117.

Stackhouse, J. (2000). Barriers to literacy development in children with speech and language difficulties. In D. V. M. Bishop & L. B. Leonard (Eds.), *Speech and language impairments in children* (pp. 73–98). Hove, East Sussex, UK: Psychology Press.

Stackhouse, J., & Wells, B. (1997). *Children's speech and literacy difficulties: A psycholinguistic framework.* London: Whurr.

Stanovich, K. (1986). Matthew effects in reading: Some consequences of individual differences in the acquisition of literacy. *Reading Research Quarterly, 21,* 360–407.

Stanovich, K. (1991). Discrepancy definitions of reading disability: Has intelligence led us astray? *Reading Research Quarterly, 26*(1), 7–29.

Sterne, A., & Goswami, U. (2000). Phonological awareness of syllables, rhymes and phonemes in deaf children. *Journal of Child Psychology and Psychiatry and Allied Disciplines, 41*(5), 609–625.

Stewart, S. R., Gonzalez, L. S., & Page, J. L. (1997). Incidental learning of sight words during articulation training. *Language Speech and Hearing Services in Schools, 28,* 115–125.

Sutton, A., Soto, G., & Blockberger, S. (2002). Grammatical issues in graphic symbol communication. *Augmentative and Alternative Communication, 18*(3), 192–204.

Teale, W., & Sulzby, E. (1987). Literacy acquisition in early childhood: The roles of access and mediation in storybook telling. In D. A. Wagner (Ed.), *The future of literacy in a changing world* (pp. 111–130). New York: Pergamon Press.

Teale, W., & Sulzby, E. (1989). Emergent literacy: New perspectives on young children's reading and writing. In D. Strickland & L. M. Morrow (Eds.), *Emerging literacy: Young children learn to read and write* (pp. 1–15). Newark, DE: International Reading Association.

Udwin, O., & Yule, W. (1990). Augmentative and alternative communication systems taught to cerebral palsied children: A longitudinal study: I. The acquisition of signs and symbols, and syntactic aspects of their use over time. *British Journal of Disorders of Communication, 25,* 295–309.

Udwin, O., & Yule, W. (1991). Augmentative communication systems taught to cerebral palsy children—A longitudinal study. 1: The acquisition of signs and symbols and syntactic aspects of their use over time. *British Journal of Disorders of Communication, 25,* 295–309.

van Balkom, H., & Donker-Gimbrére, M. (1996). A psycholinguistic approach to graphic language use. In S. von Tetzchner & M. Jensen (Eds.), *Augmentative and Alternative Communication: European perspectives* (pp. 153–170). London: Whurr.

Vandervelden, M., & Siegel, L. (1997). Teaching phonological processing skills in early literacy: A developmental approach. *Learning Disabilities Quarterly, 20,* 63–81.

Vandervelden, M., & Siegel, L. (1999). Phonological processing and literacy in AAC users and students with motor speech impairments. *Augmentative and Alternative Communication, 15,* 191–211.

Vandervelden, M., & Siegel, L. (2001). Phonological processing in written word learning: Assessment for children who use augmentative and alternative communication. *Augmentative and Alternative Communication, 17*(1), 11–26.

von Tetzchner, S., & Martinsen, H. (1996). Words and strategies: Communicating with young children who use aided language. In S. von Tetzchner & M. H. Jensen (Eds.), *Augmentative and alternative communication: European perspectives* (pp. 65–88). London: Whurr.

von Tetzchner, S., & Martinsen, H. (2000). *Augmentative and alternative communication* (2nd ed). London: Whurr.

CHAPTER 5

Assessment Principles

I. Introduction
II. General Principles of Assessment
    A. Literacy as an Integration of Skills
    B. The Focus of Assessment
    C. Literacy as a Goal-Driven Activity
    D. Literacy as a Developmental Process
    E. Implications of Assessment Adaptations
III. Summary

I. INTRODUCTION

In the previous chapters, the emphasis has been on acknowledging the complexity of literacy competence, the developmental continuum that exists from preliteracy to literacy, the social context that frames literacy achievement, and the intimate reciprocal relationships that exist between spoken and written language and between reading and writing. Given the complexity of the processes of reading and writing, assessing competence is neither easy nor quickly achieved, in any instance. When an individual has severe speech and physical impairments, the challenges are even greater. In this latter context, the stakes are also relatively higher—the attainment of literacy may unlock potential communication, learning, recreational, and leisure opportunities for individuals whose options otherwise may be curtailed. The use of graphic communication systems provides unique print experiences for many aided communicators. The attainment of alphabetic literacy provides them with access to potentially unlimited communication. The focus in this chapter is on general principles guiding assessment, with an emphasis on assessment as a step in the process of intervention.

II. GENERAL PRINCIPLES OF ASSESSMENT

Smith and Blischak (1997) suggested five principles that can be used to inform good assessment practice at all stages of literacy development. These

Literacy and Augmentative and Alternative Communication

principles are discussed in the following paragraphs, with minor modifications. In addition to these principles, however, it is important to recognize that assessment of written language skills must be framed in the context of other language and communication skills. On-going dynamic reflection is required, rather than once-off attempts to capture information.

Assessment of an activity as complex as literacy is daunting and is a task that no one individual is in a position to undertake in isolation. Effective assessment requires the organization of a team of individuals. Teams may be structured in many different ways and membership may vary. However, at a minimum, the client, family, significant communication partners, clinicians, and educators should be key members. For most individuals, the educational setting is a key environment in which learning to read and write takes place, so teachers, teaching assistants, and speech-language pathologists must work collaboratively to support both spoken and written language development. Educational psychologists may also be involved. Crucial information regarding physical functioning, seating, and positioning can be offered by physical and occupational therapists. Occupational therapists can provide invaluable support with regard to perceptual functioning and adaptations to equipment. Other important team members may be an audiologist, a neurologist, an ophthalmologist, a social worker, and a variety of other individuals at certain key points in the assessment process. The contributions of the latter team members are more likely to occur in response to specific problems encountered, unlike the contributions of the core team members including the client, family, significant communication partners, clinicians, and educators, whose roles are more ongoing. Although the size and structure of teams may vary, it is nonetheless essential that input from a wide range of resources is available, if assessment is to provide accurate and useful information. The concept of team involvement, therefore, can be regarded as an over-riding, umbrella principle of assessment.

A. Literacy as an Integration of Skills

Principle 1: *Literacy achievement represents an integration of many factors, both intrinsic and extrinsic to the individual.*

As suggested in previous chapters, successful reading and writing reflect a complex integration of many different skill domains. It makes little sense then to adopt a reductionist, static focus in assessment. Competence in literacy is not a static phenomenon. Performance on any particular literacy task, whether in reading or in writing, reflects not only the inherent task demands, but the individual's interest, motivation, familiarity, attention, and a host of other factors. To be successful, readers and writers must accommodate to different situations and demands. For a skilled reader, the accommodation required to read a difficult text may simply be to read more slowly. A less skilled reader may adapt by resorting to guesswork or by simply giving up. Assessment not only must consider the range of factors that underpin performance on any given literacy task but also must ensure that a range of contexts are explored to build a composite picture of ability, rather than a snapshot of performance.

Several models of assessment have been suggested both in educational and speech-language pathology contexts. Silliman and Wilkinson (1991) have suggested that assessments be conducted as if through a range of different lenses, from macro- to micro-oriented views of function. Each lens reveals a different perspective or snapshot, from a view of the client only, to a view of the client engaged in a particular activity, to a view of the total context of the client.

1. Selecting the Lens

a. The Wide-Angle Lens

Adopting a *wide-angle lens* requires consideration of the factors extrinsic to an individual that might have an impact on performance. This wide-angle view should encompass home, school, and community or vocational contexts and the literacy experiences and opportunities that are available within these contexts. Evidence on the typical home literacy experiences of individuals who use augmentative and alternative communication (AAC) and the impact they may have on subsequent literacy development is equivocal (Dahlgren-Sandberg 1998; Light & McNaughton, 1993). In addition, it is far from clear that a minimum requirement in terms of home support is necessary for a child to develop effective literacy skills, regardless of whether the individual is typically developing or uses AAC. What is undisputed is that the time demands on families of AAC users are sizable, and it is quite likely that their home literacy experiences are different from those of their typically developing peers. There is evidence to suggest that supportive home environments inspire AAC users to aim for literacy competence (e.g., Koppenhaver, Evans, & Yoder, 1991; McNaughton, 1998). It seems prudent therefore to include consideration of these factors in developing a fully framed picture of the literacy experiences of AAC users.

Discussion with parents and/or other family members can explore the range of reading materials available to an individual who uses AAC within the home; the range of typical literacy activities engaged in over the course of a week, both in terms of frequency and variety; the level of active participation on the part of the AAC user within those activities; and the incidental opportunities that may be latent and unexploited within the daily experiences of the families. Families of individuals using AAC may spend many hours of the day engaged in one-to-one interaction during activities related to personal care, recreation and "education." Are there any literacy experiences woven into the fabric of such interactions? Is there the potential to integrate such opportunities? What might the implications of such changes be? These are important questions to consider. Family members, however, must be supported to retain the primary roles of parents or siblings, rather than feeling obliged to subsume such roles in favor of clinician or educator roles. Adopting a wide-angle lens means viewing not only the environmental context of the individual who uses AAC, as it relates to literacy development but also that individual in a complex system of relationships, striving to meet several goals simultaneously across a range of domains. What must not be lost is the core essence of family life.

The wide-angle lens should also encompass the school or other formal learning contexts. The range, type, and amount of literacy learning opportunities offered to individuals within a structured educational context have a crucial bearing on their subsequent performance in learning to read and write. This is true for all individuals, not just for AAC users. However, because of the complex needs of individuals who use AAC, the range of demands on their time during a typical school day far exceeds the demands on most of their peers. The wide-angle lens must focus specifically on the teaching opportunities offered and their intensity, focus, and variety to develop a clear picture of the support for reading and writing genuinely available to the AAC user. Geraldine Bedell, writing in the British *Observer* newspaper, proposed that it is not so much that pupils with dyslexia have learning difficulties as it is that schools have teaching difficulties (Bedell, 2002). In fact, both types of difficulties coexist. For individuals who use AAC, it is likely that there is a combination of challenges for both teaching and learning, again underlining the complexity and the synergistic nature of literacy attainment.

b. The Regular Lens

A *regular lens* focuses on the specific activity as it relates to a child. Task demands (motor, physical, cognitive, and linguistic) are considered, not from the point of view of features of the task itself, but rather the unique demands the activity generates for a specific individual. Although an activity such as coloring a picture may have relatively stable core demands—an integration of visual, motor, and cognitive skills—the relative impact of these demands is very different for a typically developing 5-year-old than for a peer of the same age who has spastic quadriplegia and visuomotor difficulties. Similarly, writing a name requires a complex integration of visuomotor and cognitive-linguistic skills, but the nature of the motor demands is very different for an individual writing with a pencil and paper than for a child using a single switch and row-column scanning to generate text in a word processing program. The regular lens therefore looks at the activity itself and its familiarity, level of abstraction, complexity, and component skills, but then also considers the individual undertaking the task and the interaction between the task demands and the resources available to the individual. Each observation therefore yields a unique snapshot of a particular individual engaged in a particular activity.

c. The Close-up Lens

The *close-up lens* focuses primarily on an individual and the factors that affect that individual's performance in any skill area. Physical, sensory (vision and hearing), cognitive, and linguistic skills all affect performance on literacy tasks. As discussed in Chapter 4, all are vulnerable in individuals using AAC. The close-up lens explores the resources brought by the individual to the task. The picture from this lens captures the individual's specific motor, sensory, and linguistic skills, but also their prior unique experiences that affect the context of learning within which they operate—their interests, motivation, and expectations. Are there particular contexts that maximally support performance? What types of interactions seem to help more—sitting beside the child and modelling performance, or giving physical support and guiding performance? Is it better to give a verbal explanation and allow the child to work independently initially? A clear picture from a close-up lens will uncover the factors that compromise performance.

All three lenses discussed above offer different views and perspectives on intrinsic and extrinsic factors operating across the three contexts described by Pumfrey and Reason (1991)—the learning context, the language context, and the print context. Points of interest within each of these contexts are outlined in the next section.

2. Defining the Context

a. The Learning Context

The wide-angle lens captures broad information about the factors impinging on the context of learning for an individual. What resources are available to the individual within the learning context? What personnel are involved? What technology is provided? How familiar are key personnel with the resources available? What back-up systems are provided? What is the level of integration across the various systems in the individual's environment?

The regular lens keeps a focus on the activity-individual interaction—the unique task demands of a particular activity for a specific individual in a given context. Information that becomes available using this lens includes the relevance of the activity for the individual, the resource demands it presents, and the individual's motivation to participate and complete an activity.

Comparable experiences may have very different effects on two individuals. A close-up lens focuses attention on the unique context of learning for a

Table 5.1

The Learning Context: Some Considerations

Wide-Angle Lens

What resources are available in the learning environment, at home, in school or day center, employment?

    Personnel?

    Adaptive technology?

    Expertise?

    Back-up supports?

How integrated are the resources?

    Is there collaboration across the different contexts?

    Are there conflicts in terms of learning goals and expectations?

Regular Lens

What are the demands of the literacy activity, in terms of visual, motor, and linguistic characteristics?

How familiar or abstract is the material?

How complex is the material, and how many steps are involved in the task?

How many of the steps are directly related to the activity, and how many are extraneous, or due to the individual's physical needs?

What are the demands of any extraneous steps, e.g., reliable switch control, auditory scanning?

Close-Up Lens

How does the individual view self as a reader-writer?

What interests and motivators support or compromise learning for this individual?

What does this individual want to achieve from reading and writing—what is the individual's end destination of this journey?

---

particular individual. What are the self-perceptions of this individual, as a reader-writer? What are the aspirations relating to reading and writing? What is the motivator for this individual—external reinforcement; more efficient and independent communication; or the ability to read a letter, write a book, or use email?

There are many ways of formulating questions to address the views focused through each of these lenses. Examples appear in Table 5.1.

b. The Language Context

Users of AAC face many language demands. They rarely, if ever, operate within a context in which their systems of communication are the dominant sociolinguistic codes (Woll & Barnett, 1998). Significant others in the environment may have varying levels of tolerance for, understanding of, and experience with nonspeech modes of communication. A wide-angled lens can capture some information about the communication context of individuals who use AAC, shedding light on the support available in important environments for their communication and linguistic development in nonspeech modes.

For some users of AAC, independently generated written output is seen as an important source of information about expressive language abilities. If an AAC user produces "atypical" written output, interpreting that output is difficult. Do differences between the produced output and expected language forms, for example, represent underlying language difficulties, or are they simply a reflection of written language abilities? For most early reader-writers, no inferences about spoken language development would be drawn on the basis of their written language, even though as school progresses, written language becomes the primary assessment medium not only for content knowledge but also for language skills. For individuals who use AAC, the relationship between performance and competence within the linguistic domain is difficult to disentangle. Written language provides a medium through which underlying language skills can be evaluated, but written language is itself a separate focus of assessment.

Engaging in literacy activities requires a focus on language as an object in its own right. Both encoding and decoding tasks (i.e., both reading and writing tasks) require a range of metalinguistic and analytic skills, a separation of form and meaning, and attention to abstract units. A regular lens can be used to explore the match between an aided communicator's existing communication system and the target orthographic system that is the focus of learning. How similar are the language forms of the target text and the language form familiar to the aided communicator? Although many individuals using AAC both hear and understand speech, others (whom von Tetzchner and Martinsen [1992] categorized as alternative communicators) rely on nonspeech modes for both input and output. Even for those who use speech as a dominant input mode, the similarity between the internal features and structural organization of their output mode and the target orthography may have important implications for task demands (Smith & Grove, 2003).

The regular lens also captures information about the match between the language demands of the text in terms of syntactic, morphological, and semantic complexity and the language skills of the reader-writer. These latter skills are explored by switching to a view from the close-up lens to uncover the language and communication resources available to the individual.

There is broad agreement that truly efficient reading and writing skills reflect the integration of a complex and effective spoken language system. Whereas decoding of unfamiliar words may draw specifically on speech processing skills, language comprehension links more closely with reading comprehension. Nation and Snowling (2000) argued that syntactic competence is critical in facilitating easy access to text understanding. Vocabulary likewise is known to link intimately with success in reading and writing (Stanovich, 1986). Preliminary research data (Iacono & Cupples, 2003) suggest that similar spoken-written

Table 5.2

The Language Context: Some Considerations

Wide-Angle Lens

What is the environmental support available to the individual for use of the aided communication system?

What are the opportunities provided for expressive use of the aided communication system? How frequent are these opportunities?

Is input provided in the aided communication system? If yes, how complete is this input, in terms of structural organization?

Are there other individuals within the broad communication environment who use a similar system?

Regular Lens

How *linguistic* is the aided communication system, in terms of its formal structural properties?

    Is the aided communication a lexical set, or a lexical system, with built-in potential for generation of new symbols?

    Is there potential for sublexical organization within the system?

    What kind of linguistic units are included in the aided communication system—concrete naming words, actions, or function words?

    What kind of utterances can be constructed using the aided communication system?

What kind of linguistic demands are implicit within the text?

Does the individual have experience producing similar linguistic constructions using his or her own aided communication system?

How familiar might the language structures be to the individual, based on his or her input experience?

Close-up Lens

What are the language and communication resources available to the individual?

language relationships hold true for aided communicators. At the very least, therefore, we need to consider measures of vocabulary, syntax-morphology, semantics, and pragmatic abilities in terms of their impact on the understanding of differing text structures. General measures of language comprehension are of relatively little value in untangling spoken-written language relationships. The emphasis must be on exploring abilities across each of the language subskills listed above. Some suggestions are proposed in Table 5.2.

c. The Print Context

Reading and writing exist and are accessible only through the print context. It is important therefore to consider the opportunities, needs, and barriers that individuals encounter as they engage with print.

The wide-angle lens allows a view into the print environment for an individual. For early reader-writers the wide-angle lens may offer valuable information about the print supports available within the home and school environments, the range and accessibility of reading and writing materials, the time allocated to literacy-related activities, the priorities attached to print activities, and the opportunities and barriers for both formal and incidental learning. For older students, the wide-angle lens focuses on the prevailing ethos about how students learn to read and write, the instructional approach adopted, the time dedicated to formal instruction and independent literacy activities, and the value placed on such activities, as evidenced by the interruptions tolerated within dedicated learning times. Teachers and families are essential resources in focusing this lens effectively.

The regular lens permits us to examine the specific demands of a given text-student interaction. Many types of factors come into focus including visuomotor factors such as the size of print, foreground/background contrasts, motor demands for switch use, and/or physical manipulation of drawing or writing materials, as well as text demands relating to actual text features (e.g., print and linguistic complexity) and their match to the resources of the student. To focus the regular lens, support may be needed from team members such as occupational and physical therapists and possibly an ophthalmologist, psychologist, and neurologist.

The close-up lens shifts the focus of attention to within-student resources. Two main domains of functioning come under scrutiny—letter-sound relationships and competencies and whole-word competencies. In addition, print information regarding prosody (indicated by punctuation markings) must be rapidly processed, if the meaning of the text is to be accurately constructed. The close-up lens allows us to explore in more detail the functioning of the various processors proposed by Seidenberg and McClelland (1989)—the orthographic processor, the phonological processor, the meaning processor, and the context processor. The latter two processors are explored in the language context, described above, but are considered here in relation to their access through the print medium. Likewise, the phonological processor may be considered to belong more appropriately to the language context, but again it is the function of the phonological processor in relation to print that is the focus here. Examples of questions that might be considered through adoption of any of the three lenses appear in Table 5.3.

In the section above, the phonological processor gets only cursory mention, although, as suggested throughout the earlier chapters of this book, phonological processing plays a central and key role in reading and writing. Given its importance, some time will be spent here in considering the particular challenges in assessing the functioning of the phonological processor for individuals with severe speech impairments.

3. The Phonological Processor

As outlined in Chapter 2, the phonological processor's primary role relates to spoken language. In a written language context, it is activated through the

Table 5.3

The Print Context: Some Considerations

Wide-Angle Lens

What are the opportunities present in the environment that can support literacy learning?

   What is the range and availability of print materials?

   What are the formal learning opportunities?

   What are the incidental learning opportunities?

   How balanced are the opportunities across both decoding and encoding activities?

What are the barriers to participation in literacy learning activities within the environment?

   Physical?

   Sensory?

   Linguistic?

   Philosophical?

Regular Lens

What kind of text format is accessible to the individual?

   From a physical point of view?

   From a visual point of view?

   From a linguistic point of view?

What additional supports are required to make a text accessible?

   Enlargement?

   Repositioning?

   Symbol support?

   Other?

Close-up Lens

Can the letters be identified?

Are phoneme-grapheme correspondences established?

How effectively is the phonological processor functioning?

   Can simple unfamiliar words be decoded?

   Can simple nonwords be spelt—initial consonant only? All consonants? Consonants and vowels?

How effectively is the orthographic processor functioning?

   Is there a core set of sight words that can be recognized easily and quickly?

   Are there any orthographic patterns, such as "-ight" that can be recognized?

   Are punctuation conventions such as use of a question mark (?) recognized?

---

orthographic processor. As its name suggests, the phonological processor analyzes incoming speech (or visual information) as an essential link in deriving sound-meaning relationships. Underlying the successful functioning of the phonological processor is an intact speech processing system. Stackhouse and Wells (1997) used the term *speech processing* to refer to all the skills included in understanding and producing speech, including peripheral skills such as articulatory ability and hearing. The basic structure of the speech processing system they proposed comprises an input system (either auditory or visual), a representational system for stored lexical representations, and an output system, which may be oral, manual, written, or, in the case of aided communicators, of another form. Based on these

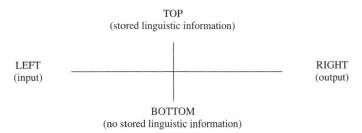

Figure 5.1. Speech processing anchor points. (From Stackhouse, J., & Wells, B. (1997). *Children's speech and literacy difficulties: A psycholinguistic framework.* London: Whurr.)

three systems, Stackhouse and Wells (1997) proposed four anchor points in their model of speech processing. Processing may be based on incoming information (input processing) or may serve to generate output (output processing). The processing activity may focus on stored information (i.e., information derived from previously stored lexical representations) or alternatively may reflect bottom-up processing, for which no such prior knowledge is required and reference to the lexical representation system is not necessary, as illustrated in Figure 5.1.

a. Speech Processing in the Developmental Context

Children with speech and/or literacy difficulties are presumed to have problems somewhere in the speech processing system, that is, in processing speech input, in developing representations of input, or in processing speech output. Stackhouse and Wells (1997) summarized the role of the speech processing system in the development of reading and spelling as follows:

> Without intact *input* skills children cannot process what they hear. If minimal pairs of words such as PIN/BIN or LOST/LOTS are not differentiated at the level of auditory discrimination and sequencing, they may not be stored as separate lexical items with distinct phonological representations. . . . An inaccurate or imprecise *phonological representation* of a word will be particularly problematic when the child wants to spell or name that word, since the phonological representation is the basis for spontaneous written or spoken production. Consistently accurate *output* skills are particularly important for rehearsing verbal material in memory. . . . Without this verbal rehearsal children find it difficult to segment utterances into their components—a necessary prerequisite for allocating letters to sounds to form spellings of new words. Literacy success is therefore dependent on coupling speech processing skills at the input, representation and output levels, with alphabetic knowledge gained through orthographic experience. (pp. 15–16)

As discussed in Chapter 4, the relationship between severe speech production impairments and the development of phonological processing skills is far from resolved. Although there is little evidence to suggest that peripheral speech production impairments interfere with all aspects of phonological processing, nonetheless the possibility remains that certain aspects of processing are assisted by the facility for verbal rehearsal (Bishop & Robson, 1989; Foley, 1989; Foley & Pollatsek, 1999; Smith, 2001). Phonological working memory seems to be one candidate for this influence. It seems clear that severe speech impairments do not necessarily cause a deficit in phonological processing. However, it is equally true that the presence of speech impairments does not preclude the presence of a phonological processing impairment. What it does is make it more difficult to *identify* such impairments.

b. Applications of Psycholinguistic Models

Psycholinguistic models, such as that proposed by Stackhouse and Wells (1997), have gained popularity, partly because of their potential to guide both assessment and intervention. "The aim of the psycholinguistic approach is to find out exactly where on this model the child's speech processing skills are breaking down, and how this might be affecting speech and literacy development" (Stackhouse & Wells, 1997, p. 9). Assessment procedures can be structured to explore input processing for both nonsense (i.e., unstored) material and stored lexical representations. For example, tasks such as deciding whether spoken stimuli /flɪt/ /blɪt/ or /wɛks/, /bɛks/ are the same or different can be completed without any reference to stored lexical representations. On the other hand, if asked to point to "socks" from an array of pictures including "fox," "socks," and "sacks," the correct picture can only be identified when individuals scan their lexicons and access the appropriate, previously stored representations.

Similarly, output tasks may require analysis or activation of stored linguistic material as, for example, in a naming task, or they may require processing of unstored information, such as in tasks requiring repetition of nonwords. Tasks requiring processing of unstored material are often regarded as shedding a relatively pure light on phonological processing capacities, because the stimuli are not "contaminated" by any representational factors. The ability to repeat nonsense words is regarded as a reliable index of phonological memory, whereas the ability to read nonwords is also considered to be a reliable index of the ability to decode phoneme-grapheme relationships (Gathercole & Baddeley, 1990).

Psycholinguistic models of speech processing have increasingly been used to focus assessment and intervention with individuals who have spoken and/or written language difficulties and have been helpful in illuminating contrasting types of difficulty in individuals with relatively similar surface presentations. One major advantage is that traditional assessment tools, such as measures of receptive vocabulary, and naming tasks can easily be slotted into the framework and used to derive information referenced to the anchor points of the model. Such measures can therefore be used not only as a *knowledge* measure (e.g., vocabulary is an important consideration in assessment of literacy skills) but also as an indicator of processing efficiency. To successfully identify a named stimulus from an array of four options, an individual must perceive and process the auditory stimulus, scan a stored lexical set, and select the unique match. Difficulty with such a task may reflect either a limited vocabulary or lexical pool or alternatively a processing difficulty. A processing difficulty can be explored by presenting arrays of phonologically similar or dissimilar items and contrasting performance across both contexts. If an individual can select "fork" from an array containing "fork," "spoon," "knife," and "plate," but is unsuccessful if the array comprises "fork," "four," "pork," and "fort," then attention must focus on processing skills, rather than the vocabulary domain. From a diagnostic point of view, therefore, processing models can be extremely helpful. Clinicians and educators can create tools relatively quickly and easily to shed light on particular areas of processing difficulty.

c. Psycholinguistic Models in AAC

There are several challenges that arise when one attempts to apply speech processing models of assessment with individuals who have severe speech and physical impairments. One problem is that most aided communicators have access to a restricted range of response options, so that presentation of tasks must be adapted. These adaptations may change the nature of the task itself (see Blischak, 1994). Because this is a general problem in all assessments of individuals with significant physical and communication difficulties, it will be discussed in further detail later, under Principle 5.

A second problem is that assessing output tasks is extremely difficult in many instances. For example, one common assessment task with individuals who have written language difficulties taps the ability to rapidly name stimuli. Many aided communicators are constrained in the external lexicon available to them. As with their speaking peers, failure to name a presented picture stimulus may reflect a naming deficit or a vocabulary limitation. Careful selection of the stimuli should allow an examiner to determine which is the more likely explanation. However, with aided communicators, such apparent failure to name items may also reflect a difficulty finding the appropriate representation in their communication systems. Aided communicators may access appropriate internal lexical representations but not have these targets in their communication systems. Another possibility is that they may not be able to recall the necessary code to select the target or they may not be able to remember where the target is stored within their systems. Although it may be possible to get around some of these difficulties by ensuring that targets selected are readily and easily accessible, such an action eliminates the potential for exploring contrasting performance across frequently and infrequently used vocabulary—a contrast that may in itself have diagnostic significance.

4. Stored–Unstored Distinctions

Psycholinguistic models contrast performance not only on input–output tasks but also on the processing of stored and unstored information. If an examiner lists a set of four words, one of which does not rhyme with the others, individuals may identify the odd word either by reference to their stored representations, or alternatively, may simply engage in "on-line" processing and treat the set of words as if they were nonwords. In contrast, if an examiner simply presents a set of pictures in which one item does not rhyme with the others, and does not name the stimuli, then the only way to complete the task accurately is for individuals to access their own lexical representations and perform comparisons. In a similar manner, individuals may be asked to repeat real words of varying length, to assess the consistency and reliability of the motor programs they have stored for these lexical items, for broad generalizations to be made about their speech motor programing in general. A more stringent assessment task requires the repetition of nonwords, for which no learning effects are in place to support performance.

Accurate repetition of a novel stimulus (i.e., a nonword) requires accurate processing and temporary storage of the input stimulus and the generation of an appropriate motor program as the basis for motor output. Nonword repetition is therefore often used as a measure of motor programing for children with speech impairments. Typically developing children perform better when they repeat real words than when they attempt to repeat nonwords (Vance, Stackhouse, & Wells, 1995). However, the contrast in performance is often significant for children with specific speech difficulties and literacy problems (Stackhouse & Wells, 1997), suggesting a particular difficulty in creating a motor program for a new word. Comparable difficulties with both tasks may reflect either pervasive processing difficulties or a lower level articulatory disorder.

In written language tasks, the ability to read novel nonwords depends on an intact phonological processor. With novel stimuli, the visual route to word identification is only of use as a secondary strategy based on analogy with known words. Hence an individual who can read nonsense words must be able to decode the individual graphemes, assign a phonemic code to each grapheme, retain the string of grapheme-phoneme correspondences in memory, and synthesize the information to generate an appropriate response. Even if analogy is being used, the individual must be able to assign the appropriate phoneme-grapheme link to the novel element of the stimulus.

Nonword stimuli therefore offer a particular window on both input and output processing efficiency. Discrepancies in performance across real and nonsense stimuli may have diagnostic significance and hence implications for management. However, for individuals with significant speech impairments, the use of nonsense stimuli is extremely problematic. Nonwords by definition do not form part of stored lexical sets. How can they be produced by individuals who rely on such stored sets? The only route to production of nonwords for individuals with severely compromised speech abilities is through generation of a written form of the target. However, it is precisely the lack of literacy skills that often prompts the in-depth assessment of speech processing and the use of nonword stimuli. Several creative tasks have been devised in an attempt to explore nonword processing abilities for individuals with severe speech impairments (e.g., Erickson, 2003; Foley & Pollatsek, 1999; Iacono & Cupples, 2003; McNaughton, 1998; Vandervelden & Siegel, 1999, 2001). We will return to these tasks in more detail when we discuss assessment practicalities (see Chapter 6).

5. A Model to Assess Participation

Most of the above discussion has focused on the assessment of an individual with complex communication needs, albeit through a range of lens perspectives that includes their immediate communication environments. A complementary approach is offered by the model of Participation Assessment proposed by Beukelman and Mirenda (1992, 1998). They suggested that (at least) three critical factors must be considered in assessment: *opportunities*, *needs*, and *barriers*. Smith and Blischak (1997) discussed the application of this model to literacy assessment.

Assessment of *opportunities* can be considered under all three contexts referred to by Pumfrey and Reason (1991). The learning context indicates the importance of a broad range of life experiences, if the reader is to be able to relate to the thoughts and purposes of the author. It is therefore worth considering the opportunities for experiencing a range of different environments available to the individual being assessed. Opportunities in the language context refer to experience with a range of language forms and uses allied with opportunities to participate in a wide range of communication situations. The print context is explored through assessment of opportunities to observe literate adults and peers engaging in reading and writing, participating actively in meaningful literacy activities, and exploring literacy materials independently. Opportunities to explore the sound system of the language and to engage in sound play, in directed activities involving rhyming, segmentation, and analysis, and in production of vocalizations or synthetic speech output should also be assessed.

Most of us read or write to fulfill definite *needs* or purposes, which dictate the nature and form of the literacy activity we select. Assessment of an individual's needs to engage in literacy activities should consider a variety of overlapping purposes of literacy such as the following:

- Self-regulation—writing a reminder to oneself
- Social interaction—writing a letter to a friend
- Education—obtaining or transmitting information
- Employment—developing a mailing list
- Recreation—enjoying poetry

It is important to identify needs that are currently being met, as well as currently unmet and future needs. A restricted range of identified needs may point to a lack of awareness of the many functions of print. Given that literacy learning ideally occurs in the context of functional, meaningful experiences, it is worth exploring what unidentified needs might be present in the life of an AAC user and then broadening the range of needs before addressing the issue of literacy learning itself.

Subtle philosophical *barriers* may relate to beliefs, policies, and practices, whereas more obvious practical barriers refer to the physical characteristics of the environment. Research to date suggests that the beliefs and expectations of parents and teachers are important in shaping the perceptions individuals have of themselves as readers-writers (Koppenhaver, Evans, & Yoder, 1991). Light and McNaughton (1993) reported that other outcomes, such as independence, may supersede literacy in the hierarchy of parental and educator priorities.

Beliefs themselves often inform policies. For example, if the expectation is that *all* children will learn to read and write, then inclusion of children with disabilities in a mainstream educational curriculum (whether in an integrated or segregated setting) is required. If expectations for academic performance are low or if physical independence is considered to be of primary importance, then withdrawal from reading class for other therapy activities is acceptable. Clearly, for individuals with complex needs, expectations and priorities must be determined on an individual basis. The formulation of policy and methods of intervention based on beliefs about a homogeneous group is inherently problematic.

Practices may closely mirror policy or may be almost in direct opposition to stated policy, even though this opposition may not be conscious or deliberate. For example, a child with a speech impairment may be placed in a mainstream class, and withdrawal for therapies may not be allowed, but there may still be little real participatory inclusion.

Careful observation of school or, for adults, work environments, should indicate whether there are philosophical barriers operating in practice, relating to beliefs about needs, ways of learning, and expectations for learning. Practical barriers may be more easily identified and include issues such as physical positioning in a classroom. For example, Eileen, described by Smith (1991), attended a small rural school with narrow aisles between desks. The only space for her wheelchair within the classroom was in the front of the class, so that she faced her peers. This positioning not only made unsanctioned peer interaction difficult, but also placed Eileen physically closer to the teacher, thereby emphasizing her exclusion from her classmates. Assessment of extrinsic barriers is best accomplished in collaboration with individuals who can actually effect change. Often, simply asking for consideration and writing down specific information regarding accessibility are sufficient to spark change. However, it is important to use both interview and direct observation to determine the interactions between beliefs and expectations, policy, and actual practice.

B. The Focus of Assessment

Principle 2: *Assessment should be time-efficient and guide intervention.*

Assessment may serve many functions. It may be undertaken to determine eligibility for service provision or to measure progress. It may be used to plot an individual's abilities on a developmental profile. However, the most important purpose of assessment is to guide intervention. Pumfrey and Reason (1991) referred to the *symbiotic relationship* between assessment and intervention—the inseparability of these two processes. For individuals with severe speech impairments and other physical, sensory, perceptual, neurological, and/or cognitive impairments, *all* activities (including participation in assessment) take longer than for their peers. A key maxim therefore must be *maximum gain for minimum pain.* In other words, assessments must be time-efficient, yielding useful information to guide intervention, rather than a list of deficits. Given the range of impairments commonly presented by individuals who use AAC, it is tempting to fall into the trap of adopting what Wolf and Glass (1992) called a *shotgun* approach to assessment. In such an approach, a full battery of assessment tools is essentially thrown at the problem, in the hope that relevant information will emerge. The implicit danger in such a scenario is that assessment itself becomes an end goal. A contrasting but equally ineffective approach to assessment is to attempt to oversimplify the process to save time and hence find that assessment has yielded little information that can be used to guide intervention.

1. Static Assessment Approaches

Although assessment must be broadly focused, in that it must be holistic and have a multiple-lens perspective, the goal of the assessment must be clearly and narrowly defined. Occasionally, it may be important to establish performance of aided communicators relative to that of their age-matched peers (perhaps for service delivery, allocation of resources, or legal reasons). The assessment tools typically used in such a situation are norm-referenced. An individual's performance is plotted against the expected performance of someone of the same age or grade level. Raw scores can be converted into standard scores of different types and sometimes into age equivalencies. An example of a norm-referenced test is the Peabody Picture Vocabulary Test (Dunn & Dunn, 1997). However, norm-referenced assessment approaches have significant limitations.

Typically these static assessments simply establish a list of deficits already apparent to those working with the individual. The tools used are product-focused. Performance is scored as correct or incorrect on a range of measures, yielding a quantitative measure of performance, possibly as a profile of strengths and weaknesses. Only those areas in which abilities are completely developed, as evidenced in a consistently accurate score, are revealed as strengths. As Westby, StevensDominguez, and Oetter (1997) pointed out, such product-focused procedures "seldom provide information concerning how the children arrived at the answers or the strategies they used to complete the activities. More importantly, such assessments provide little useful information to guide intervention" (p. 144).

In addition to the above limitations, there are many problems with using norm-referenced assessment tools with a client group having significant communication difficulties and other associated impairments. Such tools rarely include individuals with difficulties or impairments within their standardization sample, compromising the value of normative information. Assessment procedures often need to be adapted for individuals with a restricted range of response options. Time and physical fatigue factors may mean spreading the assessment over a period of time, compromising the validity of normative data. Finally, the range of assessment tools available that require only a nonverbal response is limited, so that test selection may reflect more the response modes available to the client rather than the assessment focus desired by the assessor.

An alternative to norm-referenced assessment is criterion-referenced assessment. Whereas norm-referenced assessments yield information summarizing performance relative to a normative sample, the emphasis in criterion-referenced assessments is on determining the specific knowledge or skill base acquired within a particular domain. An example of a criterion-referenced assessment tool is the Derbyshire Language Scheme (Knowles & Madislover, 1982). In this assessment tool, the outcome or product yielded is information about the number of information units within a sentence that can be accurately processed to guide a response. Although criterion-referenced assessment tools may be potentially more useful in suggesting intervention targets, they are of limited use in determining *how* intervention should proceed for maximal effectiveness.

2. Dynamic Assessment Approaches

Unlike static assessment approaches, dynamic assessment approaches focus on the process(es) by which children arrive at solutions to problems (or assessment tasks), the factors that support or compromise their performance, and the scaffolding and mediation required to maximally enhance their learning (Goldsworthy, 1996). In such an approach, assessment and intervention are intimately linked. Assessment is ongoing but is achieved actively, through intervention (Nelson, 1994). At key points, it may be necessary to focus more specifically on assessment, but even within such points, the question asked in dynamic assessment relates to the *nature* of the difficulty, rather than to its extent, and the strategies that are useful in terms of compensation for such difficulty. The emphasis is on finding the level at which success can be achieved and finding the best ways of raising that level. Adopting a dynamic assessment approach does not necessarily preclude the use of either norm- or criterion-referenced assessment tools. Rather, it shifts the focus from the score achieved on assessment tools to the actual performance of the individual—what process led to the score and what implications that process might have for future work.

3. Constraints of Assessment

For all individuals, being assessed can be tiring, somewhat stressful, and in some ways even threatening. Naturalistic assessments may attempt to mitigate the effects associated with assessment, but it is extremely difficult to eliminate them entirely. For individuals with severe physical impairments, all activities take longer than for their peers, so the emphasis must be on obtaining as much information as possible from as little performance as possible. A simple solution to this problem is to use a very small number of items within an assessment. If typical reading assessments, for example, present 20 word-picture matching tasks, the decision may be made to use only a small selection of these items when one assesses someone with significant performance constraints. The potential risk in such a strategy is a temptation to overinterpret single performances as reliable indicators of underlying abilities. This leads to a constant tension between maintaining reliability and minimizing task demands.

One approach to resolving this tension is to adapt existing test materials, either in the number of items offered (as above), the format of response required, or the physical characteristics. For example, items may be enlarged to accommodate visual difficulties or spaced to facilitate eye-pointing responses. Such adaptations cause their own difficulties in terms of interpreting responses, as discussed later, but may offer the only option in certain contexts.

A second approach is to devise assessment tools specifically to meet the performance abilities of individuals with significant impairments. Often, this is the approach adopted in research, in which specific protocols are devised, often loosely based on existing tools. The advantage here is that performance limitations are *built in* to the design of the test instrument. Generally speaking, materials and response requirements are tailored to the needs of the individual, rather than adopted from another frame and imposed on an individual. The materials can be devised to address specific questions relating to an individual, be made relevant to the individual's interests and experiences, and be improved as a result of the input from significant people in the environment.

A disadvantage of such a strategy, however, is that the assessment protocols may be used only within the specific piece of research for which they were devised or with one particular client. Generalizing findings from research becomes very difficult. Considerable time and effort may be spent by many different researchers, reinventing the same wheel, with only minor variations in the nature of the spokes. In the worst-case scenario, a completely different wheel-like structure may evolve, making it very difficult to develop and expand the knowledge base within the field. There is another potential risk—the risk of further isolating research in literacy with exceptional populations from what can be regarded as mainstream research. Despite these risks, it is likely that for many clinical assessment purposes, individually devised assessment protocols will continue to form a key part of assessment, with therapists and educators integrating findings from many different sources. As long as assessment is seen as an ongoing process, rather than as a start-up product, the limitations of nonstandardized tools can be counterbalanced by the skill of the assessor.

A third approach, one that is receiving increasing attention, is to develop literacy assessment tools that are expected to have applicability across all individuals, including those with no impairments as well as those with significant sensory, motor, or linguistic difficulties. The goal is therefore to ensure mainstream use, while not disadvantaging those with response limitations through the design of the response format (Erickson, 2003).

C. Literacy as a Goal-Driven Activity

Principle 3: *Assessment must be goal driven and reflect the varied functions of literacy for individuals using AAC.*

Reading and writing are activities that are undertaken primarily in the service of other goals. There may be times when the goal is simply to write as a therapeutic experience in itself, but generally, we write with a purpose—to make sure we complete tasks, to make contact with individuals, to apply for employment, and so on. In a similar vein, individuals who have difficulty reading and writing may decide to address their difficulties because of a particular primary need. They may seek to learn to read and write to be able to help their own children with homework or to meet a particular job requirement. The purpose is not incidental to the process of reading or writing—the purpose dictates the reading and writing strategies adopted and so is intimately connected to the skills used in any given task. To take effective notes during a lecture a person must have the ability to synthesize information, abstract key points, and then jot them down in telegraphic form, within a logical structure. Use of numbers, arrows, or other organizing symbols often makes it easier to make sense of the notes subsequently. It is generally useful also to be able to write legibly at great speed. A letter written to a friend in this format and using the same skills, however, would appear bizarre to the receiver.

Similarly, the way we read changes according to task demands. If we are reading to gain particular information about a product or an address, for example, we can effectively discard large chunks of text, with only a cursory scan to check whether or not the text contains necessary key features (perhaps the initial letters of the target name). Only when increasingly large sections of the text present with potentially useful information do we need to slow our rate and pay more conscious attention to all elements of the text. These strategies work very well, if we are searching for a phone number. However, if we use similar strategies as we proofread a text before submitting it for an assignment, then the chances are that we will miss a lot of important information that may affect a final grade. Clearly, in all of the scenarios outlined above, there are certain core processing skills that are common across all the tasks. However, there is a range of additional strategies that may be pulled into service, depending on task requirements. Assessing reading comprehension by exploring an individual's ability to answer questions on a previous text is certainly one essential component of an overall assessment. Nonetheless, it only provides information about abilities for that particular task. The point is not that all possible reading or writing tasks must be assessed, but rather that we do not assume that reading levels shown on one particular task will necessarily be transferable to other, different, tasks with different task requirements.

Similarly, assessment is undertaken for a purpose. Throughout this book, the emphasis is on assessment as a guide to intervention. The aim may be to determine where to go next, in terms of intervention, or to identify the kinds of texts that are best suited to support the development of specific skills and to offer useful and productive reading experiences. Ideally, the goals of intervention are coconstructed by the person using AAC, significant communication partners, and clinicians/educators. The purposes of assessment should be linked to the literacy goals being considered, so that the question, "What do I, as an assessor, want to find out?," is linked directly with the question, "What does this person using AAC want to achieve through reading and writing?"

Uncovering the motivational focus for individuals who use AAC may offer a very useful platform for focusing intervention. For most children within a school system, reading and writing are presented as curriculum subjects, and the balance across both depends more on the teacher's philosophy and the flexibility of the educational program than on most other factors. However, adults may approach the task of learning to read and write with different priorities. My experience with adults who use AAC has been that their initial priority is to develop spelling and writing skills. After a period of work on the output side of the continuum, their interest in developing more effective decoding skills emerges. There may be practical reasons for this focus. For many of them, reading is associated with a long history of failure and educational frustration. Their need to read in many instances is limited. Even if they achieve effective reading skills, their opportunities to read independently are few. For some, the realization that reading is necessary to use tools such as email to communicate with others, kick-starts motivation to focus on development of reading skills.

The goals of reading and writing are many for those with complex communication needs as well for those with fewer difficulties. Assessment should focus on potential literacy activities, from hitting a switch to listen to a taped story or contribute a repeated story line to joining on-line discussion groups or producing creative writing. For those with degenerative conditions (e.g., motor neuron disease or multiple sclerosis), the most relevant focus may be on an individual's ability to use word prediction or alphabet-based encoding principles to retrieve stored lexical items. Where possible, the links between written language skills and communication skills should be maximized. Although every gain in literacy abilities potentially contributes to communicative efficiency, explicit demonstration of links may be needed to harness transfer effectively. This means including a consideration of the skills that are needed to enhance communicative effectiveness throughout the literacy journey.

D. Literacy as a Developmental Process

Principle 4: *Assessment should, where appropriate, reflect the developmental nature of literacy attainment.*

Reading and writing skills develop over time, and in a fairly predictable sequence, as component skills become more automatic. Young children starting to learn to read and write draw on a different range of skills than do older children or adults who are already reading. There is an attractive logic, therefore, to use of developmental models as a frame of reference in exploring reading and writing abilities. In particular, such a framework highlights the continuum that exists from the early stage apprentice reader to the fluent independent reader-writer. Literacy skills along many points on the continuum may be explored. Such exploration provides useful indicators for possible future learning needs. There are two important caveats, however, that should be considered in applying a developmental framework. First, as with all aspects of development, "stages" of development are not discrete. Children do not retire to bed one night as alphabetic readers and emerge from slumber as orthographic readers. A more useful way of applying the developmental framework is to consider the range of different reading and writing skills that have been added to the pool of resources available to an individual. Skills that appear to emerge early are not discarded as individuals become more competent at reading and writing—even if they appear to be dormant for much of the time. Fluent readers resort to letter-by-letter decoding when the need arises, even if they appear to rarely use such strategies for their day-to-day reading activities. The focus is therefore less on plotting the developmental stage attained as an end point in itself, but rather on emphasizing the skills and resources that become available as reading and writing skills develop.

A second caveat is that the skills available to and availed of by an individual are intimately related to the specific text demands. By varying text difficulty or even the topic of the text, very different skills may become evident. Simple texts of high interest are likely to provide a window on the maximal level of performance, whereas texts of greater difficulty may provide insights into the strategies an individual falls back on when the text is less accessible.

The strength of the developmental approach is that it not only allows a profile of competence on a continuum to literacy attainment to be developed but also provides useful information about the next range of skills that need to be achieved. It allows inferences to be drawn about what is needed at each stage for an individual reader-writer. For example, for an individual at an early stage of literacy development, engaging in story-reading activities, with active participation, discussion of the language and content of the story, and opportunities to explore books and reading materials are valuable supports. Drawing attention to print-speech relationships and developing the language of stories provide support for future, more sophisticated, skills. For the apprentice writer, opportunities to draw, scribble, and attempt to write and all other ways of engaging with print provide a platform for developing print-specific concepts and future writing skills.

Phonological awareness skills are crucial to cracking of the alphabetic code. Progression to an understanding that sounds are discretely represented by particular graphemes requires some explicit instruction, ideally linking letter knowledge with tasks focusing specifically on sound properties and sound manipulation tasks. Consolidating these skills requires practice with texts that provide suitable challenges, with many opportunities for repetition with motivating texts to support the *self-teaching* proposed by Share (1995). Becoming a fluent reader requires, first and foremost, a lot of practice—with texts that are not too challenging, so that the reader can build representations of orthographic strings that can be accessed rapidly and easily, allowing speech and accuracy of reading to increase.

A developmental approach, however, is not always the most appropriate frame of reference. For older individuals, assessment must also take into account functional literacy needs. In many respects, assessment in such cases focuses on the goals of literacy attainment. For an individual with intelligibility difficulties, assessment may focus on identifying the contexts in which the individual can indicate the first sound of a word to support their intelligibility, with no intention of progressing further down the phonological recoding route. For others, the emphasis may be on determining the range of environmental print that is accessible to them—the sight words they can identify—and their immediate reading needs. Certainly, for many adolescents and adults who have difficulty with reading and writing, a developmental framework may be limited in its relevance when one considers the road map to development of more effective and functional literacy skills.

As a final point, when one considers assessment of the written language abilities of adults with complex communication needs, it is important to take into account their previous experiences with print and how these experiences might affect the context of learning for them. For many adults who use AAC, written language represents an obstacle they have never managed to overcome, and it carries with it many negative connotations and reminders of failure (Iacono, Balandin, & Cupples, 2001). The developmental path for such individuals is likely to be very different from that of children setting off on the road trail for the first time.

E. IMPLICATIONS OF ASSESSMENT ADAPTATIONS

Principle 5: *Assessment should consider the adaptations required by AAC users and the extent to which those adaptations may change task demands.*

Many individuals who use AAC have a range of additional difficulties that compromise and affect the response options available to them in assessment situations. The majority of those using aided communication have physical impairments; many also have visual, attention, and perceptual difficulties. All of these factors combined present a challenge in development of assessment tools. There are few standardized assessment tools currently available that can be used without adaptation. In some instances the adaptations are relatively minor—enlarging print or displaying items over a greater visual area, so that eye-pointing responses can be interpreted with greater reliability. In general, tools that require a nonverbal response can be modified with relatively little difficulty in this way. However, even these adaptations can represent subtle changes to the test format (Blischak, 1994). For example, it may be necessary to reduce the number of items presented to minimize the visual load or to facilitate eye-pointing responses. Additional time may be required (and *is* required in almost all cases), but this may mean that only partial information becomes available. As Stackhouse and Wells (1997) pointed out, accuracy is only one dimension of performance that is of interest in relation to processing—speed of processing is also crucial.

Of more fundamental concern are adaptations that change the nature of the task itself. On the whole, tasks that focus on input processing or on recognition and selection of targets can be modified relatively easily. Modifying output tasks, for which a speaking individual would be expected to produce a verbal response of some kind, is far more difficult. For example, in a common task measuring phonological awareness, children are asked to generate words that rhyme with a particular target (e.g., "cat"). It is difficult to use the same task with individuals who use aided communication. The range of vocabulary available on a communication board or in a device is typically very much reduced, relative to a presumed internal lexicon. Even if a participant has potential rhyming pairs available in an external lexicon, the time and effort involved in scanning and selecting a response are very different from the demands on a speaking child. Furthermore, if there is a written label accompanying the symbols displayed, rhyming words may be selected on the basis of orthographic or visual strategies, rather than on the basis of a phonologically motivated strategy.

One common adaptation is to present a set of pictures and to ask the AAC user to select the one that rhymes with the spoken target. However, this latter task is different in important ways from the first one (Blischak, 1994). It is primarily a recognition task, rather than a recall task (recall generally being regarded as the more difficult task). The recognition task, in this case, requires a child to retain a phonological string in memory while scanning distracter items, perform a comparison, and then select a response, so that the memory and processing loads are quite high. Furthermore, many typically developing children, when asked to generate a rhyming string, use a phonological strategy, rather than a lexical strategy (Stackhouse & Wells, 1997). Many produce a mix of words and nonwords (e.g., "cat," "bat," "fat," "gat," "mat," "nat," "pat," "at," and "wat"), suggesting that they do not necessarily access their own stored lexical representations to complete the task. When the task is modified to one of selecting the picture that rhymes with a spoken word, the participant is forced to use a lexical strategy.

Most output processing tasks being explored with individuals who use AAC and who do not write must be modified and in the adaptation often emerge as recognition rather than recall tasks. Blischak (1994) outlined a comprehensive list of adaptations. She pointed out, however, that task adaptations must be undertaken cautiously, or it may become difficult to separate performance on the additional task requirements from demonstration of the actual skill. It is also worth noting that, because spoken responses are not possible, the primary response mode is through pictures or occasionally spelling. Any visual perceptual difficulties will therefore exacerbate the difficulties of the task for many who use AAC to a far greater extent than for their speaking peers who have access to a broader range of response options.

Finally, fatigue is a far more central issue within the assessment process for individuals who use AAC than it is for most of their peers. Not only are the task demands different, but also testing itself creates far greater demands for those who have a range of communication, physical, and sensory difficulties. The testing demands may not be related directly to the focus of the assessment but may be central to the performance of the individual in that assessment.

III. SUMMARY

The preceding discussion has focused largely on principles that may be used to inform assessment. Primary among these principles has been the need to make use of the support of a team within assessment. The complexity of the processes involved in reading and writing must also be respected, and this complexity must be reflected in the choice of assessment tools and processes. Dynamic assessment approaches that yield information to guide intervention are far more valuable than tools that highlight a list of abilities and deficits, without reference to the strategies that support performance. Although developmental frameworks provide a key point of reference, functional approaches that emphasize sight–word abilities may assume primacy with certain individuals. Finally, assessment itself is complex, and the many adaptations that are often required to accommodate the physical needs of those who use AAC may have important implications for the nature of the tasks used and the inferences that can be drawn. These five principles are presented again in Figure 5.2.

Principle 1: Literacy achievement represents an integration of many factors, both

intrinsic and extrinsic to the individual

Principle 2: Assessment should be time-efficient and should guide intervention

Principle 3: Assessment must be goal-driven, and reflect the varied functions of literacy

for individuals using AAC

Principle 4: Assessment should, where appropriate, reflect the developmental nature of

literacy attainment

Principle 5: Assessment should consider the adaptations required by AAC users and the

extent to which those adaptations may change task demands

Figure 5.2.   Principles of assessment. (Adapted from Smith, M., & Blischak, D. (1997). Literacy. In L. Lloyd, D. Fuller, & H. Arvidson (Eds.), *Augmentative and Alternative Communication: Principles and Practices* (pp. 414–444.). London: Allyn & Bacon.)

In the next chapter, specific assessment approaches are outlined, with a greater emphasis of the practicalities of meeting the challenge of assessment.

REFERENCES

Bedell, G. (2002, March 17). Why can't Johnny read? *Observer*, p. 17.

Beukelman, D., & Mirenda, P. (1992). *Augmentative and alternative communication: Management of severe communication disorders in children and adults.* Baltimore, MD: Paul H. Brookes.

Beukelman, D., & Mirenda, P. (1998). *Augmentative and alternative Communication: Management of severe communication disorders in children and adults* (2nd ed). Baltimore, MD: Paul H. Brookes.

Bishop, D. V. M., & Robson, J. (1989). Unimpaired short-term memory and rhyme judgement in congenitally speechless individuals: Implications for the notion of "articulatory coding." *The Quarterly Journal of Experimental Psychology, 41A*(1), 123–140.

Blischak, D. M. (1994). Phonologic awareness: Implications for individuals with little or no functional speech. *Augmentative and Alternative Communication, 10*, 245–254.

Dahlgren-Sandburg, A. (1998) Reading and Spelling among nonvocal children with cerebral palsy: Influences of home and school literacy environment. *Reading and Writing: An Interdisciplinary Journal, 10*, 23–50.

Dahlgren-Sandberg, A., & Hjelmquist, E. (1997). Language and literacy in nonvocal children with cerebral palsy. *Reading and Writing: An Interdisciplinary Journal, 9*, 107–133.

Dunn, L. M., & Dunn, K. (1997). *Peabody Picture Vocabulary Test—III.* Circle Pines, MN: American Guidance Service.

Erickson, K. (2003). Evaluation techniques: The particular problem of how to assess output skills of individuals with complex communication needs and limited literacy skills. In S. von Tetzchner & M. Jensen (Eds.), *Perspectives on theory and practice in Augmentative and Alternative Communication: Proceedings of the Seventh ISAAC Biennial Research Symposium, Odense, Denmark, August 2002.* Toronto, Ontario: ISAAC, 191–196.

Foley, B. E. (1989). *Phonological recoding and congenital dysarthria.* Amherst: University of Massachusetts.

Foley, B. E., & Pollatsek, A. (1999). Phonological processing and reading abilities in adolescents and adults with severe congenital speech impairments. *Augmentative and Alternative Communication, 15*, 156–173.

Gathercole, S. E., & Baddeley, A. D. (1990). Phonological memory deficits in language-disordered children: Is there a causal connection? *Journal of Memory and Language, 29*, 336–360.

Goldsworthy, C. (1996). *Developmental reading disabilities: A language based treatment approach.* London: Singular Press.

Iacono, T., Balandin, S., & Cupples, L. (2001). Focus group discussions of literacy assessment and world wide web-based reading intervention. *Augmentative and Alternative Communication, 17*(1), 27–36.

Iacono, T., & Cupples, L. (2003). Language bases in literacy development: The challenge for people with complex communication needs. In S. von Tetzchner & M. Jensen (Eds.), *Perspectives on theory and practice in Augmentative and Alternative Communication: Proceedings of the Seventh ISAAC Biennial Research Symposium, Odense, Denmark, August 2002.* Toronto, Ontario: ISAAC, 183–190.

Knowles, W., & Madislover, M. (1982). *Derbyshire Language Scheme.* Derbyshire, UK: Derbyshire County Council.

Koppenhaver, D., Evans, D., & Yoder, D. E. (1991). Childhood reading and writing experiences of literate adults with severe speech and motor impairments. *Augmentative and Alternative Communication, 7*(1), 20–33.

Light, J., & McNaughton, D. (1993). Literacy and augmentative and alternative communication: The expectations and priorities of parents and teachers. *Topics in Language Disorders, 13*(2), 33–46.

McNaughton, S. (1998). *Reading acquisition of adults with severe congenital speech and physical impairments: Theoretical infrastructure, empirical investigation, education implication.* Unpublished doctoral dissertation, University of Toronto, Toronto, Ontario, Canada.

Nation, K., & Snowling, M. (2000). Factors influencing syntactic awareness skills in normal readers and poor comprehenders. *Applied Psycholinguistics, 21,* 229–241.

Nelson, N. W. (1994). Curriculum-based language assessment and intervention across the grades. In G. P. Wallach & K. G. Butler (Eds.), *Language learning disabilities in school-age children and adolescents: Some principles and applications* (pp. 104–131.). New York: Macmillan.

Pumfrey, P. D., & Reason, R. (1991). *Specific learning difficulties: Challenges and responses.* Berks, UK: NFER-Nelson.

Seidenberg, M., & McClelland, J. L. (1989). A distributed, developmental model of word recognition and naming. *Psychological Review, 96,* 523–568.

Share, D. L. (1995). Phonological recoding and self-teaching: *Sine qua non* of reading acquisition. *Cognition, 55,* 151–218.

Silliman, E., & Wilkinson, L. C. (1991). *Communicating for learning: Classroom observation and collaboration.* Gaithersburg, MD: Aspen.

Smith, M. (1991). Assessment of interaction patterns and AAC use—A case study. *Journal of Clinical Speech & Language Studies, 1,* 76–102.

Smith, M. (2001). Literacy challenges for individuals with severe congenital speech impairments.*International Journal of Disability, Development and Education, 48,* 331–353.

Smith, M., & Blischak, D. (1997). Literacy. In L. Lloyd, D. Fuller, & H. Arvidson (Eds.), Augmentative and Alternative Communication: Principles and Practices (pp. 414–444.). London: Allyn & Bacon.

Smith, M., & Grove, N. (2003). Asymmetry in input and output for individuals who use AAC. In J. Light, D. R. Beukelman, & J. Reichle (Eds.), *Communicative competence for individuals who use AAC: From research to effective practice* (pp. 163–195). Baltimore, MD: Paul H. Brookes.

Stackhouse, J., & Wells, B. (1997). *Children's speech and literacy difficulties: A psycholinguistic framework.* London: Whurr.

Stanovich, K. (1986). Matthew effects in reading: Some consequences of individual differences in the acquisition of literacy. *Reading Research Quarterly, 21,* 360–407.

Vance, M., Stackhouse, J., & Wells, B. (1995). The relationship between naming and word repetition skills in children age 3–7 years. Department of Human Communication Science, University College London: *Work in Progress, 5,* 127–133.

Vandervelden, M., & Siegel, L. (1999). Phonological processing and literacy in AAC users and students with motor speech impairments. *Augmentative and Alternative Communication, 15,* 191–211.

Vandervelden, M., & Siegel, L. (2001). Phonological processing in written word learning: assessment for children who use augmentative and alternative communication. *Augmentative and Alternative Communication, 17*(1), 11–26.

von Tetzchner, S., & Martinsen, H. (1992). *Introduction to sign teaching and the use of communication aids.* London: Whurr.

Westby, C., StevensDominguez, M., & Oetter, P. (1997). A performance/competence model of observational assessment. *Language, Speech, and Hearing Services in Schools, 27,* 144–155.

Wolf, L., & Glass, R. (1992). *Feeding and swallowing disorders in infancy: Assessment and management.* Tucson, AZ: Therapy Skill Builders.

Woll, B., & Barnett, S. (1998). Toward a sociolinguistic perspective on augmentative and alternative communication. *Augmentative and Alternative Communication, 14,* 200–211.

CHAPTER 6

The Practicalities of Assessment

I. INTRODUCTION

The challenges of assessment were outlined in the last chapter. Despite these challenges, careful, reflective assessment provides a cornerstone for future intervention. In this chapter, the focus is on the practicalities of assessment—the tools that can be used to explore abilities across a range of literacy-related areas. The list of tools suggested here is by no means exhaustive. Rather, in this chapter we present an overview of some of the measures referred to in research with individuals who use augmentative and alternative communication (AAC). The focus is on specific tasks used in the assessment of language, metalinguistic, reading, and writing abilities. As new resources become available, it is important that every attempt be made to consider their application for those who use AAC

Literacy and Augmentative and Alternative Communication

and the implications of any adaptations that may be necessary for the tools to be accessible. As has been discussed previously, formal measures should be used with great caution and only rarely can normative information be derived, given the limitations of the standardization and administration procedures typically implicit in such tests. As always, a key component in the assessment process is an informed clinician or educator who understands the complexity of literacy, the assessment process, and the challenges facing those who use AAC.

II. A POSSIBLE MODEL

Beukelman and Mirenda (1992, 1998), in their model of assessment of participation, set out three key realms for consideration in looking at enhancing participation in communication activities (Figure 6.1). These realms are also relevant when one thinks about participation in literacy activities. The three realms for consideration are opportunities to engage in literacy activities, needs that must be fulfilled, and barriers to participation. Arising out of this perspective, assessment can be structured to do the following:

1. Objectively evaluate the literacy learning and participation opportunities that are and that have been available to the target individual and compare these opportunities to those of peers.

2. Explore the range of literacy needs that exist and are perceived to exist for the target individual, again relating this information to the needs identified for peers.

3. Determine and quantify the barriers to participation for the target individual, considering whether these barriers relate to factors that are intrinsic or extrinsic to the individual in question.

Smith and Blischak (1997) applied this model to the assessment of literacy and set out a range of questions that might be useful in developing insights into the factors, both intrinsic and extrinsic to the individual, that may promote or limit their development of reading and writing (Tables 6.1 to 6.3).

III. TOOLS AND APPROACHES

Many tools to explore the range of skills involved in reading and writing are available. As discussed in the previous chapter, not all tools can be used with individuals with a limited range of response options. However, an attempt will be made here to outline some of the tools reported as being useful in the literature. Assessment not only must focus on outcome products, as evidenced in test

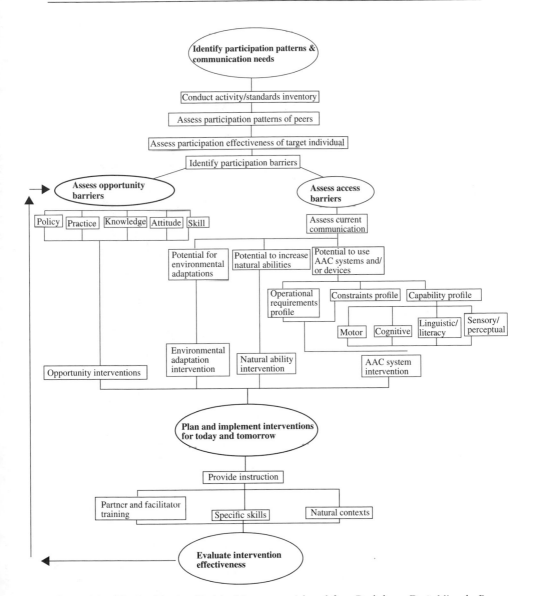

Figure 6.1. The Participation Model of Assessment. Adapted from Beukelman, D., & Mirenda, P. (1992). *Augmentative and alternative communication: Management of severe communication disorders in children and adults* (p. 102). Baltimore, MD: Paul H Brooks.

Table 6.1

Literacy Assessment of Young Preschool Children

Opportunities	Needs	Barriers
How frequently are storybooks read to the child at home? In other settings? By whom? Does the child have a favorite storybook? Are stories re-read? Does the child actively participate in the reading activity? Does the child assist in turning pages? Ask questions? Comment?	What are the different literacy needs throughout the day? How is the child encouraged to/assisted in participating? Examples include reading recipes, writing lists, looking up a telephone number, sending greeting cards, and reading a map.	What importance is attached to literacy in the home? In other environments? Do caregivers believe that the child can attain literacy? How important is literacy within the total framework of the child's needs? How is the child positioned during reading and writing activities? Can the child
Does the child handle books and other printed matter?	Does the child know the front from back of books? Top from bottom? Can the child turn the pages? Point to print vs. picture?	see the text? The reader's face?
Are there a variety of writing opportunities? Scribbling? Painting?	Does the child differentiate writing from drawing? Know that writing can be "read"? Does the child	Is an assistive communicative device used? How does the child typically communicate during
Are there opportunities to observe adults engaging in literacy activities?	understand that during reading some elements are repeated? Does the child recognize adults' mistakes in reading?	literacy activities? Are adaptations such as amplification or magnification provided?
	Does the child engage in fingerplays, rhymes, and sound play?	Are activities interesting? Relevant to the child's experiences? At a suitable language level? Are writing materials adapted?

From Smith, M., & Blischak, D. (1997). Literacy. In L. Lloyd, D. Fuller & H. Arvidson (Eds.), *Augmentative and alternative communication: Principles and practices* (pp. 414–444.). London: Allyn & Bacon.

scores, but also must consider the processes that underlie the attainment of a score. In other words, although static assessment tools may be used, a dynamic assessment approach focuses the lens through which performance is viewed. Throughout assessment, qualitative information is needed to supplement information derived through quantitative assessment measures. As a final cautionary note, McNaughton (1998) cited an analogy offered by Stanovich while lecturing to educators, which compared a score on a test to the result obtained by a physician in testing a knee reflex:

> The patient's reaction to a knee tap contributes to the physician's diagnosis of the patient's total state of health. Its relevance is dependent upon many circumstances, however, and it is but one of several indicators of the patient's general physical condition. Neither a poor reflex nor the result on a single reading skill test should be

Table 6.2

Literacy Assessment of Preschool–Early Elementary School Children

Opportunities	Needs	Barriers
Is the school environment "print-rich?" Is there a "literacy center" with available reading and writing materials? • Is the child encouraged to view educational television programs that feature explicit exposure to literacy? Independently? With adult interaction-discussion? 　Are children encouraged to engage in literacy experiences in pairs, groups, or individually? Is group discussion encouraged? 　Are visits to the library included as part of the home or school curriculum? How often? Are books purchased or borrowed? Does the child have a book collection? A favorite book?	Are reading activities built around a language theme or do they occur independently of other school activities? Does the child attend to/identify print in the environment? Examples include possessions (lunchboxes, bookbags), personal areas (lockers), areas of the school and classroom (boys, girls, exit), and environmental print (labels, signs). Does the child identify the alphabet? associate letters with sounds? recognize words by sight? demonstrate beginning "word-attack" skills? Does the child print letters to represent sounds, syllables, or words? Write from left to right? Write words? sentences? Use invented spellings? Can the child retell familiar stories? Remember and/or predict outcomes?	What is the prevailing philosophical approach to literacy development in the school? Is "readiness" considered to be important in determining when to introduce literacy materials? Are reading/writing materials physically accessible? Can application of technology provide physical access? • Can the child participate in literacy experiences to the extent that nondisabled peers do? Are appropriate communication messages available via an AAC system? How are changes in message needs managed?

From Smith, M., & Blischak, D. (1997). Literacy. In L. Lloyd, D. Fuller & H. Arvidson (Eds.), *Augmentative and alternative communication: Principles and practices* (pp. 414–444.). London: Allyn & Bacon.

considered a behavior to be directly treated. Rather, both outcomes provide one of many signals that together can lead to a plan for intervention. (pp. 310–311)

A. Qualitative Approaches

Interviews, ecological inventories, observation schedules, and questionnaires all form part of qualitative assessment resources. There are many possible interview tools that can be used.

Table 6.3

Literacy Assessment of Later Elementary School Children

Opportunities	Needs	Barriers
Does the child have opportunities to engage in different types of reading/writing activities? Does that child spend the most time on skill-building with word- or sentence-level tasks? • How often does the child produce text that is longer than a paragraph? • Does the child have opportunities to independently read text of personal interest within their ability range? Is adult guidance provided? Is the teacher aware of the child's interests? Are there opportunities for discussion of literature and suggestions for future reading?	What are the literacy needs/tasks of same-aged peers as they relate to academic, social, and extracurricular participation? Examples include content areas such as social studies, mathematics, music, art; corresponding with an electronic "pen-pal"; playing board or card games; participating in school performances such as plays or concerts; and viewing, participating in, or discussing sports. Does the child comprehend extended written text? Answer questions? Discuss what has been read? Can the child compose coherent text, with few spelling errors? Edit independently? Revise both mechanical errors and writing content/style? Can the child access dictionaries, encyclopedias, and other reference materials?	How does use of AAC link with the literacy demands of the classroom? How flexible are others in expanding or facilitating integration of technology? Are back-ups provided in the case of equipment breakdown? Are appropriate adaptations provided for test-taking, completing homework, independent study, and text production?

Smith, M., & Blischak, D. (1997). Literacy. In L. Lloyd, D. Fuller & H. Arvidson (Eds.), *Augmentative and alternative communication: Principles and practices* (pp. 414–444). London: Allyn & Bacon.

1. Questionnaires

McNaughton (1998) developed a questionnaire focusing on the current and previous literacy experiences of individuals with severe congenital speech and physical impairments. Likewise, Koppenhaver, Evans, and Yoder (1991) presented a comprehensive questionnaire in their research with adults who used AAC. The themes covered in the questionnaire include the range of literacy experiences available in childhood to the participants, information about the frequency of opportunities to read, support for reading both at home and in school, and specific instructional practices. Questionnaires like these provide valuable information about the learning context of individuals using AAC and also allow a therapist to interpret other assessment findings more realistically. Reading and writing require specific instruction, at least for the vast majority of individuals. Difficulties in demonstrating competence may be inaccurately ascribed to intrinsic limitations of the individual, unless there is a clear understanding of the teaching aids that have been available to support the development of necessary skills.

Literacy activities are undertaken for a purpose. Interviews, discussions, or questionnaires may provide useful insights into the sources of interest and motivation for children, adolescents, and adults using aided communication (Koppenhaver & Yoder, 1992; Wixson, Bosky, Yochum, & Alvermann, 1984). The Reading Comprehension Interview (Wixson et al., 1984) offers a different kind of focus. This interview format is designed for use with students who have already achieved a relatively high degree of literacy skill and focuses on their understanding of the purposes or goals of classroom reading activities. The questions allow exploration of a student's meta-insights into reading and writing within the class, addressing issues such as the following:

- What is the most important reason for reading this kind of material?
- What do you have to do to get a good grade in _____ in your class?
- Why would your teacher want you to do worksheets like these?
- If you were the teacher, what would you ask this person to do differently next time?

2. Observation

Koppenhaver and Yoder (1992) suggested that observation of literacy instruction can also provide useful information. There are several ways in which this can be accomplished. One can be termed *self-observation* or *monitoring*. Here, the educator can simply set a time alarm to go off at regular intervals throughout a school day and record the activity that is in progression at each time point, thus giving an overview of the typical realization of a day's plan.

An alternative is to use an outside observer or a videotape recorder to chart what happens at regular intervals through the day. Such observation can be unstructured, if essentially all information that is perceived by the observer to be relevant at a given point is written down. Alternatively, observation can be structured to various degrees. The person recording may simply fill in a sheet with a set of predetermined categories of likely activities (e.g., reading instruction in group, individual silent reading, class discussion, writing, mathematics, art, nursing care, and break time). A decision can be made that the sheet will be filled in every 15 minutes to give insight into the typical makeup of a day. Of course, the information obtained in such a format is limited and is specific to the time of recording; in other words, unless the task is repeated many times over, those involved must be cautious in attempting to draw any generalizations on the basis of such meager data. However, even with these limitations, it can be useful to compare such observation sheets with an educator's plan for the day. This may lead to discussion of how an educational plan can be fully implemented for even a short period within a day.

Information obtained through observation need not be restricted to ticking off of predetermined categories. Additional support information can also be recorded to describe the activity at the point of observation, thus yielding a richer description of learning opportunities. The exact nature of a literacy activity can be described, with information about the performance of the target individual within that activity.

Each of these observation approaches has limitations and strengths. Although videotape recording may be less threatening than being observed by another person, reviewing recordings is extremely time-consuming. On the other hand, the data are available for inspection over time and can be compared with data collected at other time points. Although simple ticking off of categories may appear to be the simplest approach to implement, unfortunately human behavior often fails to conform to predetermined categories. Furthermore, reliability may be a real concern with this approach to data collection. For research purposes it is unlikely to be adequate, but in other contexts, it may be acceptable.

SAMPLE OBSERVATION SCHEDULE

Name:

Class:

Date:

Time	Reading in group	Reading individually	Writing in group	Writing individually	Group discussion	Conversation with peer	Bathroom	At therapy	Other

Figure 6.2. Sample observation schedule. Copyright © Martine Smith.

B. Quantitative Approaches

There are many headings under which quantitative (essentially number-based) information may be sought. As discussed in the previous chapter, it may be possible to convert raw scores on a test to a range of normative scores, including standard scores, age-equivalent scores, or percentile rankings, so that performance can be compared to that of peers. Despite its limitations, at times quantitative information is important in highlighting areas of strengths or need. The headings considered in the next section relate to four main areas for which quantitative information may be sought: (a) language skills, (b) reading skills, (c) spelling, and (d) writing skills. The section concludes with consideration of more general print-related skills.

IV. ASSESSMENT OF LANGUAGE-RELATED SKILLS

Vellutino (1993) listed seven language subskills that are components in the reading process:

1. Vocabulary knowledge
2. Comprehension of syntax
3. Pragmatic knowledge
4. Name encoding and name retrieval
5. Metalinguistic awareness
   A. Syllable and phoneme awareness
   B. Ability to judge the grammaticality of phrases and sentences
6. Facility with inflectional morphemes
7. Facility with derivational morphemes

In the next sections, specific assessment approaches targeting each of these areas are considered. Some assessment tools have been used successfully with individuals who use AAC and whose response modes are reduced relative to those of their peers. However, the caveat mentioned previously about the need to interpret performance cautiously bears repeating. Some of the suggestions are drawn from commercially available assessment tools and others from research papers. One web-based assessment, the Assessment of Phonological Awareness and Reading (APAR), was developed by Iacono and Cupples (2000), and free software can be downloaded from http://www.elr.com.au/.

A. Vocabulary Knowledge

Receptive vocabulary can be assessed using any tool for which the format requires the selection of a target from a display of a range of possible choices.

Typical examples are the Peabody Picture Vocabulary Test (PPVT) (Dunn & Dunn, 1997) and the British Picture Vocabulary Scales-Revised (BPVS-R) (Dunn, Dunn, Whetton, & Burley, 1997).

B. Comprehension of Syntax

The Test of Reception of Grammar (TROG) (Bishop, 1983), the Test of Auditory Comprehension of Language (TACL-3) (Carrow-Woolfolk, 1999), and the Clinical Evaluation of Language Fundamentals (CELF-R) (Semel, Wiig, & Secord, 1987) all provide tasks measuring understanding of syntactic structures. The first two tests do not require any verbal responses and so are particularly easily adapted to accommodate the needs of individuals using aided communication.

The APAR (Iacono & Cupples, 2000) also provides a subtest that focuses on receptive syntactic abilities. In the listening comprehension subtest, participants are presented with a series of 20 test sentences. The task is to determine whether the sentence is plausible or not. Although obviously drawing on a wide range of language skills, successful performance also draws on understanding of argument structure, as well as world knowledge.

In discussing assessment of grammatical competence in individuals who use AAC, Sutton, Soto, and Blockberger (2002) argued for the need to include evidence from a range of assessment approaches (e.g., grammaticality judgment tasks and picture selection tasks) in building a comprehensive picture of grammatical abilities.

C. Pragmatic Knowledge

Included under this heading are tasks measuring comprehension beyond the level of the individual sentence, typically assessed through presentation of an extended piece of narrative, followed by questions. The CELF-R (Semel *et al.*, 1987) provides such an assessment, as does the APAR (Iacono & Cupples, 2000).

D. Name Encoding and Name Retrieval

Naming tasks are among the most difficult to adapt to suit the needs of individuals who use aided communication, partly because of the constraints of the external lexicon and the undetermined relationship between an individual's internal mental lexicon and the external aided lexicon. An additional consideration is the negative effect that timed tasks create for individuals with physical impairments. Few individuals have considered the benefits to outweigh the difficulties, and this is an aspect of assessment rarely, if ever, undertaken with individuals who use aided communication.

V. ASSESSMENT OF METALINGUISTIC AWARENESS

Two main domains of metalinguistic awareness are considered in this section: (a) phonological awareness and (b) morphological awareness.

A. PHONOLOGICAL AWARENESS

There are many different ways to categorize tasks that tap awareness of the sound structure of language and the relationship between the orthographic code and the sound structure of the language it represents. Stackhouse and Wells (1997) categorized such phonological awareness tasks as ranging along a continuum from implicit awareness to explicit awareness. In addition, the size of the phonological unit under examination can vary from word, to syllable, to phoneme levels. In developmental terms, children gradually become more able to focus more and more explicitly on units of decreasing size (Blachman, 2000). Using this framework, phonological awareness tasks can be categorized according to the degree of explicit attention required and also the size of the unit of analysis.

Vandervelden and Siegel (1999, 2001) distinguished between tasks that assess retrieval of whole word phonology, phoneme awareness, and phonological recoding and also presented detailed information about the development of these skills and the degree of difficulty associated with tasks within each of these categories. Tasks measuring retrieval of whole-word phonology tap the ability to access and retrieve phonological lexical representations. They used the term *phoneme awareness* to refer to the ability to analyze spoken words and syllables into their constituent phonemes and to manipulate phonemes in spoken words. *Phonological recoding* they defined as "the use of systematic relationships between the graphemes (single letters or letter sequences) of written language and the phonemes underlying spoken language, to recognize or read unknown printed strings, or to spell" (Vandervelden & Siegel, 1999, p. 192).

In the following section, summaries of both phonological awareness and phonological recoding tasks are offered for consideration. Phonological awareness tasks are categorized primarily in terms of the size of unit for analysis, using the distinction offered by Bradley and Bryant (1983), that is, tasks focusing on three levels: the syllable level, the intrasyllabic level (onset-rime tasks), and the phoneme level. In addition, input tasks are distinguished from output tasks. What follows is simply a sample of some of the tasks that have been used and found useful, when these skills are measured in individuals with both speech and physical impairments. A summary of the levels considered, and some of the tasks used at each level are presented in Tables 6.4 to 6.7.

1. Input Tasks at the Syllable Level

a. Syllable Segmentation

In typical syllable segmentation tasks, the student indicates how many syllables a spoken word has (e.g., the subtest on syllable segmentation in the Queensland University Inventory of Literacy (QUIL) (Dodd, Holm, Oerlemans, & McCormick, 1996)). For those using AAC, this task can be modified by presenting a response sheet with numbers displayed on the sheet. Students respond by selecting the correct number on the sheet. A similar task can be found in the Preschool Inventory of Phonological Awareness (PIPA) (Dodd, Crosbie, McIntosh, Teitzel, & Ozanne, 2000), in which the child indicates the number of syllables by pointing to the number of drums corresponding to the number of syllables within the stimulus.

Table 6.4

Summary of Tasks Used to Measure Phonological Awareness: Syllable Level

Syllable level: Input tasks
Syllable segmentation
  Syllable counting
  Syllable identification
Syllable deletion

Syllable level: Output tasks
Syllable deletion

Table 6.5

Summary of Tasks Used to Measure Phonological Awareness: Intrasyllabic Level

Intrasyllabic level: Input tasks
Rhyme judgment
  Spoken pairs of words
  Spoken sequence of words: odd-one-out tasks
  Pairs of pictures: no spoken stimulus
  Set of pictures for matching tasks, no spoken stimulus

Intrasyllabic level: Output tasks
Rhyme production

Table 6.6

Summary of Tasks Used to Measure Phonological Awareness: Phoneme Level

Phoneme level: Input tasks
Phoneme discrimination
  Homophone judgment tasks (same/different judgments)
  Lexical determination ("Is this a 'voy'?")
  Lexical decision tasks
Phoneme identification
  Initial position
    Alliteration judgment (spoken or picture stimulus)
    Odd-one-out tasks (spoken or picture stimulus)
    Does "sock" have /s/?
    Phoneme to picture matching ("which picture starts with
      /b/?")
  Initial, medial, or final position
    Does "sock" have /s/?
    Does "bus" have /s/?
    Does "missing" have /s/?
  Presence and position judgments
    Does "sock" have /s/? Is it at the beginning, middle, or end
    of the word?
Phoneme manipulation
  Phoneme substitution: "ghost"; change the /g/ to /t/, and
    what do you get?
  Phoneme deletion: "fred"; take away the /f/, and what is left?
Phoneme segmentation
  Counting number of phonemes
  Word length judgment tasks
  Phoneme matching across word pairs
Phoneme synthesis
  Word identification
  Recognition of nonwords

Table 6.7

Summary of Tasks Used to Measure Phonological Awareness: Phonological Recoding

Phonological recoding: Input
Pseudoword speech-to-print matching
Pseudoword reading
  Pseudohomophone judgement
  Alliteration
  Pseudoword rhyme judgement
  Judging homophony of word pairs with regular spelling
  Judging homophony of word pairs, irregular spelling
  Judging homophony of word-nonword pairs
  Judging homophony of two-syllable nonword-nonword pairs
  CVC-nonconventional word task

b. Syllable Identification

Students must recognize whether two spoken words have the same syllable at the beginning or the end of the word or whether the two words have no matching syllable [e.g., QUIL (Dodd *et al.*, 1996)]. Symbols can be used to represent beginning, ending, and nothing with children or adults who use aided communication.

2. Output Tasks at the Syllable Level

a. Syllable Deletion

Here, students must delete one syllable from a multisyllable word and produce the remaining segments of the word. For example, "The word is cowboy. Take away 'cow.' What is left?" This task can be modified to include only targets that are present and known in the external lexicon available to the student being assessed.

3. Input Tasks at the Intrasyllabic Level

a. Rhyme Judgment: Spoken Stimulus

In this task the examiner produces a pair of spoken words. The student must decide whether or not the words rhyme, indicating a yes/no response. Pictures can be used as well as the spoken stimulus to reduce memory load (Dodd *et al.*, 2000; Vandervelden & Siegel, 1999).

b. Rhyme Judgment: Spoken Stimulus, Odd-One-Out

In odd-one-out tasks, a series of pictures is presented and labeled, and the student must identify which of the series does not rhyme with the others (Dodd *et al.*, 2000).

c. Rhyme Judgment: Visual Stimulus Only

When the stimuli are spoken for the individual, the decision as to whether or not they rhyme can be completed without reference to internal phonological representations. Several authors (Dahlgren-Sandberg, 2001; Dahlgren-Sandberg & Hjelmquist, 1996a, 1997; Vandervelden & Siegel, 1999, 2001) have explored the performance of individuals in detecting rhymes for which the stimulus is not spoken. Vandervelden and Siegel (2001) presented the task by showing two pictures and asking the child to indicate yes or no in response to the question, "Do these words rhyme?" (Figure 6.3). This version of the task requires access to internal phonological representations, because the tester does not speak the word.

Figure 6.3. Sample task for rhyme judgment: Do the names of these things rhyme?

Dahlgren-Sandberg (Dahlgren-Sandberg, 2001; Dahlgren-Sandberg & Hjelmquist, 1996a, 1997) used a slightly more complex version of the task, which involved an array of 10 pictures, comprising 5 rhyming pairs. The task was to indicate the pictures that made up the rhyming pairs. An example of this kind of task is given in Figure 6.4.

4. Output Tasks at the Intrasyllabic Level

a. Rhyme Generation Tasks

Typically these kinds of tasks require the student to generate lists of words that rhyme with a spoken stimulus ("Tell me as many words as you can that rhyme with rat"). For individuals using aided communication, it may be possible to offer opportunities to produce words that rhyme with a spoken target, but it is unlikely that more than a few rhyming words will be available within the aided system. It is important to recognize the additional processing load that is implicit in scanning an internal lexicon to find rhyming words, comparing possible responses with the available response set in the external lexicon and selecting the target responses (Blischak, 1994). In addition, young speaking children often include nonwords in the strings they produce, suggesting that this is a task that may be completed without reference to phonological representations (Stackhouse & Wells, 1997). Using a device or communication board forces processing to the level of real words.

5. Input Tasks at the Phoneme Level

a. Phoneme Discrimination Tasks

Usually these tasks require a judgment about whether or not two words spoken by the examiner are the same—using real or nonwords, e.g., "siff"-"sieve"

Which ones rhyme? (fish, hat, clock, dish, bat, rock)

Figure 6.4. Sample task for rhyme matching: Which picture matches the rhyme?

(Bishop, 1985; Bishop, Byers-Brown, & Robson, 1990). In the Bishop (1985) study, a total of 36 word pairs and 36 nonword pairs were presented as spoken stimuli, with contrasting phonological features across the word pairs. (Matched pairs were presented as written stimuli, hence the spelling forms.) Examples from the set of stimuli are presented in Tables 6.8 to 6.10.

Table 6.8

**Homophone Judgment Tasks: Sample from
Homophone List**

Real Words		Nonwords	
won	one	wrup	rup
not	knot	pight	pite
write	right	broove	bruve
tax	tacks	kaze	kays
daze	days	dax	dacks
nose	knows	nop	knop
would	wood	fid	phid
sure	shore	cobe	coab
hymn	him	quead	kweed
hole	whole	feks	fheks
guest	guessed	coim	koym
groan	grown	bew	bue

Bishop, D. V. M. (1985). Spelling ability in congenital dysarthria: Evidence against articulatory coding in translating between phonemes and graphemes. *Cognitive Neuropsychology, 2*(3), 249–250.

Table 6.9

**Homophone Judgment Tasks: Sample from
Fricative/Affricate Contrasts**

Real Words		Nonwords	
fan	van	fup	vupp
safe	save	pife	pyve
sewn	zone	sook	zuke
peas	piece	kass	kaz
fort	thought	roat	thote
deaf	death	meef	meath
ship	chip	shupp	chup
cash	catch	wush	wutch
chin	gin	chiss	jis
ridge	rich	fidge	fitch
sift	shift	suft	shuft

Bishop, D. V. M. (1985). Spelling ability in congenital dysarthria: Evidence against articulatory coding in translating between phonemes and graphemes. *Cognitive Neuropsychology, 2*(3), 249–250.

Table 6.10

Homophone Judgment Tasks: Sample of Plosive/Nasal
Contrasts

Real Words		Nonwords	
come	gum	koome	goom
duck	dug	hoyg	hoick
port	bought	porst	borst
cub	cup	thibb	thip
touch	dutch	taib	dabe
heart	hard	vutt	vud
mad	bad	mool	bool
bob	bomb	meeb	meam
tail	nail	newk	tuke
nut	none	shote	shoan
mock	knock	marp	knarp
lane	lame	ume	oon

From Bishop, D. V. M. (1985). Spelling ability in congenital
dysarthria: Evidence against articulatory coding in translating
between phonemes and graphemes. *Cognitive Neuropsychology, 2*(3),
250.

b. Phoneme Discrimination Task: Picture Stimulus

Bishop *et al.* (1990) also used a task modified from Locke (1980) to assess
phoneme discrimination, while minimizing memory load. In this version, the
participant was shown a picture stimulus and asked whether the stimulus spoken
by the examiner matched the picture stimulus, the spoken stimulus varying from
the target in a sequence of graded phonological dimensions (Figure 6.5).

c. Phoneme Discrimination: Lexical Decision Tasks

Smith (2001) reported a task similar to that above, in which participants
were presented with a series of spoken targets and were required to determine
whether or not the spoken stimulus was a real word. The target list was balanced
for nonwords containing permissible sequences of phonemes for English and
words that contained illegal sequences, that is, sequences of phonemes that could
not occur in English, such as "bakp." Although tasks such as this require processing at the level of the phoneme, successful performance is based on the ability
to retrieve a full phonological representation and perform a comparative analysis. The list of stimuli used by Smith (2001) is presented in Table 6.11.

Figure 6.5. Sample task for lexical determination. Copyright © Martine Smith.

Table 6.11

Spoken Stimuli for Lexical Decision Task

map	/ŋgʌp/	get	ship
/dɪt/	/gɛn/	lit	/hɛt/
/sɛp/	sing	/fot/	bin
/mɪp/	cup	/ʒɪm/	hot
/bʌdi/	ticket	gallop	/lɛkɛt/
/rʌntou/	lady	/palɛg/	window
/skap/	frog	treat	/mlʌt/
/triːn/	scar	/pfʌg/	plate
lamp	sɛnk	dust	/sɪmp/
/lakp/	wasp	/dʌnb/	milk

From Smith, M. (2001). Literacy challenges for individuals with severe congenital speech impairments. *International Journal of Disability, Development and Education, 48,* 331–353.

d. Phoneme Identification: Initial Position

In alliteration tasks, the focus is on whether or not words share an initial phoneme, based on either a spoken stimulus and/or a picture stimulus. Typically, the examiner asks a question such as "Do these words start with the same sound: corn, cat?" Manipulating the number of phonemes that occur within the onset (for example, "cat," "clock"; "cat," "skate") increases task complexity. If the tester does not speak the stimuli, then the task is more difficult, because the participant must access internal phonological representations. Similarly, the task can be modified, as an odd-one-out task, in which the participant must identify the word that does not belong in a sequence, based on alliteration patterns (Figure 6.6).

e. Phoneme Identification: Initial Position

Dahlgren-Sandberg (Dahlgren-Sandberg & Hjelmquist, 1996a,b; Dahlgren-Sandberg, 2001) described a series of tasks in which the participant was required to identify whether or not a word contained a target phoneme. For example, questions such as the following can be asked:

- "Does 'sock' have /s/?"
- "Does 'sun' have /f/?"

f. Phoneme Identification: Medial and Final Positions

The preceding task can be modified to focus attention on other phoneme positions within the word:

Do these start with the same sound?

Which one does not belong? (cap, camel, apple*)

Figure 6.6. Sample tasks for phoneme identification. Copyright © Martine Smith.

- "Does 'sock' have /k/?"
- "Does 'sun' have /m/?"
- "Does 'hammer' have /m/?"
- "Does 'ticket' have /p/?"

g. Phoneme Identification: Word Pairs

In the APAR (Iacono & Cupples, 2000), a task is provided, in which the examiner labels a pair of pictures. The examiner then produces a phoneme, and the task for the student is to select the word containing the target phoneme. (An example of this kind of task is provided in Figure 6.7.)

h. Phoneme Identification: Complex Task

Dahlgren-Sandberg (2001) modified the phoneme identification task described above by adding a further layer of complexity. In the more complex

In the following example, the examiner labels the two pictures, and

then produces the target phoneme /b/. The task for the participant is

to select the picture containing the target phoneme (bee).

Figure 6.7.   Example of phoneme identification task format in APAR. Copyright © Martine Smith.

version of the task, participants not only were required to judge whether or not a spoken word contained a target phoneme but also had to indicate whether the target phoneme occurred at the beginning, middle, or end of the spoken word.

i. Phoneme Manipulation Tasks: Deletion and Substitution

In these tasks, participants are presented with a spoken target and are required to generate a new response, based on either deleting a phoneme or substituting a phoneme within the target word. In the version of the task used by Vandervelden and Siegel (2001), participants were presented with a set of three picture stimuli. They were told, for example: "Listen, /ghost/. Change the /g/ to /t/. What is the new word?" The target response and two distracters were presented for each item. A similar task was used to assess the ability to delete phonemes (e.g., "Listen, fred. What is fred without the /f/?").

Dahlgren-Sandberg (2001) likewise used an array of four pictures for a phoneme deletion task, with each array containing the target response, one phonological foil, and two distracter items.

j. Phoneme Segmentation and Analysis Tasks

Both the QUIL (Dodd et al., 1996) and the PIPA (Dodd et al., 2000) contain subtests focusing on phoneme segmentation, in which the task for the participant is to segment a target word into phonemes and to count the phonemes. This task can be modified for individuals using AAC, by using a display containing numbers, so that participants can indicate the number of phonemes in spoken stimuli by pointing to the correct number.

The APAR likewise contains subtests addressing the ability to count phonemes, with a set of targets specifically for adults and another set for children. The stimuli contain between three and five phonemes, and the task includes a picture stimulus. The instructions follow the format: "I'm going to show you a picture. I will tell you its name. I want you to listen to the word and tell me how many sounds you can hear. Remember, listen for the number of sounds. Don't worry about the number of letters you would need to spell the word, but rather the number of sounds you hear." In the version for children, no word contains more than four phonemes, and the instructions are modified somewhat to allow the child to indicate a response by pointing to a number matching the number of phonemes.

k. Phoneme Analysis: Word Length Judgment

Dahlgren-Sandberg (Dahlgren-Sandberg & Hjelmquist, 1996a,b, 1997; Dahlgren-Sandberg, 2001) included a word length judgment task, in which participants were shown an array of three pictures. Their task was to select the picture that represented the word containing the most sounds. Each array contained the target response, a semantic foil (a word representing a large object), and another foil. Dahlgren-Sandberg labeled the pictures before the participant attempted the task. An example of the kind of stimuli that might be included in such a task is presented in Figure 6.8.

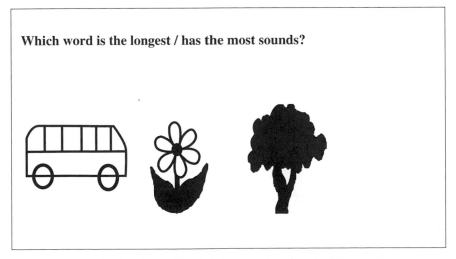

Which word is the longest / has the most sounds?

Figure 6.8. Sample word length judgment task. Copyright © Martine Smith.

l. Phoneme Segmentation Task

Dahlgren-Sandberg (2001) reported a further segmentation task, comprising lists of word pairs. The task was to indicate whether the initial, middle, or final phonemes were identical across the word pairs.

m. Phoneme Synthesis Tasks

In phoneme synthesis tasks, participants are presented with a sequence of phonemes to retain in memory and to synthesize to generate a target word. In the version of the task used by Dahlgren-Sandberg (2001), participants were presented with an array of pictures containing the target, along with phonological and semantic foils. A similar task is included in the APAR, in which three pictures are shown to the participant. The examiner produces the target word, phoneme by phoneme, and the student identifies the correct picture. Each set of pictures includes the target, a distracter word with the same initial sound as the target, and a semantic distracter. The maximum number of phonemes to be retained and synthesized is five.

n. Phoneme Synthesis: Nonwords

In addition to real word synthesis, the APAR also includes a subtest involving synthesis of nonwords. The examiner first produces a set of phonemes (two to four phonemes) and then produces a nonword. The task for the client is to determine whether the nonword produced matched the sequence of phonemes. The instructions from the examiner are "I am going to say some made-up or nonsense words. I will say each nonsense word one sound at a time; then I will put the sounds together. I want you to tell me 'yes' if that was the nonsense word made by the sounds and 'no' if it was a different nonsense word." Sample items include /p/ /ar/ /l/. "Did I say 'porf'?"

6. Output Tasks at the Phoneme Level

Many of the tasks described earlier, when used with speaking children, are also used as output tasks. For example, children are often asked to segment words into constituent phonemes, to produce words that start with the same sound, or to say the word arising out of a sequence of phonemes presented individually. In some instances it may be possible to explore output abilities in individuals with aided communication systems by careful evaluation of the available lexicon within the system and by knowing also the familiarity of items. However, in all such instances, there are considerable additional cognitive and motor processing demands, when compared to those for speaking children, and so caution must be exercised in interpreting performance on such tasks.

7. Phonological Recoding: Input Tasks

Phonological recoding, as used by Vandervelden and Siegel (2001), refers to the ability to make use of the systematic relationship between letters or letter sequences of a written language and the phonemes underlying spoken language to read sequences of letters and for spelling tasks. Phonological recoding abilities are typically assessed through performance on reading and spelling nonsense words. Typical tasks can be found in the Nonword Reading and Nonword Spelling subtests of the QUIL (Dodd et al., 1996). Usually, such tasks are accomplished through oral reading and independent writing. For obvious reasons, the former is not possible for individuals using aided communication, and so tasks must be modified. The most common modification is to adapt the task to one of recognition rather than recall. For example, students can be presented with a spoken nonword and an array of possible orthographic matches. Distracter words displayed can be selected to differ by initial sound, final sound, and both initial and final sounds. Participants must select the correct orthographic match. Similar adaptations are found in many of the tasks in the next sections.

a. Pseudoword Speech-to-Print Matching

After presentation of a spoken pseudoword (e.g., /sot/), the student selects the match from a set of three printed pseudowords (e.g., "fep" "sut," "pom") (Vandervelden & Siegel, 2001).

b. Pseudoword Reading

In the following tasks, the student or participant must access a phonological representation independently of the examiner, because the examiner does not speak the pseudowords or nonwords. Many of the tasks are taken from the papers published by Foley and Pollatsek (1999) and Vandervelden and Siegel (1999, 2001). In pseudohomophone judgment tasks, the student is presented with a pair of pseudowords (e.g., "ked," "sed"). The task is to select the one that sounds like a real word (Foley & Pollatsek, 1999; Vandervelden & Siegel, 1999, 2001). In alliteration tasks, the student is presented with a pseudoword (e.g., /gam/) and a picture (gun). The student must read the pseudoword and indicate whether or not it starts with the same sound as the name of the picture (Vandervelden & Siegel, 2001). Finally, in pseudoword rhyme judgment tasks (Vandervelden & Siegel, 2001), the student is presented with a pseudoword (e.g., /gat/) and a set of three pictures (e.g., gate, hat, tap). The instructions are to "Read this silly word; does it rhyme with the name of this picture?"

c. Judging Homophony of Word Pairs with Regular Spelling

Participants are presented with a pair of words and must decide whether or not the words are homophones, that is, sound the same ("rays"-"raise" versus "rats"-"raise") (Foley & Pollatsek, 1999; see also Bishop, 1985, for real and nonword pairs, such as "see"-"sea").

d. Judging Homophony of Word Pairs, Irregular Spelling

As with the task above, participants must decide whether or not pairs of words presented (e.g., "dough"-"doe") constitute homophones (Foley & Pollatsek, 1999).

e. Judging Homophony of Word–Nonword Pairs

Again the task here requires participants to decide whether word pairs are homophones, but one word in each pair is a real word and the second is an orthographically plausible sequence of letters that may or may not yield a homophone pair (e.g., "ocean"-"oshun") (Foley & Pollatsek, 1999).

f. Judging Homophony of Two-Syllable Nonword–Nonword Pairs

Participants are presented with pairs of nonwords and must decide whether or not they sound the same (e.g., "frelame"-"phrelame") (Foley & Pollatsek, 1999).

g. Consonant-Vowel-Consonant-Nonconventional Word Task

McNaughton (1998) reported on a phonological recoding task, involving explicit instruction in a nonconventional spelling rule—lengthening of a vowel. A print cue—a thick line over the vowel—was also used to support recoding. The task for participants involved recognition of an orthographic target for a spoken nonword stimulus from an array of five items.

8. Phonological Recoding: Output Tasks

In phonological recoding output tasks, individuals must use the systematic relationships between letters and phonemes to generate written output. The most common measure of output phonological recoding is nonword spelling tasks, for which the examiner presents a spoken nonword target for the participant to spell. Many sources of nonword spelling lists are available. The QUIL (Dodd et al., 1996) Nonword Spelling subtest contains a list of stimuli of increasing complexity, and raw scores can be converted to standard scores for normative comparison, should such information be required. As previously noted, however, the additional task constraints for students using aided communication and writing systems must be considered. Vandervelden and Siegel (2001) assessed pseudoword

Table 6.12

Sample from Nonword Spelling Word List

mɪʃ	gɔθ	ʃɔip
nɪv	fouð	dʒeɪt
pɛŋ	vam	woen
bɑg	sjuk	rʌs
teɪf	zɑb	hɪŋ
dɒtʃ	θaid	tʃʌl
kudʒ	ðɛz	lar

From Bishop, D. V. M. (1985). Spelling ability in congenital dysarthria: Evidence against articulatory coding in translating between phonemes and graphemes. *Cognitive Neuropsychology, 2*(3), 251.

spelling using a set of 10 one-syllable pseudowords ("fep," "mip," "ful," "bof," "dak," "dulp," "snom," "flup," "himp," and "sket"). Bishop (1985) constructed a list of 21 consonant-vowel-consonant (CVC) nonwords to include a wide range of English phonemes in initial and final positions. These words are presented in Table 6.12. In most cases in such tasks, scores are awarded for each correct letter included in the spelling attempt.

B. Morphological Awareness

Vellutino (1993) suggested that a second aspect of metalinguistic awareness deserving of attention is the ability to judge the grammaticality of phrases and sentences. Grammaticality judgment tasks are included in the APAR, in which a total of 18 sentences are presented. Grammatical errors include word order errors (e.g., "The glass on broke the floor"), verb tense errors (e.g., "The baby was have a bath"), or errors of subject-verb agreement (e.g., "The farmer milk his cows every day").

McNaughton (1998) used a set of 35 sentences derived from an unpublished thesis by Gottardo (1995) for a grammaticality judgment task. Errors within the sentences derived from word order changes, subject-verb agreement errors, and prepositional errors (e.g., "We went at school").

Dahlgren-Sandberg (2001) reported on a task she used to tap awareness of syntactic completeness, adapted from a test of syntactic acceptability constructed by Nauclér and Magnusson in 1994 (as cited by Dahlgren-Sandberg, 2001, p. 17). This task consisted of nine phrases, four with fully accurate syntax and five containing syntactic simplifications intended to approximate the kinds of syntactic immaturities typical in the speech of a young child aged approximately 2 years. The phrases were presented as comments made by either a mother or a child in a conversation. Participants were required to determine which utterances in the conversation were likely to have been produced by the mother and which by the child. To complete this task successfully, participants had to make a judgment about the syntactic accuracy of the utterances and assign the less grammatically complete utterances to the child.

1. Facility with Inflectional Morphemes

The third and fourth language areas identified by Vellutino (1993) as being important in consideration of reading skills relate to skills in inflectional and derivational morphology. Morphological knowledge can greatly support spelling (Masterson & Apel, 2000), and performance on morphological judgment tasks has been found to correlate significantly with general measures of spelling (Fowler & Lieberman, 1995). Research evidence to date suggests that individuals who use aided communication may have difficulty dealing with aspects of English morphology (Blockberger & Sutton, 2003; Sutton & Gallagher, 1993; Sutton et al., 2002).

Several commercially available tests provide subtests measuring these skills for speaking children. Comprehension of inflectional morphology is typically assessed through tasks asking participants to point to the picture that matches a stimulus spoken by the examiner. For example, an array may contain pictures of a boy running, boys running, and a boy sleeping, with the spoken stimulus "The boy runs." For individuals with limited response options, subsections of the following tests can be easily adapted to support eye-gaze or gross pointing responses:

1. Test of Reception of Grammar (TROG) (Bishop, 1983)
2. Test of Auditory Comprehension of Language (TACL-3) (Carrow-Woolfolk, 1999), particularly Section 2, Grammatical Morphemes
3. Clinical Evaluation of Language Fundamentals (CELF-R) (Semel et al., 1987)

2. Facility with Derivational Morphemes

The preceding tests also provide possibilities for assessing the ability to generate derivational morphemes (e.g., "piano," "pianist"; "teach, "teacher"). However, many individuals using aided communication will have little access to derivational morpheme options within their communication system.

VI. ASSESSMENT OF READING SKILLS

It is beyond the scope of this text to review all possible reading assessments that might be used, and thus only a small selection are considered here. In terms of commercially available resources, those mentioned in the following sections are the most commonly referred to in the AAC literature for assessment of individuals who speak English.

A. Formal Measures of Reading

There is a vast and ever-growing range of reading assessments available for screening and diagnostic purposes. For assessment of reading at least three types of tasks must be considered: (a) assessment of letter knowledge and of phoneme grapheme correspondences; (b) assessment of single word decoding; and (c) assessment of comprehension of connected text. In relation to the latter, it may be worth considering contrasting performance on connected texts that are literary in nature versus texts that are used for informational purposes (Mulis, Martin, Gonzalez, & Kennedy, 2003).

1. Letter Knowledge

To assess letter knowledge or phoneme–grapheme knowledge, no formal standardized test is necessary. However, many commercially available tests measuring early reading abilities provide materials for the assessment of letter knowledge and phoneme-grapheme correspondence. Tests include the Test of Early Reading Ability (Reid, Hresko, & Hammill, 2001), the Woodcock Reading Mastery Tests—Revised (Form G) (Woodcock, 1998), the Aston Index (Newton, 1994), and the PIPA (Dodd et al., 2000).

2. Single Word Decoding and Reading Comprehension

The following tests have all been used in research with individuals who use AAC.

The Test of Reading Comprehension (TORC) (Brown, Hammill, & Wiederholt, 1995) was used by Foley and Pollatsek (1999) and McNaughton (1998). The third edition of this test (TORC-3) (Brown et al., 1995) has a target age range of 7 years through 17 years and 11 months. The test comprises eight subtests grouped under the General Reading Comprehension Core (general vocabulary, syntactic similarities, paragraph reading, and sentence sequencing) and four diagnostic subtests.

The stated age range for the Woodcock Reading Mastery Tests-Revised (Woodcock, 1998) is wide, ranging from 5 years to 75 years. There are two test forms, G and H, that can be used for test-retest purposes or to add to the pool of diagnostic information available. Individual subtests support assessment of visual-auditory learning, letter identification, word identification, word attack, word comprehension, and passage comprehension.

The Peabody Individual Achievement Test (Dunn & Markwardt, 1970), a reading comprehension subtest, was used by Foley and Pollatsek (1999) and McNaughton (1998).

Dahlgren-Sandberg and Smith (research in progress) used the Wordchains Test (Guron, 1999), a test that focuses on orthographic knowledge, as students identify potential word boundaries within strings of letters.

The SPAR Group Reading and Spelling Test (Young, 1987) was used by Smith (1989, 2001). This test comprises two sections, one involving word identification, based on selecting the correct word to match to a picture, and the second assessing sentence-level reading comprehension, based on a Cloze procedure.

B. ADDITIONAL MATERIALS REPORTED

In addition to the preceding formal, commercially available materials, several tasks have been devised to tap specific reading abilities in students with specific response limitations. Among these additional assessment resources are tasks focusing on single word decoding, comprehension of connected text, and proofreading tasks, as outlined in the following sections.

1. Decoding Single Words

Many researchers have developed lists of single words from various sources to use as assessment tools for students at particular stages. Typically, the task for the student is to point to the picture from an array of four that matches a printed word. An alternative version requires the selection of a correct word from an array of several to match a presented picture (Dahlgren-Sandberg & Hjelmquist, 1996a,b, 1997; Dahlgren-Sandberg, 2001; Vandervelden & Siegel, 2001). When tasks such as this are devised for specific students, the level of difficulty can be manipulated by increasing the similarity of distracter items. For example, "Compare the following set of stimuli, where the target word in each case is 'soap': 'soap,' 'duck,' 'boot'; 'swim,' 'sock,' 'soap'; 'speak,' 'snip,' 'soap'; 'soap,' 'soup,' 'sip.' "

When one works with individuals using aided communication, it may also be helpful to consider using words taken from the communication display to determine whether any incidental learning of sight word vocabulary has occurred through exposure to these items in communicative contexts.

2. Primary Word Reading Task

McNaughton (1998) adapted a single-word reading task from Vandervelden (1992) that was based on a list of 60 primer words, selected sequentially to a

Grade 1 reading level from a range of commercial tests: "no," "up," "yes," "you," "the," "go," "we," "jump," "is," "book," "see," "stop," "yellow," "red," "play," "dog," "in," "come," "green," "look," "eat," "it," "mom," "dad," "run," "big," man," "cat," "to," "work," "was," "me," "milk," "and," "bed," "are," "ball," "boy," "car," "girl," "like," "little," "pig," "sleep," "good," "help," "all," "fast," "fish," "rug," "said," "swim," "this," "with," "away," "him," "name," "day," "two," "she." When used with individuals using AAC, the task was simplified to 30 words only by eliminating every second word. Participants identified words by pointing to the equivalent symbol on their display, by giving a synonym, or by placing the word in a sentence to demonstrate they had read the word's meaning. Again, the demands implicit in such adaptations mean that the task itself becomes far more than a word reading task. However, such adaptations demonstrate how creative approaches to assessment can yield important information regarding abilities.

3. Lexical Decision Tasks

In this task, as described by Dahlgren-Sandberg (Dahlgren-Sandberg & Hjelmquist, 1996b; Dahlgren-Sandberg, 2001), students were presented with written stimuli. The students sorted the stimuli into those that were real words and those that were not real words. In Dahlgren-Sandberg's studies, real words were placed in an attractive box, whereas nonwords were placed in a box resembling a trash bin.

4. Proofreading

Proofreading is another task described by Dahlgren-Sandberg (Dahlgren-Sandberg & Hjelmquist, 1996b; Dahlgren-Sandberg, 2001). In this task, students were shown a set of sentences in which half contained words that were spelled incorrectly, but that were phonologically plausible. The students were required to indicate which words were spelled incorrectly. Because all the words were phonologically plausible, identification of error words was presumed to draw on orthographic rather than phonological strategies.

5. Comprehension of Connected Text

Comprehension of connected text can be measured in a range of ways. Questions may be placed at the end of a set of connected text, as is the case in the APAR Comprehension of Written Texts subtest (Iacono & Cupples, 2000). In this subtest, the questions all require only a "yes" or "no" response. Other tests addressing similar abilities require more content-heavy responses. Comprehension may also be assessed through plausibility judgments. For example, in the Comprehension of Written Sentences subtest in the APAR, the student is presented with a series of sentences and must determine whether or not each is sensible. An example of an implausible sentence is "The flowers slammed the door." Again, such tasks tap a wide range of skills.

6. Reading Cloze

This is a commonly used technique to assess comprehension of connected text. Typically, in such tasks, students are presented with a sentence in which one word is missing. Their task is to select the correct word, from an array of several choices, to complete the sentence. Task difficulty can be modified by increasing the complexity of the target words or the sentence stimulus, by varying the contextual support, and/or by increasing similarity across distracter items. Harrison-Harris (2002) referred to this as a maze reading assessment technique and suggested providing three alternative words in random order at each blank space (correct choice, incorrect choice of the same part of speech, and incorrect choice of a different part of speech). The scale of reading proficiency most often used for informal reading assessments such as this is 90% accuracy, indicating that the student is reading at an independent level; 60% to 80% accuracy, indicating that the student needs more instruction and below 60%, indicating that the student is reading at a frustration level.

VII. SPELLING AND WRITING ASSESSMENTS

Although there are many commercially available tests designed to measure reading abilities, traditionally far less attention has been paid to assessing spelling and writing. Kamhi and Hinton (2000) lamented what they called the lack of respect that spelling has received. Reading and spelling are intimately related and may in fact be construed as two sides of a coin (Ehri, 2000). However, it is also the case that spelling places additional demands on the system. As Ehri (2000, p. 24) pointed out "more information is needed to produce a correct spelling than to produce a correct reading." Knowledge of spelling draws on many different sources of information—phonological information to be able to segment a word into target phonemes; morphological information to recognize the need to use consistent orthographic forms such as "-ed" despite variable pronunciation; and orthographic information to determine common within-word patterns.

In the earlier section on phonological recoding, many tasks that involve spelling skills were outlined—including spelling of real words with spoken or picture stimuli, spelling of nonwords, and proofreading tasks. The discussion in this section seeks to broaden the view of spelling from one that focuses only on the phonological information encoded in attempts at spelling, but that also addresses the other layers of information implicit in accurate spelling.

Ehri (2000) proposed that there are at least three distinct ways to read and spell words: by memory, by invention, and by analogy. Highly familiar words can be stored as wholes. For apprentice writers, the potential store of memorized forms may be very limited, and thus they are forced to rely on additional attack strategies. Invention strategies involve segmenting pronunciations, detecting sound units, and assigning graphemes in plausible letter sequences. When one uses analogy, reference is made to apparently similar words held in store. However, the possible limited size of the memory store necessarily limits the effectiveness of this strategy for early readers and writers (Ehri, 2000). In addition, the nature of English spelling means that there is likely to be more than one candidate for analogy. For example, "Should the analogy for [/treɪn/] be 'rain' or 'lane'?"

When one undertakes assessment of spelling ability, therefore, it is important to consider the full range of skills required to generate "correct" spellings and the insights that spelling abilities can shed on an individual's understanding of not only the sound structure but also the morphological structure of language. As Templeton and Morris (2000) pointed out, spelling represents three layers of information:

1. The alphabetic layer, where letters and sounds are matched in a left-to-right fashion (e.g., /pat/ = p-a-t)

2. The pattern layer, reflecting both within-syllable and between-syllable information. An example of a within-syllable pattern in English is seen with long and short vowels. A vowel/consonant/silent e pattern signals a long vowel, such as "tape," in contrast to the short vowel in "tap." For a between-syllable pattern in bisyllabic English words, if the vowel in a stressed syllable is long, it is usually followed by a single consonant (e.g., "pilot"), whereas if it is short (e.g., "pillow"), it is often followed by a double consonant.

3. The meaning layer, reflects "the fact that words parts that are related in meaning are usually spelled consistently, despite changes in pronunciation: solemn/solemnity, paradigm/paradigmatic" (p. 527).

Spelling offers a window not only on the effectiveness of phonological processing and the specificity of phonological representations but also on a range of other aspects of language functioning. It is regarded by some researchers (Ehri, 2000) as the pacemaker for reading and for the development of phonemic awareness in the early stages of reading and writing, and thus merits close attention. For many individuals using aided communication, the ability to spell is crucial to development of an open communication system. There is also some evidence to suggest that for this client group, spelling lags even further behind other abilities than does reading (Dahlgren-Sandberg, 2001) and so requires particular attention. For those with acquired communication difficulties, spelling may represent a crucial communication and recreational link with their previous lives.

A. Spelling and Writing Tasks

Masterson and Apel (2000) described three basic methods used to determine spelling skills.

> In the first, dictation, the examiner reads aloud a list of words and the student is instructed to write the spelling for each. In the second, connected writing, the student is asked to generate text in response to a picture or as a story to retell. In the third, recognition, the student is given a group of words that contain the correct spelling along with a few misspellings, or foils. The student is asked to indicate which spelling is correct. (p. 51)

For each of these methods, the authors offer a selection of possible tools to be used and give a useful critique of the various possibilities that may be considered.

1. Dictation

The Test of Written Spelling-3 (Larson & Hammill, 1994), the Test of Written Language-3 (Hammill & Larson, 1996), and the Wide Range Achievement Test-3 (Wilkinson, 1995) all contain dictated word lists, and all have been reviewed and have met the minimal standards of the American Psychological Association for technical adequacy (Moats, 1994). The Schonell Spelling Test (as part of the Aston Index [Newton, 1994]), and the Diagnostic Spelling Test (Vincent & Claydon, 1983) may be more widely used in the United Kingdom and Ireland. Word lists can also be found in textbooks on spelling (Bear, Invernizzi, Templeton, & Johnston, 2000; Henderson, 1990). Word lists can be structured to explore different spelling features, from simple CVC structures to the use of digraphs, diphthongs, morphological derivations, and others. Although not strictly dictation tasks, other single word tasks have also been included in research with individuals with severe speech impairments. Bishop (1985), for example, asked participants in her study to spell their own names and to write any other words they knew they could spell.

a. Scoring

Approaches to scoring can also vary. Many tests apply all or nothing scoring, in which only fully correct spellings receive a score. If the purpose of assessment is to identify those with spelling difficulties, this approach may be efficient. However, for many individuals with severe communication difficulties and those with early emerging spelling abilities, such scoring systems offer little useful diagnostic information. Alternate scoring approaches, giving credit for the number of correct graphemes included or the approximation to the phonological form of the target word may be more informative and useful. Dahlgren-Sandberg (Dahlgren-Sandberg & Hjelmquist, 1996b; Dahlgren-Sandberg, 2001) and Vandervelden and Siegel (1999, 2001) all reported alternate scoring approaches, with the aim of yielding a more sensitive measure of emerging spelling abilities than a simple correct/incorrect approach. Treiman and Bourassa (2000) provided a detailed description of their scoring protocol, in which individual target words were assigned potential scores ranging from 0 to between 8 and 11 points. Although 0 points were awarded for strings that did not contain any letters, children were awarded 1 point if they attempted a spelling that incorporated letters, even if those letters were not related to the word, and if other symbols such as numbers also appeared in the string. For example, for the word "lap" 4 points were awarded for responses that included two of the three target phonemes represented by either the correct or by related graphemes (e.g., "l-o" or "l-a"). A total of 8 points was awarded for conventional spelling of the target word in this case.

b. Modality Issues

As is often the case, the issue of modality of presentation of materials and of production of responses requires consideration, when one works with people with significant response limitations. In typical dictation tasks, the tester speaks the stimulus, and the student writes down the spelling. In such a task, the student may be directed by the spoken stimulus to a stored representation of the word or may use either of the other two strategies referred to by Ehri (2000)—invention or analogy—to spell the word. As the tester speaks the stimulus, the student does not necessarily need to refer to internal phonological representations—even if that is typically what happens. In contrast, if the tester does not speak the target word, then the student must access his or her own internal phonological representation to attempt the spelling. Dahlgren-Sandberg (2001) contrasted the performance of speaking children and children using AAC on two spelling tasks—one in which the stimulus words were spoken and one in which the stimuli were presented as pictures. For both groups, the picture context was more difficult. However, for the children with severe speech impairments, the contrast in performance across both conditions was far greater than that for their speaking peers. These findings suggest that the additional load of referring to self-generated phonological representations may have a more devastating effect on performance for at least some individuals using aided communication. Smith (2001) reported similar contrasts in performance across spoken and picture stimulus assessment contexts for adults using aided communication.

Taken together, these findings suggest that it is important to explore not only whether or not an individual can generate a spelling but also the conditions under which that spelling can be generated. For communicative purposes, the crucial skill is the ability to generate at least some of the letters of a target word. Understanding the conditions under which that ability can be demonstrated may have important implications for intervention. The question is not so much "How well can this individual spell single words?" but rather "Under what conditions can this individual spell the initial letter, the consonant letters, or all the target letters in a word?" This focus echoes back to Principles 2 and 3, referred to in the previous chapter—that reading and writing occur for a purpose and that assessment must reflect the multiple purposes of engaging with written language and serve to guide intervention.

A second modality question arises in relation to the modality of response. In most dictation tasks, students are expected to write down their attempted spellings. There is some evidence to suggest that asking students to spell words orally is more difficult, at least after the very early stages of spelling (Treiman & Bourassa, 2000). For individuals using aided communication, it is therefore important that their attempts to spell are recorded and remain on view to them as they attempt to complete the task. If the assessment is completed using a computer with a visual display that is visible during the process, this should not be a problem. However, for individuals who use communication boards, each letter selected should be written down and displayed for review as the task is completed.

2. Connected Writing

Few speaking individuals learn to spell single words as an end in itself. For most individuals, it is important to also consider how skills in tasks such as single-word spelling transfer to contexts in which the demands are higher. Two issues should be separated in this context—spelling ability in connected writing and the ability to generate connected writing texts. To consider spelling first, accuracy in single-word tasks does not always transfer to longer text situations, such as writing in the class (Moats, 1995). Moats pointed out that spelling accuracy (similar to reading accuracy) might be influenced by the topic, motivation, attention to task, and response mode. Although some tests (e.g., the Test of Written Language [Hammill & Larson, 1996]) provide subtests designed to measure spelling skills in connected writing, Masterson and Apel (2000, p. 52) proposed that "unfortunately, such subtests simply do not contain a sufficient number of words representing the necessary orthographic patterns to make the scores meaningful or helpful." They described an alternate strategy, for which four to five target error patterns evidenced on single-word dictation tasks are selected and are woven into simple stories. The student writes the story as narrated by the examiner. The same story can be used repeatedly to monitor progress over time.

The second issue referred to above in relation to spelling in connected texts is the ability to generate written output beyond the level of single words. To write a piece of narrative or even a sentence, a whole range of language skills, well beyond mere spelling skills, are brought into play. An idea must be formulated, mapped into a language structure, with appropriate vocabulary, and retained in memory while each individual word in the overall structure is spelled and written down. Problems may arise at any or all of these levels. Table 6.13 outlines some of the steps involved in the process, and some of the factors that may influence performance.

Many of the component skills or elements referred to in Table 6.13 are vulnerable in individuals using aided communication. For example, most speaking individuals come to the task of writing with a relatively long history of creating extensive texts in spoken language. These language experiences provide a platform for the generation of ideas and sequences for print-based texts. However, many individuals using aided communication have only limited experience in generating long utterances using their aided communication system (Kraat, 1987; Smith, 1998; Udwin & Yule, 1991; van Balkom & Donker-Gimbrére, 1996; von Tetzchner & Martinsen, 1996). Phonological working memory may be vulnerable (Dahlgren-Sandberg, 2001; Foley & Pollatsek, 1999), making it difficult to retain a planned language sequence in memory long enough to be able to record it in print, particularly given the typically slow rate at which

Table 6.13

Levels Involved in Developing Connected Text

Processes	Potential influences	Suggested strategies to explore
Generate an idea	Motivation Interest Attention Experience Familiarity Cognitive abilities	Provide a basis for the text—e.g., the opening line of a story. Use a familiar story. Provide a visual prop such as a photograph.
Select an appropriate language form	Language abilities in the areas of syntax, morphology, semantics, and pragmatics	Specify the language form. Select the topic together, but give the language structure.
Implement the underlying language form into print	*Memory* retention of total planned language form *Spelling* of individual words *Reading* of words already in print and comparison with total planned language form *Physical* realization of writing, whether with pen and paper or with computer	Provide spoken feedback, either personally or through software. • Use visual feedback. Monitor levels of physical comfort.
Monitoring of accuracy of print generated	Proofreading ability Physical access Memory and language skills	Leave text on display. Use voice output to support feedback.

print is generated by aided communicators. Beyond even language experiences, the day-to-day living experiences of individuals with significant physical impairments may differ in crucial ways from those of their speaking peers, making it more difficult for them to generate ideas to write about. Exploring abilities to generate connected text has the potential to yield far more information than simply gathering data about spelling ability.

3. Recognition

Spelling recognition tasks are similar to proofreading tasks and are typically explored by asking participants to select the correct spelling from a range of possibilities (e.g., "rain," "rane," "rayne") or to identify whether or not a word is spelled correctly. Many authors have expressed reservations about the value of recognition tasks in uncovering spelling abilities (e.g., Ehri, 2000; Moats, 1995). Although the task of proofing is clearly different from spelling production tasks (Masterson & Apel, 2000), nonetheless, such tasks may yield useful information about the orthographic strategies and knowledge resources available to an individual. Many reader-writers will recognize that both skills come into play when they try to spell problem words. Often a final decision about how a word is spelled can only be made when the possibilities have been written down for "proofing." Such phenomena attest to the close interrelatedness of reading and writing—the two sides of a coin phenomenon referred to by Ehri (2000).

4. Print-Related Skills

There are other print-related skills that do not fit neatly in any of the above headings and that may be relevant in working with individuals using aided communication. One such skill is related to processing of print information. Many individuals using aided communication may also be at risk for visual perceptual difficulties that may interfere with efficient processing of print. There are several commercially available tests that include subtests exploring visual perception and visual memory skills are available, e.g., the Aston Index (Newton, 1994) and the Carrow Auditory Visual Abilities Test (CAVAT) (Carrow-Woolfolk, 1981). However, given the range of assessment possibilities with this client group, such assessments should only be undertaken when there is a concern that visual perceptual abilities are interfering in a significant way with the development of literacy.

In a slightly different vein, it has been pointed out by many researchers (Bishop, Rankin, & Mirenda, 1994; McNaughton, 1993; McNaughton & Lindsay, 1995) that individuals using aided communication have experience with the print medium, and there may be aspects of that experience that influence their acquisition of literacy skills. McNaughton (1998) looked more specifically at processing of graphic symbols, specifically Blissymbols. She devised two tasks, both using

Blissymbols of increasing levels of difficulty and with increasing numbers of components. In the first task, visual matching, participants were first given an explanation of a stimulus symbol. They were then presented with a sequence of five symbols, including the target, and were asked to indicate whether or not each symbol in the sequence matched the original stimulus symbol. The second task, a visual analysis retrieval task used the same set of symbols, presented in a different order to the first task. In this task, the stimulus symbol was first presented, discussed, and then placed facedown, while the distracter symbols were presented. Again, the task was to indicate whether or not a presented symbol matched the stimulus symbol. McNaughton (1998) reported that within her group of adults who used Blissymbols, those who were categorized as print readers achieved significantly higher scores on the visual retrieval task compared with scores of those who were categorized as Bliss readers. Such findings indicate that exploring literacy within the graphic symbol medium may yield useful information.

Erickson (2003) pointed out that a print-related skill, which is often overlooked but contributes significantly to silent reading comprehension, is the ability to process information rapidly. Word identification skills are clearly important. However, if comprehension of a text is to be maintained, then word identification not only must be accurate, but also must be sufficiently quick to support on-going processing of the meaning of the text. One other context for which rapid processing may be critical is in the use of text prediction to support both written output and face-to-face communication for aided communicators. Unless a reader can rapidly scan the word options offered after a selection of a letter and make a decision to accept or reject the options presented, text prediction may be minimally useful as a rate-enhancing technique.

Finally, few, if any, individuals using aided communication are able to physically write with a pen and paper. In most assessment and learning situations, they produce text using a computer. Distinguishing literacy-related skills from computer-related skills may be difficult. Scanning responses may be unreliable because of either motor, perceptual, or spelling difficulties. A switch may have moved, so that responses are delayed or inaccurate, yielding errors that have little to do with reading or writing ability. Throughout all assessment tasks it is important therefore to be cognizant of the many factors impinging on performance. Some factors may be centrally related to performance and others may be more peripheral. It is worth remembering that competence and performance are two very different animals.

VIII. SUMMARY AND CONCLUSIONS

Many examples of assessment tools have been considered in this chapter. These examples represent just a few of a wide range of possibilities, a range that is constantly expanding. There is no doubt that assessment could fill many days, months, or even years. However, this is not the approach advocated here. Our view is that assessment must be meaningful. It should be goal oriented and problem driven, so that it yields useful information that will guide intervention and provide real benefit to the client. Assessment is not a finite process, yielding a static product. Rather it should be viewed as an ongoing process of hypothesis testing, woven into the process of intervention, guiding, and honing the focus of intervention. In the next section of this book, we turn our attention to the intervention process and consider some general principles to structure and guide intervention (Chapter 7) before exploring some practical strategies (Chapter 8).

REFERENCES

Bear, D., Invernizzi, M., Templeton, S., & Johnston, F. (2000). *Words their way: Word study for phonics, vocabulary, and spelling instruction* (2nd ed.). Upper Saddle River, NJ: Prentice Hall.

Beukelman, D., & Mirenda, P. (1992). *Augmentative and alternative communication: Management of severe communication disorders in children and adults.* Baltimore: Paul H. Brookes.

Beukelman, D., & Mirenda, P. (1998). *Augmentative and alternative communication: Management of severe communication disorders in children and adults.* (2nd ed.). Baltimore: Paul H. Brookes.

Bishop, D. V. M. (1983). *Test for reception of grammar.* Published by the author and available from the Age and Cognitive Performance Research Centre, University of Manchester.

Bishop, D. V. M. (1985). Spelling ability in congenital dysarthria: Evidence against articulatory coding in translating between phonemes and graphemes. *Cognitive Neuropsychology, 2*(3), 229–251.

Bishop, D. V. M., Byers-Brown, B., & Robson, J. (1990). The relationship between phoneme discrimination, speech production, and language comprehension in cerebral-palsied individuals. *Journal of Speech & Hearing Research, 33,* 210–219.

Bishop, K., Rankin, J., & Mirenda, P. (1994). Impact of graphic symbol use on reading acquisition. *Augmentative and Alternative Communication, 10,* 113–125.

Blachman, B. A. (2000). Phonological awareness. In M. Kamil, P. Mosenthal, P. D. Pearson, & R. Barr (Eds.), *Handbook of reading research* (Vol. 3, pp. 483–502.). London: Erlbaum.

Blischak, D. M. (1994). Phonologic awareness: Implications for individuals with little or no functional speech. *Augmentative and Alternative Communication, 10,* 245–254.

Blockberger, S., & Sutton, A. (2003). Toward linguistic competence: Language experiences and knowledge of children with extremely limited speech. In J. Light, D. R. Beukelman, & J. Reichle (Eds.), *Communicative competence for individuals who use AAC: From research to effective practice* (pp. 63–106.). Baltimore: Paul H. Brookes.

Bradley, L., & Bryant, P. E. (1983). Categorising sounds and learning to read: A causal connection. *Nature, 310,* 419–421.

Brown, V. L., Hammill, D. D., & Wiederholt, J. L. (1995). *The Test of Reading Comprehension* (3rd ed.). Circle Pines, MN: AGS.

Carrow-Woolfolk, E. (1981). *Carrow auditory visual abilities test.* Austin, TX: DLM Teaching Resources.

Carrow-Woolfolk, E. (1999). *Test of Auditory Comprehension of Language-3* (3rd ed.). Circle Pines, MN: AGS.

Dahlgren-Sandberg, A. (2001). Reading and spelling, phonological awareness and short-term memory in children with severe speech production impairments—A longitudinal study. *Augmentative and Alternative Communication, 17,* 11–26.

Dahlgren-Sandberg, A., & Hjelmquist, E. (1996a). A comparative, descriptive study of reading and writing skills among non-speaking children: A preliminary study. *European Journal of Disorders of Communication*, *31*, 289–308.

Dahlgren-Sandberg, A., & Hjelmquist, E. (1996b). Phonologic awareness and literacy abilities in non-speaking preschool children with cerebral palsy. *Augmentative and Alternative Communication*, *12*(3), 138–154.

Dahlgren-Sandberg, A., & Hjelmquist, E. (1997). Language and literacy in nonvocal children with cerebral palsy. *Reading and Writing: An Interdisciplinary Journal*, *9*, 107–133.

Dodd, B., Crosbie, S., McIntosh, B., Teitzel, T., & Ozanne, A. (2000). *The preschool and primary inventory of phonological awareness. P.I.P.A.* London: Psychological Corporation.

Dodd, B., Holm, A., Oerlemans, M., & McCormick, M. (1996). *Queensland University Inventory of Literacy.* Department of Speech Pathology and Audiology, University of Queensland.

Dunn, L. M., & Dunn, K. (1997). *Peabody Picture Vocabulary Test—III.* Circle Pines, MN: American Guidance Service.

Dunn, L. M., Dunn, K., Whetton, P., & Burley, T. (1997). *The British Picture Vocabulary Scales* (2nd ed.). Windsor, Berks, UK: NFER-Nelson.

Dunn, L. M., & Markwardt, F. C. (1970). *Peabody Individual Achievement Test.* Circle Pines, MN: American Guidance Service.

Ehri, L. C. (2000). Learning to read and learning to spell: Two sides of a coin. *Topics in Language Disorders*, *20*(3), 19–36.

Erickson, K. (2003). Evaluation techniques: The particular problem of how to assess output skills of individuals with complex communication needs and limited literacy skills. In S. von Tetzchner & M. Jensen (Eds.), *Perspectives on theory and practice in Augmentative and Alternative Communication: Proceedings of the Seventh ISAAC Biennial Research Symposium, Odense, Denmark, August 2002.* Toronto, Ontario: ISAAC, 191–196.

Foley, B. E., & Pollatsek, A. (1999). Phonological processing and reading abilities in adolescents and adults with severe congenital speech impairments. *Augmentative and Alternative Communication*, *15*, 156–173.

Fowler, A. E., & Lieberman, I. Y. (1995). The role of phonology and orthography in morphological awareness. In L. B. Feldman (Ed.), *Morphological aspects of language processing* (pp. 189–209.). Hillsdale, NJ: Erlbaum.

Gottardo, A. (1995). Syntactic and phonological processing in children with language impairments, children with reading disabilities and normally achieving children. Unpublished doctoral dissertation, University of Toronto, Ontario, Canada.

Guron, L. (1999). *Wordchains.* London: NFER-Nelson.

Hammill, D. D., & Larson, S. (1996). *Test of Written Language-3.* Austin, TX: PRO-ED.

Harrison-Harris, O. (2002). AAC, literacy and bilingualism. *ASHA Leader*, *7*(20), 4–5, 16–17.

Henderson, E. (1990). *Teaching spelling.* Boston, MA: Houghton Mifflin.

Iacono, T., & Cupples, L. (2000). *Assessment of phonological awareness and reading.* Retrieved April 23, 2003 from http://www.elr.com.au/apar.

Kamhi, A., & Hinton, L. N. (2000). Explaining individual differences in spelling ability. *Topics in Language Disorders*, *20*(3), 37–49.

Koppenhaver, D., Evans, D., & Yoder, D. E. (1991). Childhood reading and writing experiences of literate adults with severe speech and motor impairments. *Augmentative and Alternative Communication*, *7*(1), 20–33.

Koppenhaver, D., & Yoder, D. E. (1992). Literacy issues in persons with severe speech and physical impairments. In R. Gaylord-Ross (Ed.), *Issues and research in special education* (Vol. 2., pp. 156–201). New York: Columbia University Teachers College Press.

Kraat, A. (1987). *Communication interaction between aided and natural speakers: An IPCAS study report.* Madison: Trace Research and Development Center, University of Wisconsin-Madison.

Larson, S., & Hammill, D. D. (1994). *Test of Written Spelling—Revised*. Austin, TX: PRO-ED.

Locke, J. L. (1980). The inference of speech perception in the phonologically disordered child. Part II. Some clinically novel procedures, their use, some findings. *Journal of Speech and Hearing Disorders, 45*, 445–468.

Masterson, J., & Apel, K. (2000). Spelling assessment: Charting a path to optimal intervention. *Topics in Language Disorders, 20*(3), 50–65.

McNaughton, S. (1993). Graphic representational systems and literacy learning. *Topics in Language Disorders, 13*(2), 58–75.

McNaughton, S. (1998). Reading acquisition of adults with severe congenital speech and physical impairments: theoretical infrastructure, empirical investigation, education implication. Unpublished doctoral dissertation, University of Toronto, Toronto, Ontario, Canada.

McNaughton, S., & Lindsay, P. (1995). Approaching literacy with AAC graphics. *Augmentative and Alternative Communication, 11*, 212–228.

Moats, L. C. (1994). Assessment of spelling in learning disabilities research. In G. R. Lyons (Ed.), *Frames of reference for the assessment of learning disabilities* (pp. 333–350.). Baltimore: Paul H. Brookes.

Moats, L. C. (1995). Spelling development, disability, and instruction. Baltimore: York Press.

Mulis, I., Martin, M., Gonzalez, E., & Kennedy, A. (2003). *PIRLS 2001 international report: IEA's Study of Reading Literacy Achievement in Primary School in 35 Countries.* Boston: International Study Center, Boston College.

Newton, M. (1994). *The Aston Index*. London: LDA.

Reid, D. K., Hresko, W. P., & Hammill, D. D. (2001). *Test of Early Reading Ability*. Circle Pines, MN: AGS.

Semel, E., Wiig, E. H., & Secord, W. (1987). *Clinical Evaluation of Language Fundamentals—Revised.* New York: Psychological Corporation, Harcourt Brace Jovanovich.

Smith, M. (1989). Reading without speech: A study of children with cerebral palsy. *Irish Journal of Psychology, 10*, 601–614.

Smith, M. (1998). *Pictures of language: The role of PCS in the language acquisition of children with severe congenital speech and physical impairments.* Unpublished doctoral dissertation, Trinity College, Dublin, Ireland.

Smith, M. (2001). Literacy challenges for individuals with severe congenital speech impairments. *International Journal of Disability, Development and Education, 48*, 331–353.

Smith, M., & Blischak, D. (1997). Literacy. In L. Lloyd, D. Fuller & H. Arvidson (Eds.), *Augmentative and alternative communication: Principles and practices* (pp. 414–444.). London: Allyn & Bacon.

Stackhouse, J., & Wells, B. (1997). *Children's speech and literacy difficulties: A psycholinguistic framework.* London: Whurr.

Sutton, A., & Gallagher, T. (1993). Verb class distinctions and AAC language encoding limitations. *Journal of Speech & Hearing Research, 36*, 1216–1226.

Sutton, A., Soto, G., & Blockberger, S. (2002). Grammatical issues in graphic symbol communication. *Augmentative and Alternative Communication, 18*, 192–204.

Templeton, S., & Morris, D. (2000). Spelling. In M. Kamil, P. Mosenthal, P. D. Pearson, & R. Barr (Eds.), *Handbook of reading research* (Vol. 3, pp. 525–543.). Mawah, NJ: Erlbaum.

Treiman, R., & Bourassa, D. (2000). Children's written and oral spelling. *Applied Psycholinguistics, 21*, 183–204.

Udwin, O., & Yule, W. (1991). Augmentative communication systems taught to cerebral palsy children—A longitudinal study. 1: The acquisition of signs and symbols and syntactic aspects of their use over time. *British Journal of Disorders of Communication, 25*, 295–309.

van Balkom, H., & Donker-Gimbrére, M. (1996). A psycholinguistic approach to graphic language use. In S. von Tetzchner & M. Jensen (Eds.), *Augmentative and alternative communication: European perspectives* (pp. 153–170). London: Whurr.

Vandervelden, M. (1992). *Phonological recoding and phonological analytical skills in early literacy learning: A developmental approach.* University of Toronto, Toronto, Ontario, Canada.

Vandervelden, M., & Siegel, L. (1999). Phonological processing and literacy in AAC users and students with motor speech impairments. *Augmentative and Alternative Communication, 15,* 191–211.

Vandervelden, M., & Siegel, L. (2001). Phonological processing in written word learning: Assessment for children who use augmentative and alternative communication. *Augmentative and Alternative Communication, 17*(1), 11–26.

Vellutino, F. R. (1993). *What speech and language therapists can do to facilitate assessment and remediation of reading difficulties.* Paper presented at the annual convention of the American Speech-Language Hearing Association, Anaheim, CA.

Vincent, D., & Claydon, J. (1983). *The Diagnostic Spelling Test.* London: NFER-Nelson.

von Tetzchner, S., & Martinsen, H. (1996). Words and strategies: Conversations with young children who use aided language. In S. von Tetzchner & M. Jensen (Eds.), *Augmentative and alternative communication: European perspectives* (pp. 65–88.). London: Whurr.

Wilkinson, G. S. (1995). *The Wide Range Achievement Test-3.* Wilmington, DE: Jastak Associates.

Wixson, K. K., Bosky, A. B., Yochum, M. N., & Alvermann, D. E. (1984). An interview for assessing students' perceptions of classroom reading tasks. *The Reading Teacher, 37,* 346–352.

Woodcock, R. (1998). *Woodcock Reading Mastery Tests—Revised.* Circle Pines, MN: AGS.

Young, D. (1987). *The SPAR Group Reading and Spelling Tests.* Sevenoaks, Kent, UK: Hodder & Stoughton Educational.

CHAPTER 7

Principles of Intervention

I. INTRODUCTION

There are few topics that have been more widely discussed, disputed, researched, analyzed, and reported on over the past few decades than the topic of reading and writing development and disorders. There are many reasons for this emphasis on success in learning to read and write. Reading is one of the most important abilities acquired by children as they progress through school,

Literacy and Augmentative and Alternative Communication

laying the foundation for learning across all subjects. Reading and writing are not simply educational goals; they can form the basis for recreation and for personal growth. In the view of the United Nations,

> . . . literacy is about more than reading and writing—it is about how we communicate in society. It is about social practices and relationships, about knowledge, language and culture. Literacy—the use of written communication—finds its place in our lives alongside other ways of communicating. . . . Those who use literacy take it for granted—but those who cannot use it are excluded from much communication in today's world. Indeed, it is the excluded who can best appreciate the notion of "literacy as freedom." (http://portal.unesco.org/education/ev.php)

Getting agreement that attainment of literacy is desirable is not difficult. Far more challenging is reaching a consensus about how best to achieve the goal of creating successful readers and writers. Debates have raged about whether the primary emphasis should be on the function and meaning aspects of reading and writing or whether instead children should be taught through an emphasis on sounds and letter patterns, until these aspects of print information have become fluent and effortless. Approaches that emphasize meaning come under the umbrella term of *top-down* or *meaning-centered approaches*. These approaches highlight the higher-order cognitive processes involved in fluent reading. The alternative print-focused approaches are often termed *bottom-up* or *skill-centered approaches*, because they emphasize the individual building block skills that yield the information required to access and construct meaning.

Over the last few decades there has been increasing recognition that, in fact, no single approach offers all the answers (Butler & Wallach, 1995; Ellis, 1993; Goldsworthy & Pieretti, 2004). Reading and writing involve the complex integration of many different skills. Each child is also unique. Reading demands differ across contexts, and skills change over time. Although many skills are necessary to be able to read fluently, fluent reading is characterized by a lack of awareness of these component skills while reading. Snow, Burns, and Griffin (1998) summarized the position of the Committee for the Prevention of Reading Difficulties in Young Children as follows:

> Briefly put, we can say that children need simultaneous access to some knowledge of letter-sound relationships, some sight vocabulary, and some comprehension strategies. In each case, "some" indicates that exhaustive knowledge of these aspects is not needed to get the child reading conventionally; rather, each child seems to need varying amounts of knowledge to get started, but then he or she needs to build up the kind of inclusive and automatic knowledge that will let the fact that reading is being done fade into the background, while the reasons for reading are fulfilled. (pp. 79 and 94)

Although there are shared features that are common across many effective instructional approaches, there can also be many differences. One of the crucial determinants of success is the teacher or facilitator (Frost, 2000); a second is the extent of opportunities for, and barriers to, the student engaging with the task of learning to read and write. In the book *Waves of Words: Augmented Communicators Read and Write,* it is clear that the experiences of augmented communicators who learn to read and write are many and varied. How they learn to read and write, why they embark on the journey, and by which criteria they measure their successes differ across all the individuals profiled. In part, these differences reflect the fact that many factors can influence the process of developing *some* knowledge of letter-sound relationships, *some* sight vocabulary, *some* comprehension strategies, and the further development and integration of these knowledge bases to support fluent reading and writing. These factors are discussed in this chapter with reference to the contexts outlined by Pumfrey and Reason (1991): the learning context, the language context, and the print context. We then turn attention to some general principles that underpin intervention, before considering the unique experiences of individuals who use augmentative and alternative communication (AAC). Approaches to instruction are reviewed, with suggestions for some specific applications with younger children, adolescents, and adults.

II. CONTEXTS FOR CONSIDERATION

A. THE LEARNING CONTEXT

The learning context encompasses our cognitive set and purpose, our expectations of a text and of the experience of either creating or reading a text, the knowledge we bring to an encounter with text, and a focus on constructing meaning within a text (Pumfrey & Reason, 1991). The learning context is shaped by previous and present life experiences, by expectations of enjoyment and competence, by the unique meaning system of the individual, and by the extent to which an author or an intended target audience share background knowledge with the reader or writer. Thus, it is subject to the influences of sociocultural factors, developmental factors, and educational experiences. It is also affected by an individual's interests and motivation and by what Guthrie and Wigfield (2000) called *engagement* with the learning process.

1. Sociocultural Considerations

According to the United Nations, literacy extends beyond mere reading and writing: "it is about social practices and relationships, about knowledge, language and culture" (http://portal.unesco.org/education/ev/php). Rassool (1999) proposed that literacy has potent symbolic value and, thus, is a social and cultural artifact. "As a communication practice embedded in society and culture, literacy is deeply implicated in the lives of people, cultural transmission and cultural reproduction. That is to say, it provides the means *par excellence*, by which cultures make, and remake themselves" (p. 3).

Cultures differ in the roles and importance they ascribe to literacy and to different literacy activities. Within each culture, individual family units also operate with a set of values, and these values have the potential to affect perceptions of the roles, worth, and meanings of written language. Snow and Tabors (1996) suggested four mechanisms of intergenerational transfer of literacy that can occur within families:

1. Simple and direct transfer of literacy skills, through participation in activities such as storybook reading and immersion in print-rich environments, whereby parents often unconsciously engage in *proto-teaching*;

2. Participation in literacy practice, whereby children learn the functional uses of literacy through their experiences of everyday life in the family;

3. Enjoyment and engagement, whereby parental enthusiasm about literacy activities creates a set for the child to become an active motivated participant in literacy experiences;

4. Linguistic and cognitive mechanisms, whereby the family structures activities that lay the foundation for skills subsequently important to literacy development. For example, simple activities such as recounting the day's activities at mealtime offer opportunities for the development of sequencing, memory, and linguistic skills, as well as development of a narrative framework.

Families differ in the extent to which these mechanisms for transferring literacy skills are used. Each child coming to the task of formally learning to read and write exists within and represents a unique learning context. As outlined in Chapter 4, families of individuals who use AAC have many different and competing demands on their time and their energies. Mechanisms of intergenerational literacy transfer may operate quite differently for children who use aided communication than for their siblings. Furthermore, if there is a social or cultural entity such as "individuals who use aided communication" (Woll & Barnett, 1998), one of the characteristics that may be common across many members of the group is difficulty acquiring effective literacy skills. This feature may have implications for the self-identity of the group and also for the expectations of those outside this particular social group.

Effective literacy intervention successfully addresses the learning context. Rasinski and Padak (2000) proposed that a key to development of effective literacy instruction is the creation of authentic and engaged classrooms. By *authenticity* these authors mean that "what students read, how they read it, and how they respond to what they read (and write) (*is*) connected to the children's interests and lives, connected to the real world, and connected to other areas of the curriculum" (Rasinski & Padak, 2000, p. 4). By *engaged* they mean that students are active, enthusiastic participants in reading and writing. The goal of intervention in their view is "not simply to develop students who *can* read, but those who *want* to read and *choose* to read" (p. 5). In a similar vein, Guthrie and Wigfield (2000, p. 404) argued that "a person reads a word or comprehends a text not only because she can do it, but because she is motivated to do it." Motivation in this framework is seen as being crucial to engagement, because it is motivation that activates behaviors, whether those behaviors constitute looking for a book to read, attempting to apply decoding strategies, or creating additional text in a written activity. Harnessing and developing this motivation are critically important for apprentice readers and writers who use aided communication, given the many challenges they face in all aspects of their educational development.

3. Developmental Considerations

Although wanting and choosing to read are always important, what children understand by "reading" or "writing" and what they *can* choose to read and write change over time (Smith & Warwick, 1997; Snow *et al.*, 1998). As outlined in Chapter 3, the learning needs of children change as they make the journey from apprentice to expert readers and writers. For early readers and writers, learning contexts that offer multiple, rich opportunities to engage with print are needed, so that a child can engage in meaningful, enjoyable reading and writing activities, supported by expert readers and thus can develop both spoken and written language skills and metaskills (Frost, 2000; Snow *et al.*, 1998). Progression from this stage requires a learning context that continues to be authentic and engaged (Rasinski & Padak, 2000), but within which explicit instruction is provided to crack the code of the alphabetic principle (Snow *et al.*, 1998). Children can approach a reading task by simply memorizing words, but to progress to productive reading, they must move to a level of explicit analysis of words. At this stage of development, therefore, learning is heavily dependent on exogenous factors; the instructional context provided is crucial. As children master a bank of sight words and gain insights into sounds, sound-letter correspondences, and orthographic patterns, literacy learning becomes increasingly endogenous or self-generated and self-driven (Stanovich, 1994). Clearly supports are still needed from the environment, but a range of other cognitive and learning skills become increasingly implicated and meshed with literacy achievements. Most crucial at this stage is access to interesting, accessible print materials to encourage the ongoing engagement of the apprentice reader-writer. Only such regular engagement can offer the repeated opportunities necessary to develop fluency, to *self-teach*, and to foster the automaticity needed to free cognitive space for focusing on what is being read, rather than the activity of reading itself.

The factors discussed in this section indicate a need to consider not only the sociocultural factors impinging on the learning context for each apprentice reader-writer, but also the necessary changes in learning context that occur, as apprentice readers and writers encounter new life experiences, acquire and develop new knowledge bases, problem-solving skills, and interests, and face new learning demands. Because much of the formal experience of learning to read and write occurs in the structured classroom, a key influence in the learning context is the educational context.

4. Educational Considerations

Considerable evidence is available to support a view that children coming from home backgrounds in which literacy is valued, prominent, and promoted have an advantage when it comes to developing skills in reading and writing (Smith & Warwick, 1997; Snow et al., 1998; Teale & Sulzby, 1987, 1989). However, when children start school, they encounter a whole new social context, in which learning demands and expectations differ greatly from those of the home environment and, crucially, the shared common background so embedded in the home context is replaced by widely varying levels of common background (Smith & Warwick, 1997). An educational context that provides rich, frequent, and authentic literacy experiences can do much to overcome potential differences in home experiences presented by each child learner. Wilkinson and Silliman (2000, p. 337) suggested that the classroom is a unique context for learning and exerts a profound effect on students' development of language and literacy skills, particularly in the early years.

Instructional approaches also vary considerably across and within schools. For some children, the educational context may encourage experimentation, risk-taking, and creativity. For others, accuracy and attention to detail may be perceived as more important (Clay, 1991). These contrasting approaches may exert considerable influence on the learning strategies adopted by children, their enthusiasm for the task, their construct of "learning," and their expectations of future learning experiences (Wilkinson & Silliman, 2000). For individuals with significant physical, sensory, or motor difficulties, the priorities within the educational context may be perceived as being very different from the priorities for their typically developing peers, even within the same classroom (Koppenhaver, 1991; Koppenhaver & Yoder, 1993; Mike, 1995). Thus, the learning context, both at home and in school, needs consideration when one plans intervention strategies.

B. THE LANGUAGE CONTEXT

Reading and writing are essentially processes of constructing meaning from and in print. As such, they are implicitly linguistic activities. Pumfrey and Reason

(1991) emphasized that written language is intimately linked to spoken language abilities, drawing on all aspects of linguistic and metalinguistic knowledge, across domains of semantics, syntax, morphology, pragmatics, and phonology. Clearly, understanding of the vocabulary, concepts, and linguistic structures contained within a text is important. However, productive reading involves more than simply understanding the individual words and sentences within a text (Snow *et al.*, 1998). It also demands reflective purposive understanding of the underlying meaning of the text. In this respect, productive understanding requires metacognitive or reflective control of comprehension—a constant self-monitoring of understanding, of linking to what has been previously read, and of checking that the inferred meaning makes sense in the context of the rest of the text (Tattershall, 2002).

There is a great deal of overlap between spoken and written language development. Written language also draws on unique domains of knowledge and indicates development in ways different from spoken language. Just as spoken language provides a platform for the development of written language skills, written language itself opens up new and important language learning experiences of considerable importance to the development of spoken language. The language demands of print, including vocabulary demands, are higher than the demands in spoken language (Hayes & Ahrens, 1988). Stanovich, West, Cunningham, Cipielewski, and Siddiqui (1996) argued that "even children with limited comprehension skills will build vocabulary and cognitive structures through immersion in literacy activities" (p. 29). As individuals progress through the later school years and adolescence, written language becomes an increasingly important source of vocabulary learning, as well as aspects of language use, such as idioms, similes, and figurative language (Nippold, Allen, & Kirsch, 2001). Thus, whereas the relationship between spoken and written language changes over time, it remains an intimately interconnected relationship, with reciprocal benefits for language and literacy development.

Pumfrey and Reason (1991) proposed three kinds of ingredients that influence the unique language context each reader and writer brings to encounters with print:

1. Familiarity and facility with the range of purposes of language;
2. Familiarity and facility with the range of purposes of print; and
3. Competence and skills in relation to all aspects of language structure.

1. The Range and Purposes of Language

Many instructional approaches, particularly those associated with top-down approaches advocate an emphasis on building spoken language skills, as preliminary to and in addition to development of specific written language skills. These approaches stress the importance of integrating speaking, reading, and writing as intimately connected activities (Christie, Enz, & Vukelich, 1997). Planned writing activities may be developed and elaborated on first in spoken language, through a mixture of class discussion, story telling and retelling, and perhaps dramatization (Yaden, Rowe, & MacGillivray, 2000), so that language concepts are fully consolidated in spoken language. The outcomes of these discussions serve as the focus for a writing activity, so that a tightly woven tapestry of spoken and written language emerges.

As outlined in Chapter 4, the communication and language learning experiences of individuals who use aided communication may differ from those of their naturally speaking peers. The effects and significance of these different experiences are as yet unclear. Evidence to date suggests that the use of aided communication systems tends to be restricted, in terms of frequency of communication (Kraat, 1987; Light, Collier, & Parnes, 1985b; Light & Kelford-Smith, 1993; Soto & Toro-Zambrana, 1995), in terms of the kinds of expressions produced (Smith, 1996; Sutton, Gallagher, Morford, & Shahnaz, 2000; Sutton, Soto, & Blockberger, 2002; Udwin & Yule, 1990), and in terms of the communicative functions fulfilled (Grove & Smith, 1997; Light, Collier, & Parnes, 1985a). Taken together, it seems reasonable to suggest that individuals who use aided communication come to literacy learning with different levels of "familiarity and facility with the range of purposes of language" than do their speaking peers.

Although there are clearly both shared and unique dimensions of spoken and written language for natural speakers, for those using aided communication the distinction between these two modalities is not as clear-cut. Both "spoken" and "written" expressive communication occur within the same modality—the visual graphic modality. Even if voice output is also produced, the means of accessing the spoken output is usually through the visual graphic modality. Another unique aspect of the language learning experience of many aided communicators relates to the asymmetry in input and output communication modalities (Grove & Smith, 1997; Smith & Grove, 1999, 2003). Many individuals who use graphic symbols to communicate expressively hear and understand spoken language around them. Their primary input modality is therefore spoken language. However, when it comes to generating output, they must either translate an underlying spoken message into an alternative modality at the point of transmission or construct the message within the alternative modality from the start (Smith & Grove, 2003). Each attempt to communicate expressively represents a metalinguistic challenge, quite different from the communication challenges faced by speaking children. The discussion at the start of this section about the complementary and increasingly differentiated roles of spoken and written language is just as relevant for those using aided communication, but these complementary competencies may be difficult to disentangle.

2. The Range and Purposes of Print

Individuals who have experience with a wide range of print uses are better able to understand the many ways language can be encoded in print and the formats and types of language structures that are effective and efficient in a range of different writing contexts. Consequently, they can adapt a flexible approach to language use in print. They recognize the need for particular schema in story narration and the contrasting structure of expository text. Just as a tennis player improves the odds by increasing his or her pool of possible shots, so also a reader-writer with experience across a wide range of uses of language and of print has an advantage when it comes to creating meaning in print or constructing meaning from print.

Intervention approaches that highlight the varied and contrasting uses of print have many possible advantages. First, the chance of engaging a reader-writer is better with such approaches, because it is likely that there will be at least one purpose that is perceived as being more motivating and rewarding. For example, anecdotal evidence suggests that many aided communicators are motivated initially to write for communication purposes or to share their own story, with reading taking a secondary position of importance. Second, by offering a wide range of experiences to apprentice reader-writers, such approaches provide a whole new set of learning experiences, extending far beyond mere text decoding, and have the potential to feed directly into developing "spoken" language as well as written language skills. Such experiences may be particularly crucial for individuals using aided communication in developing their expressive communication as well as their literacy skills.

3. Competence and Skill In Language Structure

The third aspect of the language context mentioned by Pumfrey and Reason (1991) is competence and skills in relation to all aspects of language structure. There have been many questions raised about the impact of severe speech impairments on the development of the morphosyntactic aspects of language (Blockberger & Sutton, 2003; Soto & Toro-Zambrama, 1995; Sutton & Gallagher, 1993; Sutton et al., 2002). Many graphic communication systems do not offer structural organization below the level of the word unit (Smith, 1998). Generating expressive output through manipulation of sublexical units such as morphemes may be an experience aided communicators have for the first time through written language. In this respect, they are very different from their speaking peers, who typically have several years' experience in just this type of problem solving. In the early stages of language acquisition, speaking children receive feedback relating to the content of their communication. Over time, however, the focus shifts to issues of accuracy. Increasingly, speaking children receive explicit feedback about the structural accuracy of their communication contributions, fostering an awareness of language structure as a focus in its own right and as something separate from the meaning of a message.

In contrast, for individuals using aided communication, expectations for structural accuracy of communication messages are typically very different. Partner feedback is more likely to focus on accuracy of physical access or symbol choice than on specific aspects of language structure. Many factors, including a drive for communicative efficiency or modality-specific influences may have an impact on the structure of messages (Smith & Grove, 2003), and the relationship between spoken language competence and performance within an alternative modality may be far from transparent. In light of all of these factors, the language context for such individuals must be considered as a unique and poorly understood ingredient in the literacy mix and one needing particular attention in intervention.

C. The Print Context

The print context is interpreted here to encompass all aspects of print—understanding and familiarity with letters and with phoneme-grapheme correspondences, sight word vocabulary, and the facility to rapidly and simultaneously process all aspects of print, including punctuation. At some point, all instructional approaches must grapple with the specific skills necessary to engage with print. The emphasis placed on print-specific skills may differ in top-down and bottom-up approaches, but clearly the most fundamental difference between spoken and written language is that the latter can only be accessed through print itself. These skills can be embedded in rich, naturalistic language learning experiences. Alternatively, they can be presented as a "prerequisite" set of skills to be consolidated before or parallel with reading and writing activities. Either way, beginning readers and writers need explicit instruction in the alphabetic principle to crack the code. In 1998, the Committee on the Prevention of Reading Difficulties in Young Children published their report *Preventing Reading Difficulties in Young Children*, a wide-ranging review of literature on reading instruction (Snow *et al.*, 1998). They concluded that, "explicit teaching and application of the alphabetic principle and writing are the instructional components whose importance is most strongly supported by research. They also correspond to the abilities that are found to be differentially underdeveloped in students with reading difficulty" (p. 197). Whatever the guise under which such instruction is introduced, it is unavoidable that specific print-related skills must be fostered.

We have already considered the many different ways in which severe congenital speech impairments may influence the development of speech and print processing skills. Other factors affecting the print context for individuals who use aided communication may be associated sensory and/or perceptual impairments and relatively limited print-related experiences because of the many demands of personal care. On the other hand, individuals who use graphic symbols are exposed to "print" often from an early age and in a communicative context. Typically, written words accompany their graphic symbols or a written word is generated on a display on a voice output communication aid. Once again, therefore, the unique print context of individuals who use augmentative or alternative communication must be acknowledged.

The ingredients of literacy outlined by Pumfrey and Reason (1991) undoubtedly are just as relevant for those using AAC as they are for natural speakers. However, compiling and collecting the ingredients together and establishing the most effective and appropriate balance across the ingredients requires constant review and reflection and a respect for the complexity of challenges faced by those with difficulties communicating in conventional ways. Setting aside these challenges, certain principles of intervention in literacy learning can be said to be relevant to all apprentice reader–writers.

III. GENERAL PRINCIPLES

After many decades of research, there is still no definitive evidence to indicate *the* most effective approach to literacy instruction (Aihara *et al.*, 2000; Foorman & Torgesen, 2001; Frost, 2000). This limitation does not suggest that there is no consensus regarding general principles that characterize good instructional practice (Foorman, Francis, Fletcher, Schatschneider, & Mehta, 1998; Foorman & Torgesen, 2001). In the *Literacy Bill of Rights* drawn up by Erickson, Koppenhaver, and Yoder (2002), included in Chapter 1 of this book, essential features of intervention programs are set out, both explicitly and implicitly. Smith and Blischak (1997, pp. 429–431) outlined four principles to be considered in developing literacy intervention programs for individuals using AAC. These principles are revisited in the following sections.

A. DEFINING GOOD INTERVENTION

Principle 1: *Good literacy intervention practice applies across all types of literacy instruction with clients with all types of abilities.*

Good literacy instruction is required by *all* children (Snow *et al.*, 1998). There is no research evidence to suggest that children experiencing difficulties require radically different supports or techniques to achieve mastery of literacy, although clearly they are likely to need more intensive support. Snow *et al.* concluded that "good instruction seems to transcend characterizations of children's vulnerability for failure; the same good early literacy environment and patterns of effective instruction are required for children who might fail for different reasons" (p. 2) and further that "excellent instruction is the best intervention for children who demonstrate problems learning to read" (p. 3).

What features characterize "excellent" instruction? Smith and Blischak (1997, p. 430) suggested the following:

1. A view of reading and writing as interactive, constructive processes, with which the reader-writer is actively engaged (Christie *et al.*, 1997; Clay, 1991; Dechant, 1991; Galda, Cullinan, & Strickland, 1993; Gavelek, Raphael, Biondo, & Wang, 2000).

2. A primary focus on meaning (Guthrie & Wigfield, 2000; Pumfrey & Reason, 1991; Rasinski & Padak, 2000).

3. An emphasis on the integration of language skills, both oral and written, while building on life experiences and knowledge (Foley, 1993; Pumfrey & Reason, 1991). This component incorporates the first two ingredients outlined by Pumfrey and Reason (1991). Crucially, consideration must also be given to the final segment, encompassing analytic skills relating to grapheme-phoneme correspondences. It has been reported that of all the various aspects of language arts instruction in the kindergarten, only the proportion of time devoted to ana-lyzing the internal structure of spoken and written words reliably predicts dif-ferences in reading achievement at the end of first grade (Scanlon & Vellutino, 1996). Thus, an instructional program built around this model requires the inte-gration of both holistic and analytic components.

4. Dual recognition of the importance of the *functions* and *forms* of print (Galda *et al.*, 1993; Koppenhaver, Coleman, Kalman, & Yoder, 1991; Teale & Sulzby, 1987).

5. A focus on providing strategies rather than on teaching splinter skills. Galda *et al.* (1993) suggested, "As children acquire strategies, they automatically acquire skills" (p. 106).

6. Consideration of the linguistic/communication context of literacy learning, as well as the social and physical contexts. Active participation in com-munication surrounding literacy activities is encouraged (Erickson *et al.*, 2002; Galda *et al.*, 1993; Koppenhaver & Erickson, 2003), perceptions and expectations for reading and writing are addressed (Koppenhaver & Yoder, 1992a; Mirenda, 2003), and, the availability and accessibility of literacy materials and literate models are considered.

7. A focus on the individual learning style of the "apprentice" reader-writer (Erickson, Koppenhaver, Yoder, & Nance, 1997; Koppenhaver & Erickson, 2003; Koppenhaver & Yoder, 1993) rather than on the adoption of a prescriptive approach to reading-writing instruction.

8. Recognition of both the similarities and the differences between oral and written language (Gillam & Johnston, 1992).

9. Fostering of "safe" learning—building on success and current levels of functioning (Forester, 1988)—with the goal of allowing the learner to control his or her own learning. Effective literacy instruction programs develop and encourage intrinsic motivation for reading and writing, so that learners seek out literacy opportunities and enjoy the challenge of literacy learning. In contrast, instructional approaches that emphasize extrinsic motivation, whether the motivator is praise, recognition, or tangible incentives, are associated with a desire to complete a task rather than to understand or enjoy a text or a task (Guthrie & Wigfield, 2000). If the self-teaching process proposed by Share (1995) is to be initiated, then the learner must actively engage with his or her own learning.

10. Provision of materials that are of personal interest (Forester, 1988) and appropriate difficulty (Erickson *et al.*, 2002; Koppenhaver & Yoder, 1992b; Steelman, Pierce, & Koppenhaver, 1993).

Determining appropriate levels of difficulty is important with the recognition that task demands and difficulty levels interact with learning opportunities. Three levels of difficulty can be considered when one selects texts for apprentice readers (Snow *et al.*, 1998). *Independent reading level* texts support the most fluent levels of reading. At this level, there are few if any errors of word identification or decoding, comprehension and recall are appropriate, and no or minimal assistance is required by the reader. At the *instructional reading level*, texts offer more challenges, and errors are more common. However, with supervision, support, and appropriate preparation, comprehension and recall are adequate, and reading accuracy is high. The level of errors does not interfere with text processing, and there are sufficient opportunities for new learning to occur. At the *frustration level*, predictably, reading skills break down, errors are so common that they interfere with text comprehension, recall is poor, and often signs of discomfort or stress are also obvious. As a general rule, frustration levels occur if a reader makes errors on one or more words of every 10 words in a text, although this rule should not be taken as being written in stone. The frustration thresholds of individuals differ. The challenge for the educator is to balance the tension between providing texts that allow independent reading, while ensuring that there are still sufficient opportunities for a reader to encounter new learning opportunities within those texts. Constant assessment and monitoring are therefore essential, leading to the next principle.

B. THE ASSESSMENT BASIS

Principle 2: *Intervention programs should be based on appropriate assessment.*
Because moves to require evidence of the effectiveness of intervention are increasing across all health-related and educational arenas, through evidence-based

practice (EBP) (e.g., Schlosser, 2003), the focus on appropriate and efficient assessment approaches has become more sharp. Ideally, assessment and intervention are inextricably linked, in a dynamic, context-grounded focus (Goldsworthy, 1996; Wallach & Butler, 1994). In such a framework, intervention is not postponed while exhaustive assessment is undertaken. Rather, both occur simultaneously or in a fluid interchange of focus. Task-based observations replace static assessment tools. Reading and writing skills are recognized as existing on a continuum of expertise, influenced by task and context factors. Accepting the symbiotic relationship between assessment and intervention also safeguards against the temptation to postpone intervention until exhaustive (and frequently exhausting) assessment has taken place.

C. Contrasting Developmental and Functional Frameworks

Principle 3: *Although reading and writing emerge in a developmental sequence, application of a developmental framework is not always the most appropriate choice.*

One of the insights yielded by developmental approaches to literacy is that the repertoire of literacy skills changes over time; another is that needs differ as apprentice reader-writers progress along the path to expertise. In the initial stages, exposure to print, both for reading and writing, in meaningful and enjoyable contexts, is important. If these experiences are linked with exploration of the sound system of the language and with opportunities in playful contexts to link these sound explorations to written language, then the stage is well set for development of decoding skills. To crack the alphabetic principle, explicit, direct instruction in letter-sound relationships is required. Writing may be a critical catalyst in prompting and driving analytic attention to sound structure and to letter-sound relationships at this stage (Snow *et al.*, 1998; Templeton, 2002; Templeton & Morris, 2000).

Progressing to a stage of fluency in reading depends on a variety of factors. Snow *et al.* (1998, p. 4) suggested the following:

- Having a working understanding of how sounds are represented alphabetically;
- Having sufficient practice in reading to achieve fluency with different kinds of texts;
- Having sufficient background knowledge and vocabulary to render written texts meaningful and interesting;
- Having control over procedures for monitoring comprehension and repairing misunderstandings; and
- Having continued interest and motivation to read for a variety of purposes.

By fourth grade, students are expected to be sufficiently expert in reading that they are able to read independently to learn. Reading to learn requires the application of higher-order comprehension skills and the activation of a range of background knowledge. A critical transition in skills is presumed to occur across the second and third grades and is contingent on lower-level skills developing to a sufficiently automatic level that they no longer consciously impinge on the reader. In this way, cognitive effort can be directed to the *content* rather than to the *process* of reading or writing.

Reading approaches that draw on developmental information are appealing, following as they do an apparently transparent road map. Such approaches typically focus on a range of skills, simultaneously addressing decoding and encoding, sight word recognition, and comprehension, with varying emphasis, depending on the skill level of the learner and the apparent "stage" of learning.

Such approaches can be contrasted with *functional* or *sight word* approaches to instruction. To some extent, this contrast is unfortunate, because it may lead to the inference that developmental approaches are somehow nonfunctional or that sight word vocabulary is not relevant within the latter approach. Such a dichotomization is unfair on both approaches. Functional approaches to literacy instruction typically emphasize the development of a store of sight words, with little attention being paid to decoding skills. Thus, they are sometimes criticized for failing to provide strategies for apprentice readers to deal with unfamiliar words. Most typically, such approaches are considered with learners who have particular learning difficulties (Belfiore, Skinner, & Ferkis, 1995; Browder & Shear, 1996; Conners, 1992; Lalli & Browder, 1993) or with adults who have a history of failure in traditional reading instruction approaches. They are based on a careful analysis of an individual's needs to support independence within his or her own community (Browder & Xin, 1998; Schloss et al., 1995). Target words may differ considerably in their internal complexity, and they are selected on the basis of their importance to the individual, rather than on any predetermined criterion of difficulty. *Deodorant* may be prioritized over *cat,* for example, or favorite TV program names may be selected as targets, over and above more apparently simple, regular, words. Sight word approaches have been used for specific activities of daily living, such as grocery shopping and household chores (Lalli & Browder, 1993) or reading product warning labels (Collins & Stinson, 1995). Browder and Xin (1998) conducted a review of the research on sight word instruction using meta-analysis of published research and concluded that this approach can be highly effective in establishing a sight word vocabulary. However, they pointed out that few research studies published (less than 10% of all the studies they included in their review) made any attempt to measure comprehension of sight words in real life contexts. Most typically, "success" in sight word identification was measured through table-top activities, with specific instructional materials. These authors expressed their concern that "although word finding can assist students in learning words, it is not a functional outcome."

They argued that the outcome of focus should be that students can perform an activity they could not master without knowing the word targets. The importance of contextualizing sight word learning in real life situations was supported by a further finding of their review—instructional approaches that applied sight words to real materials and activities positively influenced learning outcomes.

Functional or sight word approaches to instruction have many possible applications for individuals using AAC. Given the range of perceptual and potential processing difficulties presented by many individuals using aided communication, acquisition of analytic decoding skills may be particularly challenging. Addressing environmental and social literacy needs through the introduction of sight words can promote success and harness motivation to persist with other aspects of literacy mastery.

It is also possible that many individuals using graphic-based communication systems develop particular strengths in visual processing of gestalt images or visual analytic skills. McNaughton (McNaughton, 1998; McNaughton & Lindsay, 1995) has long argued that graphic representational systems may differ in the supports they offer to the development of literacy skills. In this view, symbols that have the potential for sublexical analysis may yield important benefits when it comes to developing skills in reading and writing. Despite the intuitive appeal of this argument, to date there has been insufficient research evidence to definitively support this hypothesis.

Incidental learning of words paired with graphic symbols may act as a potential bootstrap for further literacy developments. A sizeable sight word vocabulary may be needed for some individuals to trigger representational redescription (Karmiloff-Smith, 1992) through application of analytic processing. Berninger et al. (1999) have demonstrated that even "pure" whole word approaches can stimulate children to abstract elements of the alphabetic principle. The documented success of sight word instructional approaches with individuals with learning difficulties suggests that such approaches have much to offer. There is already some evidence to support this approach as a useful strategy with those who use AAC as a bridge to analytic decoding or as a primary learning strategy (Ratcliff & Little, 1996). As with most considerations in dealing with clients with complex impairments, it is unlikely that a single solution will meet all needs, and individualization of intervention to meet each person's needs is critical to success.

D. CONSIDERING INTRINSIC AND EXTRINSIC FACTORS

Principle 4: *Intervention programs should consider factors intrinsic and extrinsic to the individual, with the ultimate goals of maximizing opportunities to participate in* *literacy activities, while minimizing barriers to active participation, in a format that is tailored to the needs of each individual AAC user.*

This final principle emphasizes the fact that reading and writing are activities that are affected by multiple factors, all of which must be accounted for in our interventions. These factors include those intrinsic to the individual, such as sensory, physical, cognitive, and linguistic factors, as well as extrinsic factors, such as the range, frequency, and nature of the available learning experiences and the demands implicit in each literacy activity. The approach to intervention suggested here is adopted from a model of assessment described by Beukelman and Miranda (1992, 1998), focusing on opportunities, needs, and barriers to participation. Research evidence to date suggests that the literacy learning opportunities available to individuals who use aided communication are reduced compared with those for their speaking peers (Koppenhaver, 1991; Koppenhaver, Evans, & Yoder, 1991; Light, Binger, & Kelford-Smith, 1994; Light & Kelford-Smith, 1993; Light & McNaughton, 1993). This reduction in opportunities spreads across both home and school environments and extends across the range of literacy learning needs, including participation in storybook reading activities, direct instruction in print skills, and opportunities for independent reading and writing. Even when such opportunities are provided, there are many barriers to full participation, including issues of physical access, language and communication resources, and linguistic skills. Thus, for most individuals who use aided communication, opportunities to learn to read and write are reduced, barriers to participation in such opportunities are increased, and yet literacy learning needs remain comparable, if not elevated, compared with those of their speaking peers. Literacy intervention with individuals who use aided communication can be successful, as has been increasingly evident over the last decade (Blischak, 1994; Erickson *et al.*, 1997; Foley & Staples, 2003; Koppenhaver & Erickson, 2003; McNaughton, 1998; Miranda, 2003). Successful intervention approaches focus on multimodal techniques to address the complex mix of skills and needs brought to the learning task by those using nonconventional means of communication and interweave communication and literacy instruction as mutually dependent and complementary processes.

IV. AAC LITERACY AND PRINT LITERACY

The relationship between spoken and written language skills is well recognized and is increasingly drawn on in development of instructional approaches. One factor that is unique to individuals using aided communication is a duality of literacy skills that exists in their communication and their orthographic activities. Individuals using graphic symbols to communicate generate messages in symbols, in a process that is strikingly similar to traditional writing. It is difficult to determine the extent of overlap between their language skills, as evidenced through symbol-based messages, and the skills evident in traditional orthography. If, for example, someone typically relies on two-symbol combinations for expressive communication, should instruction in writing similarly be based on such constructions? Alternatively, should writing attempts be used to extend expressive language skills? Should there be a dual emphasis? Should initial instruction focus on the words included in a symbol display, and should symbols gradually be replaced by written words as sight vocabulary increases? These questions are as yet far from resolved. Although there are many advocates of using vocabulary that is drawn from communication displays in literacy instruction programs (Blau, 1986), there is also an argument against confusing the role of a communication board with that of an educational tool (Smith, 1991).

There are no simple answers to the question of where graphic communication systems "fit" in the overall journey to achievement of effective literacy skills. A prudent approach would seem to be to draw on as many possible avenues of learning as are available, including integrating communication and written language skills, while remaining mindful of the unique role played by graphic communication systems.

V. A FRAMEWORK FOR INTERVENTION: PARTICIPATION

As outlined in the preceding section, the approach advocated here is one that emphasizes participation in literacy activities as the key to effective instruction. Individuals learn to read and write by reading and writing in meaningful and motivating contexts. Active, engaged participation in authentic activities is a crucial catalyst for the emergence of self-directed learning. This emphasis, of necessity, requires broadening the focus from the individual learner to the contexts in which learning may occur. As Beukelman and Mirenda (1992, 1998) outlined, participation by an individual in communication or literacy events does not occur in a vacuum and cannot be measured in the abstract. Instead, a point of reference must be established to determine what might be typical levels of participation of others in the same context. Assessment therefore focuses on the range of literacy learning opportunities available to individuals using aided communication *relative to those for their speaking peers in the same environment* (Beukelman & Mirenda, 1992, 1998). The aim of intervention is to increase participation not to a predetermined abstract level but rather to a level commensurate with that of peers who have no additional impairments. The participation model therefore requires consideration of the social, cultural, and educational context of an individual.

At the same time, sensitivity and flexibility are important. If an individual comes from a background in which literacy skills are not valued or from a home in which no one can read or write, the aspiration is not that the target individual should demonstrate comparably constrained skills in this area. There may be cultural issues associated with literacy acquisition that directly influence the levels of participation in literacy learning opportunities and that may have either a positive or negative impact on progress. For example, story reading may not be a valued home activity, whereas joint reading of religious materials may be a central and highly prized activity.

A key point is that learning to read and write takes place in particular contexts and with particular activities, and neither of these can be considered neutral players in the learning process.

VI. APPROACHES TO INSTRUCTION

A. READING

1. Skill-Centered Approaches

Approaches to reading instruction vary primarily in their emphasis on the bottom-up skills involved in reading and the top-down meaning processes motivating reading. Skill-centered approaches identify the many subskills required in reading, including letter identification, phoneme-grapheme correspondences, identification of orthographic patterns beyond the grapheme level, sight word identification, attention to punctuation, and so on. Typically, such approaches utilize basal readers, establish a clear sequence of difficulty, rely on educator-directed instruction, and measure success in terms of skill attainment. Phonics approaches to instruction may be considered to come under the broad heading of skill-based instruction. The ingredients of literacy outlined by Pumfrey and Reason (1991) are all addressed within such approaches, but the weighting of importance of each ingredient effectively inverts the triangle in Figure 2.1, as more "space" is allocated to the print context than to the language or learning contexts. Skill-based instructional approaches have been criticized (Christie *et al.*, 1997) for placing too much emphasis on skill-and-drill activities, with little connection to real reading of meaningful stories. Low-interest materials and an emphasis on table-top activities may encourage a passive approach to reading. Reading may be treated as a compartmentalized subject within the curriculum and may be taught in isolation from other subjects, including writing. Perhaps most damaging of all, skill-centered approaches may mistakenly build on a premise that reading equals the sum of its subskills.

2. Meaning-Centered Approaches

In contrast, top-down approaches to instruction focus on the construction of meaning that is implicit in effective reading. Language processing and active engagement of prior knowledge are highlighted. Such approaches incorporate the ingredients of learning, language, and print, but the shape of the triangle matches that proposed by Pumfrey and Reason (1991). Apprentice readers are encouraged to take control of their own reading materials and to make choices, fostering a sense of ownership of the reading process and the learning involved. Skills are taught because children need them to do specific reading and writing activities rather than on the basis of a predetermined hierarchy of difficulty. Reading is integrated with writing and other subject areas. Whole language approaches sit comfortably under the heading of meaning-centred instruction. Priority is given to the child's construction of meaning, with the teacher acting as facilitator, rather than as director of learning, and specific skills are addressed opportunistically as determined by the focus and the activity in question.

Such approaches are not without limitations. Although activity-embedded skill instruction maximizes the functional value of skills addressed, it may be difficult to address all necessary skills in ways that are accessible and appropriate for readers (Christie et al., 1997). The focus on meaning may overshadow the critical print-related skills without which effective reading is not possible. As Snow et al. (1998, p. 198) pointed out, "explicit teaching and application of the alphabetic principle and writing are the instructional components whose importance in most strongly supported by research."

The popularity of each of the above approaches has waxed and waned over the past few decades. In reviewing reading research in the United States, Gaffney and Anderson (2000) reported on trends evident in two major reading journals, *Reading Research Quarterly* and *The Reading Teacher*. Within these two journals, they found a steady decline in the number of references to subword units such as letters or syllables from the 1960s through to the early 1980s, but a steady rise since then, especially in *Reading Research Quarterly*, perhaps explained by the rise in interest in phonological awareness. The numbers of references to whole text units, in contrast, were low in the 1960s, but rose dramatically in both journals between 1966 and 1970, and between 1986 and 1990, in line with increasing interest in reading as a process of constructing meaning (Gaffney & Anderson, 2000).

One of the difficulties for practitioners is that comparative studies have not been very useful in determining which approach is more effective in helping children learn to read. A key reason for this apparent lack of clear direction is what can be termed the *teacher-factor* (Frost, 2000). Teachers who are prepared to be involved in research evaluating the effectiveness of their instructional approach are likely to be the ones who are most interested, motivated, and effective. Such a motivated, enthusiastic teacher is a key extrinsic influence in the learning context. Foorman et al. (1998) attempted to separate the relative benefits of skills instruction versus whole language. In their large-scale study across eight elementary schools, they contrasted the progress of 258 students considered to be at risk of reading failure, based on one of three different instructional approaches: direct code instruction, embedded phonics instruction, and whole language approaches. The students receiving the direct code instruction improved more quickly in word reading and had higher word recognition than the others. This group was the only group in which a normal distribution in gains in word reading over the school year was recorded. Each of the other two groups had a percentage of children who made no measurable gains. However, these researchers also found that the students in the whole language group had more positive attitudes toward reading and hence may experience greater benefits over time. These findings support the proposition that gains in skill may be achieved at the expense of interest in reading and highlight again the complexities of instruction.

3. Balancing or Integrating?

Attempting to resolve the dilemma of choosing the most effective instructional approach has led many to suggest that, just as reading simultaneously draws on bottom-up and top-down skills, so also instructional approaches must combine skill instruction with meaning construction (Christie et al., 1997). Such interactive approaches encourage motivation through the use of meaningful stimulating materials, with some degree of choice for the apprentice reader. The construction of meaning is grounded in spoken language interaction before and after reading activities. Readers are encouraged to interact with extended texts in many different ways, including silent reading, to monitor their own understanding. Direct instruction on specific print skills is incorporated in structured teaching activities, but these skills are then embedded in meaningful text activities. Decoding is recognized as an essential component of the reading process. This means that it is a skill that must be acquired but not as an end in itself. Decoding only makes sense if it serves a reading need. Christie et al. (1997, p. 185) proposed that several tenets underlie effective instruction. To support connected reading, they highlighted the importance of regular daily experiences, with opportunities for reading aloud, and for silent reading from self-selected texts. Texts should be of high literary value. Discussion should be used (the language context) to support the activation and development of prior knowledge (the learning context). Decoding instruction (the print context) should be linked to the texts being read, with an integration of reading and writing throughout, to promote attention to print features. An emphasis on strategies rather than on splinter skills is recommended, with attention to provision of a broad range of learning contexts—solitary, peer partner–based, and teacher-led groups.

Snow et al. (1998) stressed that in following such eclectic approaches, an attempt may be made to *balance* skill instruction and meaning construction (as suggested by Christie *et al.*, 1997) or to *integrate* skill instruction within meaning construction. Rejecting a simple balancing act, they argued:

> "Balance" is not the right metaphor to carry our message, and we certainly did not suggest an approach that involved 'a little of this and a little of that.' "Balance" could mean splitting one's time evenly across activities designed to practice the alphabetic principle and activities designed to support comprehension. "Integration" means precisely that the opportunities to learn these two aspects of skilled reading should be going on at the same time, in the context of the same activities, and that the choice of instruction activities should be part of an overall, coherent approach to supporting literacy development, not a haphazard selection from unrelated, though varied, activities. (pp. vii–viii)

In their view, effective reading instruction integrates attention to the alphabetic principle (the print context) with attention to the construction of meaning and opportunities to develop fluency (the language and learning contexts). Returning to the participation model of intervention outlined earlier, reading instruction for individuals who use AAC should therefore consider the following:

1. Maximizing the opportunities for individuals using aided communication to integrate attention to the alphabetic principle with attention to the construction of meaning and to develop fluency;

2. Expanding and developing reading needs within the environment for those who use AAC; and

3. Minimizing the barriers to participation in the increased opportunities to meet expanded needs.

B. WRITING

Although it was argued earlier that reading and writing should be considered together in an integrated approach to literacy development, there are also aspects of developing writing and spelling skills that merit consideration on their own. Writing is an extraordinarily complex activity. Thoughts are formulated into language, captured in particular sequences of words, and processed through a complex motor and cognitive collaboration, with dual attention to the potential reader and the match between the intended expression and the form that appears on a page. During the process of writing, attention must also be paid to conventions such as punctuation, capital letters, spacing, and spelling. As writers write, they read what they have written. Although the process of writing involves generating ideas, formulating linguistic structures, generating spellings, monitoring punctuation as well as the motor act of forming letters or typing letter sequences, and checking for legibility and accuracy, none of these component skills by itself constitutes writing. Writing, in its essence, requires the synergistic engagement of cognitive, linguistic, sensory, and motor knowledge. Each of these skills is necessary, but none is sufficient on its own.

Writing instruction can be interpreted in many ways. It may mean instruction in letter formation, in penmanship, in planning a narrative structure, in creating poetry, in editing texts, in reporting concisely and accurately, in synthesizing and developing a coherent thesis, and in many other possible actions. Writing instruction can involve any or all of these activities. If a young child announces that he or she is learning to write in school, it is likely that this statement will be interpreted differently from the same statement made by a professional adult attending a summer course in a university. Despite these different interpretations, however, there is a core element of common meaning in both. Learning to write is a multifaceted process that can extend indefinitely. Learning to write does not simply imply component skill mastery, although certain skills are fundamental to the process. Learning to write implies some level of instruction, but it involves more than teaching—it also involves active learning.

Approaches to writing instruction have undergone significant changes over the last few decades. Traditional approaches to instruction focused on writing as a product (Christie *et al.*, 1997; Smith & Warwick, 1997). Instruction emphasized regular practice with topics set by a teacher and planned in advance. Clear, legible, accurate products were the main emphasis, and Smith and Warwick (1997) argued that as a result, children became gradually disenchanted with writing as an activity. A gradual loss of enthusiasm and motivation with the process of writing led to disengagement for many apprentice writers, with the inevitable outcome that they wrote less often, which set in motion a spiral of difficulties. Through the 1980s, interest in the process of writing gradually emerged, in line with the general rise in constructivist approaches in education (Christie *et al.*, 1997). Educators began to explore the processes children go through as they write. Interest in increasing motivation and guiding the journey of writing became the central focus. A key driver of this change in focus was the work of Donald Graves (1983, 1994). Graves advocated an approach in which children were encouraged to write often about meaningful topics of interest to themselves, effort was reinforced, and the specific demands of writing for an audience were highlighted through discussions of the written product from the point of view of a reader, within a setting of a writing workshop. Smith and Warwick (1997) outlined five core concepts implicit in process writing:

1. *Ownership:* Children are encouraged to choose their own topic for writing and to consider themselves as the authority on what they are writing about.

2. *Drafts and revisions:* Children are encouraged to view writing as "work in progress" requiring some risk taking. Accuracy is not central to the process.

Although writing occurs as a solitary activity, exploring possible revisions is a shared activity, with peers who act as a real audience.

3. *Conferencing:* In the conference, educators and children discuss the writing done, with the educator acting as an editor, asking predictable questions, and offering support.

4. *Publishing:* The final product is "published" in some form, whether as a printout from a computer, a display for a classroom wall, or an entry in a class book. Publishing is considered to validate the investment of the child in the product and to acknowledge the social value of the work.

5. *Teacher modeling of writing:* Teachers are expected to demonstrate "master writing" while at the same time verbalizing the process, offering the children a window on the thinking behind the writing.

Aspects of process writing have found their way into many classroom situations, and many other developments in writing instruction were spawned from the work of Graves. However, perhaps the most lasting legacy of Graves' work is recognition of writing as a creative process with a social dimension, a process that, while requiring many subskills, cannot be considered as simply the sum of those subskills. These insights have led to a harnessing of spoken language abilities as a platform for developing written language and an increased emphasis on creating connected, meaningful, personal texts, and on sharing these authentic texts with engaged readers.

For individuals who use aided communication, opportunities for generating written texts may be extremely limited. Physical access to effective writing tools may be difficult. Although typically developing children may have to cope with the demands of learning the motor skills for letter formation, those with physical impairments may have to contend with the complexities of switch control, scanning systems, and a range of different display possibilities. Fatigue may have a significant impact on opportunities to generate extended texts. The opportunities to engage in spoken discussion both before and after the creation of a text may be extremely limited, and inferences about the underlying language abilities of someone using a communication board may be problematic because of the intrinsic constraints of the communication system. Intervention may be needed to address both "spoken" language and written language development. However, if effective instructional principles recognize that individuals learn to write by writing, then clearly attention must be focused first and foremost on maximizing the writing opportunities for those using aided communication and minimizing the barriers to effective participation in such writing opportunities. Most writers fulfill many needs through their writing—behavior regulation, recreational diversion, vocational requirements, and distance communication. For aided communicators, however, in addition to these needs, writing may serve fundamental and crucial expressive communication functions. One component skill in this process is the ability to spell.

C. THE SPECIAL CASE OF SPELLING

For individuals who use aided communication, spelling plays a unique communicative role. Being able to spell means that words not available or accessible within an aided communication system can nonetheless be communicated. Even first letter cues to words can greatly increase the range of words that can be successfully communicated. For example, if a child selects a picture symbol *BOY* and then the letter *J*, the range of possible names is greatly narrowed, and the chance of successfully conveying a message is proportionately enhanced. For many older individuals who use aided communication, such concerns serve as a primary motivation for learning to read and write. To complete even these simple tasks, however, the individual must first be able to access a stable internal phonological representation of the target word, retain that representation long enough to be able to search for the appropriate grapheme, and hold on to that information until the grapheme has been successfully communicated to a partner. For many individuals, accessing an internal phonological representation seems to be a particular challenge. Many children and adults with severe speech impairments seem to perform far more successfully on spelling tasks if the target word is labeled for them (the traditional approach in spelling instruction and assessment) than they do if they are simply shown a picture of a target word and are required to generate the phonological form from their own internal representation (Dahlgren-Sandberg, 2001; Dahlgren-Sandberg & Hjelmquist, 1996; Smith, 2001). This is a puzzling phenomenon and a worrying one, because the ability to generate and retain for analysis an internal phonological representation is precisely what is required to functionally use spelling skills to enhance communication. It seems plausible that for some individuals, a degree of motor information is important for establishing and stabilizing internal phonological representations (Smith, 2003). Instructional approaches that supplement or make explicit such motor information may offer useful support for developing awareness of motor plans, even if such plans may not be directly accessible to the individual.

As representations become more stable and accessible, attention can then focus on more traditional aspects of spelling. Contrary to earlier views that spelling is a skill best learned through rote memorization and somewhat divorced from "true" reading and writing, it is now increasingly recognized that spelling is a linguistic skill (Kamhi & Hinton, 2000; Zutell, 1996) with a close relationship to reading and writing ability (Ehri, 2000; Groff, 2001). Early attempts to spell offer a unique insight into the phonological processing abilities of apprentice readers and writers, offer a window into their emerging abilities to pay attention to the sound structure of language (Ehri, 2000), and provide an important context for their development of explicit awareness of phonological and morphological dimensions of words (Ehri, 2000; Frost, 2000; Snow *et al.*, 1998; Templeton & Morris, 2000). For example, children learning to apply "-ed" to mark the past tense on verbs must first draw on their metalinguistic knowledge in relation to verb tense, detect the necessary past tense marking in spoken language, and affix the "-ed" ending to verbs such as "climbed," "wanted," "used," and "talked," despite the phonetic differences across these verbs. In addition, they must also learn that certain verbs are marked differently for past tense, for example, "hear"-"heard" and "sleep"-"slept." There is increasing evidence that apprentice writers can apply morphologically based strategies to determine the most appropriate spelling in such contexts (Bryant, Nunes, & Snaith, 2000), highlighting the inherently linguistic nature of spelling.

Spelling is often considered the pacemaker for early reading (Perfetti, Beck, Bell, & Hughes, 1987; Templeton & Morris, 2000). Spelling instruction offers opportunities to draw attention not only to the specific sound structure of words but also to possible orthographic patterns and, in English at least, to the morphological links uncovered through shared spelling patterns (e.g., "nation," "national," and "nationality"). In this way, spelling should perhaps be construed more as an activity of word study rather than merely of memorization of letter string sequences. On the other hand, some memorization of orthographic patterns is important for efficient processing of print both in decoding and encoding.

There are differing views on how best to establish the most appropriate level for spelling instruction. Target words can be selected from standard spelling lists, typically divided according to anticipated grade level. Such lists present relatively generic sets of words, ranked according to measures of difficulty such as transparency, frequency of occurrence, or regularity. Alternatively, words or word patterns may be selected as they are encountered within a text context. The problem with the former approach is that such lists are often divorced from any functional relationship to an individual's identified learning needs. Children may be required to spend time focusing on words that are well established within their repertoire. On the other hand, the second approach, based on encounters with word patterns in texts, overlooks the fact that spelling is a developmental skill and requires direct facilitation and instruction in some coherent framework. A compromise position sets out word patterns in a targeted developmental sequence and capitalizes on preplanned encounters with these target patterns in meaningful print contexts. Templeton (2000) suggested that at least 50% of words selected for study should be familiar to support searches for patterns across words. Others suggested the use of as much as 80% "old" information to contrast with only 20% new information in any activity of word study (Moats, 1995).

In summary, given the unique communicative role played by spelling for aided communicators, it is important that specific attention be paid to spelling development. An explicit focus on the motor and perceptual cues relating to sounds may be an important component of instruction, supporting the development of stable, internal phonological representations. Such work should be linked directly to explicit instruction in correspondences between sounds and orthographic patterns beyond the level of the single letter (Berninger *et al.*, 1999). Invented spelling attempts should be encouraged and carefully evaluated to shed light on an individual's awareness of the sound structure of target words. Explicit analysis and generalization of spellings should be fostered (Templeton & Morris, 2000) and linked to the uncovering of word meanings and word relationships.

D. LITERACY WORKING TOGETHER

Throughout this chapter, the emphasis has been on reading and writing as integrated activities. The particular case of individuals using aided communication has highlighted the overlap between their expressive communication and their reading and writing. For these individuals, *writing* may be accomplished by selecting symbols on a communication display or through sending symbols to a message display panel on an electronic communication device. Monitoring the accuracy of a message may require *reading* of two-dimensional symbols, similar in many ways to print, and in many instances incorporating printed words. It seems logical that harnessing these resources maximizes the effectiveness of an instructional approach.

VII. SPECIFIC APPLICATIONS

A. YOUNG CHILDREN

Through their comprehensive review of approaches to reading instruction, Snow *et al.* (1998) identified core skills to be achieved across kindergarten and first grade. They suggested that by the end of kindergarten, children should:

1. Be familiar with the structural elements and organization of print, be familiar with forms and format of books and other print resources, be able to recognize and write most of the alphabet; and have established basic phonemic awareness; and

2. Have established perspectives and attitudes on which learning about and from print depend; that is, they should be motivated and interested and view themselves as successful readers and writers.

Many techniques can be used to develop these core skills. Those suggested by Snow *et al.* (1998, p. 189) include the following:

1. Oral language activities for fostering growth in receptive and expressive language and verbal reasoning
2. Reading aloud to foster appreciation and comprehension of text and literature
3. Reading and book exploration by children for developing print concepts and basic reading knowledge and processes
4. Writing activities for developing children's appreciation of the communicative dimensions of print and for practicing printing and spelling abilities
5. Thematic activities for giving children opportunities to integrate and extend their understanding of stories
6. Print-directed activities for establishing children's ability to recognize and print the letters of the alphabet
7. Phonemic analysis activities
8. Word-directed activities to acquire a sight vocabulary and understand the alphabetic principle

B. OLDER CHILDREN

By first grade, more specific instruction in print-related skills becomes necessary to provide the resource set to foster independent reading and writing and kick-start the process of self-teaching. The key components of first grade instruction identified by Snow *et al.* (1998) are the following:

1. Providing explicit instruction and practice with sound structures that lead to phonemic awareness
2. Developing familiarity with spelling-sound correspondences and common spelling conventions and their use in identifying printed words
3. Expanding sight recognition of frequent words
4. Fostering independent reading, including reading aloud
5. Providing time, materials, and resources (a) to consolidate independent reading ability through daily reading of texts of interest and beneath the frustration level and (b) to promote advances in reading through support reading and rereading of texts that are slightly more difficult in wording or in linguistic, rhetorical, or conceptual structure
6. Promoting comprehension by building on linguistic skills and concepts
7. Providing explicit instruction on strategies, such as summarizing, predicting events, drawing inferences, and monitoring for comprehension
8. Using invented spelling and correct spelling

To develop these skills they suggested that educators use the following techniques:

1. Create a literate environment
2. Present explicit instruction in authentic and isolated practice
3. Provide multiple opportunities for sustained reading practice in a variety of formats
4. Apply a careful choice of reading materials from a wide range of subjects
5. Adjust the mode of presentation and explicitness of instruction to meet the unique needs of individual learners
6. Encourage self-regulation of reading and writing, so that learners assume responsibility for, and ownership of, their learning. This point links to the view of Stanovich et al. (1994) that motivation and responsibility must become endogenous as apprentice readers and writers move toward greater expertise.

Last but not least, Snow et al. suggested that educators must provide "masterful" management of activity, behavior, and resources.

For older children for whom previous experiences have proved unsuccessful or of limited success in developing literacy skills, supplementary intervention is necessary. Some general principles have emerged from research with this group over the past few decades. From their review of the literature on effective instruction for children at risk for reading failure, Foorman and Torgesen (2001) outlined three central elements:

1. *Phonemically explicit* interventions are more effective than interventions that are less phonemically explicit (p. 208). There is now converging evidence that systematic instruction to build phonemic awareness and phonemic decoding skills is especially beneficial for students with demonstrated weaknesses in print-related knowledge and skills. Writing activities are particularly important in bootstrapping print-related skills (Snow et al., 1998) and should be incorporated in a systematic framework that acts as a complement to reading activities.

2. Supportive interventions must be *intensive*—daily, according to Snow et al. (1998). Foorman and Torgesen (2001) found no advantage for individual work over small group work in their review of research and indeed found some positive benefits from working with small groups of up to three or four children.

3. Instruction for children at risk for reading failure must also be more *supportive*, both emotionally and cognitively (Foorman & Torgesen, 2001, p. 209), than instruction for their typically developing peers. To maintain interest and motivation, careful attention to materials is crucial, with carefully graded *phonologically protected* (Snow et al., 1998) texts that are of high interest.

Difficulties can be encountered in finding materials that are sufficiently easy to be accessible for older children and young adolescents, yet are age appropriate in their focus and topic. This is even more of a challenge if additional learning difficulties need to be taken into account. Nonetheless, finding materials that continue to engage interest is essential to future progress. A range of literacy activities should be offered, with varying emphasis on continuous text, word study, and decoding. Careful monitoring of performance and appropriate modifications of materials or activities are central to supporting successful learning.

Although they do not mention it as a core feature of successful interventions, Foorman and Torgesen (2001) also highlighted the crucial importance of ongoing professional development opportunities for all those involved to maintain motivation, interest, and skills, a view echoed also by Snow *et al.* (1998).

C. ADULTS

Older adolescents and adults require many of the same features of literacy instruction as do younger children—they need to develop alphabetic skills; they require fluent access to a sight word bank, they need analytic skills to decode and encode unfamiliar targets, and they need sufficient experience and practice with materials of appropriate interest so they can develop automatic and fluent skills. In addition to these needs, older adolescents and adults who use aided communication typically bring to the literacy experience a very particular learning context. On the negative side, many have endured repeated experiences of failure, often piecemeal, stop-start approaches to instruction, and constant reinforcement of their difficulties, leading to low self-esteem. On the other hand, most bring a clear insight into their goals in learning to read and/or write, a keen internal motivation, a sense of ownership of their own learning needs and potential, and an ability to reflect on the learning process and to evaluate its effectiveness in light of their needs. If these positive factors can be harnessed, much can be gained.

VIII. SUMMARY AND CONCLUSIONS

This chapter started with an outline of key ingredients in effective approaches to literacy instruction and explored the contexts of learning, language, and print that have an impact on literacy experiences for individuals. It is clear that there are many possible routes to mastery that may be forged by individuals and that we are far from identifying *the* most effective way to support apprentices along the journey to mastery. It is likely that, given the heterogeneity and ingenuity of individuals, we will never reach a stage of outlining a definitive path to literacy mastery. That is not to say that we know little about what characteristics of instruction offer important supports and signposts along the path to mastery. Some of the more robust research findings have been reviewed here. As outlined in Principle 1, effective literacy instruction should apply for all apprentice readers and writers. It builds on appropriate and effective assessment and is not slavishly devoted to a developmental framework. Effective intervention addresses the range of factors that affect literacy learning, those intrinsic to the individual, as well as those that exist within the environment. These principles are summarized in Figure 7.1. Finally, incorporating the suggestions culled by Snow *et al.* (1998) from a vast range of literature provides a solid basis for developing appropriate instructional approaches for those with additional needs. Further specific suggestions are provided by Smith and Blischak (1997, pp. 434–435, 437–438, 440) and are discussed in Chapter 8, in which we turn attention to specific intervention strategies and practical applications of some of the concepts raised in this chapter.

Principle 1: Good literacy intervention practice applies across all types of literacy instruction, with clients with all types of abilities.

Principle 2: Intervention programs should be based on appropriate assessment.

Principle 3: Although reading and writing emerge in a developmental sequence, application of a developmental framework is not always the most appropriate choice.

Principle 4: Intervention programs should consider factors intrinsic and extrinsic to the individual, with the ultimate goals of maximizing opportunities to participate in literacy activities while minimizing barriers to active participation, in a format tailored to the needs of each individual AAC user.

Figure 7.1. Principles of intervention. (Adapted from Smith, M., & Blischak, D. (1997). Literacy. In L. Lloyd, D. Fuller, & H. Arvidson (Eds.), *Augmentative and alternative communication: principles and practices* (pp. 414–444). London: Allyn & Bacon.)

REFERENCES

Aihara, K., Au, K., Carroll, J., Nakanishi, P., Scheu, J., & Wong-Kam, J. (2000). Skill instruction within a balanced approach to reading. *The Reading Teacher, 53*(6), 496–498.

Belfiore, P. J., Skinner, C. H., & Ferkis, M. A. (1995). Effects of response and trial repetition on sight-word training for students with learning disabilities. *Journal of Applied Behaviour Analysis, 28,* 347–348.

Berninger, V., Abbott, R., Zook, D., Ogier, S., Lemos-Britten, Z., & Brooksher, R. (1999). Early intervention for reading disabilities: Teaching the alphabet principle in a connectionist framework. *Journal of Learning Disabilities, 32*(6), 491–503.

Beukelman, D., & Mirenda, P. (1992). *Augmentative and alternative communication: Management of severe communication disorders in children and adults* (1st ed.). Baltimore: Paul H. Brookes.

Beukelman, D., & Mirenda, P. (1998). *Augmentative and alternative communication: Management of severe communication disorders in children and adults* (2nd ed.). Baltimore: Paul H. Brookes.

Blau, A. F. (1986). The development of literacy skills for severely speech- and writing-impaired children. In S. Blackstone (Ed.), *Augmentative communication: An introduction* (pp. 293–299). Rockville, MD: American Speech-Language-Hearing Association.

Blischak, D. (1994). Thomas the Writer: Case study of a child with severe physical, speech, and visual impairments. *Language Speech and Hearing Services in Schools, 26,* 11–20.

Blockberger, S., & Sutton, A. (2003). Toward linguistic competence: Language experiences and knowledge of children with extremely limited speech. In J. Light, D. R. Beukelman, & J. Reichle (Eds.), *Communicative competence for individuals who use AAC: From research to effective practice.* (pp. 63–106). Baltimore: Paul H. Brookes.

Browder, D. M., & Shear, S. M. (1996). Interspersal of known items in a treatment package to teach sight words to students with behaviour disorders. *The Journal of Special Education, 29,* 400–413.

Browder, D. M., & Xin, Y. P. (1998). A meta-analysis and review of sight word research and its implication for teaching functional reading to individuals with moderate and severe disabilities. *Journal of Special Education, 32*(3), 130–153.

Bryant, P. E., Nunes, T., & Snaith, R. (2000). Children learn an untaught rule of spelling. *Nature, 403,* 157.

Butler, K., & Wallach, G. P. (1995). Language learning disabilities: Moving in from the edge. *Topics in Language Disorders, 16*(1), 1–26.

Christie, J., Enz, B., & Vukelich, C. (1997). *Teaching language and literacy: Preschool through the elementary grades.* London: Longman.

Clay, M. M. (1991). *Becoming literate.* Portsmouth, NH: Heinemann Education Books.

Collins, B. C., & Stinson, D. M. (1995). Teaching generalized reading of product warning labels to adolescents with mental disabilities through the use of key words. *Exceptionality, 5,* 163–181.

Conners, F. A. (1992). Reading instruction for students with moderate mental retardation: Review and analysis of research. *American Journal on Mental Retardation, 97,* 577–597.

Dahlgren-Sandberg, A. (2001). Reading and spelling, phonological awareness and short-term memory in children with severe speech production impairments—A longitudinal study. *Augmentative and Alternative Communication, 17,* 11–26.

Dahlgren-Sandberg, A., & Hjelmquist, E. (1996). A comparative, descriptive study of reading and writing skills among non-speaking children: A preliminary study. *European Journal of Disorders of Communication, 31,* 289–308.

Dechant, E. V. (1991). *Understanding and teaching reading: An interactive model.* Hillsdale, NJ: Erlbaum.

Ehri, L. C. (2000). Learning to read and learning to spell: Two sides of a coin. *Topics in Language Disorders, 20*(3), 19–36.

Ellis, N. (1993). *Reading, writing and dyslexia: A cognitive analysis* (2nd. ed.). Hove, UK: Erlbaum.

Erickson, K., Koppenhaver, D., & Yoder, D. E. (2002). *Waves of words: Augmented communicators read and write.* Toronto, Ontario, Canada: ISAAC Press.

Erickson, K., Koppenhaver, D., Yoder, D. E., & Nance, J. (1997). Integrated communication and literacy instruction for a child with multiple disabilities. *Focus on Autism and Other Developmental Disabilities, 12*(3), 142–151.

Foley, B. E. (1993). The development of literacy in individuals with severe congenital speech and motor impairments. *Topics in Language Disorders, 13,* 16–32.

Foley, B. E., & Staples, A. (2003). Developing augmentative and alternative communication and literacy interventions in a supported employment setting. *Topics in Language Disorders, 23*(4), 325–343.

Foorman, B. R., Francis, D. J., Fletcher, J. M., Schatschneider, C., & Mehta, P. (1998). The role of instruction in learning to read: Preventing reading failure in at-risk children. *Journal of Educational Psychology, 90,* 37–55.

Foorman, B. R., & Torgesen, J. K. (2001). Critical elements of classroom and small-group instruction promote reading success in all children. *Learning Disabilities Research and Practice, 16*(4), 203–212.

Forester, A. D. (1988). Learning to read and write at 26. *Journal of Reading, 31*(7), 604–613.

Frost, J. (2000). From 'Epi' through 'Meta' to Mastery. The balance of meaning and skill in early reading instruction. *Scandinavian Journal of Educational Research, 44*(2), 125–144.

Gaffney, J., & Anderson, R. C. (2000). Trends in reading research in the United States: Changing intellectual currents over three decades. In M. Kamil, P. Mosenthal, D. Pearson, & R. Barr (Eds.), *Handbook of reading research* (Vol. 3, pp. 53–74). London: Erlbaum.

Galda, L., Cullinan, B., & Strickland, D. (1993). *Language, literacy and the child.* London: Harcourt Brace Jovanovich College.

Gavelek, F. R., Raphael, T. E., Biondo, S. M., & Wang, D. (2000). Integrated literacy instruction. In M. Kamil, P. Mosenthal, D. Pearson, & R. Barr (Eds.), *Handbook of reading research* (pp. 587–608). London: Erlbaum.

Gillam, R. B., & Johnston, J. R. (1992). Spoken and written language relationships in language/learning-impaired and normally achieving school-age children. *Journal of Speech & Hearing Research, 35,* 1303–1315.

Goldsworthy, C. (1996). *Developmental reading disabilities: a language based treatment approach.* London: Singular Press.

Goldsworthy, C., & Pieretti, R. (2004). *Sourcebook of phonological awareness activities.* London: Singular Press.

Graves, D. (1983). *Writing: teachers & children at work.* Exeter, NH: Heinemann Educational Books.

Graves, D. (1994). *A fresh look at writing.* Portsmouth, NH: Heinemann.

Groff, P. (2001). Teaching phonics: Letter-to-phoneme, phoneme-to-letter, or both? *Reading and Writing Quarterly, 17,* 291–306.

Grove, N., & Smith, M. (1997). Input output asymmetries in AAC. *ISAAC Bulletin, 50,* 1–3.

Guthrie, J., & Wigfield, A. (2000). Engagement and motivation in reading. In M. Kamil, P. Mosenthal, D. Pearson, & R. Barr (Eds.), *Handbook of reading research* (Vol. 3, pp. 403–424). London: Erlbaum.

Hayes, D. P., & Ahrens, M. G. (1988). Vocabulary simplification for children: A special case of "motherese"? *Journal of Child Language, 15*(2), 395–410.

Kamhi, A., & Hinton, L. N. (2000). Explaining individual differences in spelling ability. *Topics in Language Disorders, 20*(3), 37–49.

Karmiloff-Smith, A. (1992). *Beyond modularity: A developmental perspective on cognitive science.* Cambridge, MA.: MIT Press, A Bradford Book.

Koppenhaver, D. (1991). *A descriptive analysis of classroom literacy instruction provided to children with severe speech and physical impairments.* Chapel Hill: University of North Carolina. *Unpublished doctoral dissertation.*

Koppenhaver, D., Coleman, P. P., Kalman, S. L., & Yoder, D. E. (1991). The implications of emergent literacy research for children with developmental disabilities. *American Journal of Speech-Language Pathology, 1*(1), 38–44.

Koppenhaver, D., & Erickson, K. (2003). Natural emergent literacy supports for preschoolers with autism and severe communication impairments. *Topics in Language Disorders, 23*(4), 283–292.

Koppenhaver, D., Evans, D., & Yoder, D. E. (1991). Childhood reading and writing experiences of literate adults with severe speech and motor impairments. *Augmentative and Alternative Communication, 7*(1), 20–33.

Koppenhaver, D., & Yoder, D. E. (1992a). Literacy issues in persons with severe speech and physical impairments. In R. Gaylord-Ross (Ed.), *Issues and research in special education* (Vol. 2., pp. 156–201). New York: Columbia University Teachers College Press.

Koppenhaver, D., & Yoder, D. E. (1992b). Literacy learning of children with severe speech and physical impairments in school settings. *Seminars in Speech and Language, 12*, 4–15.

Koppenhaver, D., & Yoder, D. E. (1993). Classroom literacy instruction for children with severe speech and physical impairments (SSPI): What is and what might be. *Topics in Language Disorders, 13*(2), 1–15.

Kraat, A. (1987). *Communication interaction between aided and natural speakers: An IPCAS study report* (2nd ed.). Madison: Trace Research & Development Center, University of Wisconsin-Madison.

Lalli, J. S., & Browder, D. M. (1993). Comparison of sight word training procedures with validation of the most practical procedure in teaching reading for daily living. *Research in Developmental Disabilities, 14*, 107–127.

Light, J., Binger, C., & Kelford-Smith, A. (1994). Story reading interactions between preschoolers who use AAC and their mothers. *Augmentative and Alternative Communication, 10*, 255–268.

Light, J., Collier, B., & Parnes, P. (1985a). Communicative interaction between young nonspeaking physically disabled children and their primary caregivers: Modes of communication. *Augmentative and Alternative Communication, 1*, 125–133.

Light, J., Collier, B., & Parnes, P. (1985b). Communicative interaction between young nonspeaking physically disabled children and their primary caregivers: Discourse patterns. *Augmentative and Alternative Communication, 1*, 74–83.

Light, J., & Kelford-Smith, A. (1993). The home literacy experiences of preschoolers who use augmentative communication systems and of their nondisabled peers. *Augmentative and Alternative Communication, 9*, 10–25.

Light, J., & McNaughton, D. (1993). Literacy and augmentative and alternative communication: The expectations and priorities of parents and teachers. *Topics in Language Disorders, 13*(2), 33–46.

McNaughton, S. (1998). *Reading acquisition of adults with severe congenital speech and physical impairments: theoretical infrastructure, empirical investigation, education implication.* Unpublished doctoral dissertation, University of Toronto, Toronto, Ontario, Canada.

McNaughton, S., & Lindsay, P. (1995). Approaching literacy with AAC graphics. *Augmentative and Alternative Communication, 11*, 212–228.

Mike, D. G. (1995). Literacy and cerebral palsy: Factors influencing literacy learning in a self-contained setting. *Journal of Reading Behaviour, 27*(4), 627–642.

Mirenda, P. (2003). "He's not really a reader. . . ." Perspectives on supporting literacy development in individuals with autism. *Topics in Language Disorders, 23*(4), 271–282.

Moats, L. C. (1995). *Spelling development, disability, and instruction.* Baltimore: York Press.

Nippold, M., Allen, M., & Kirsch, D. (2001). Proverb comprehension as a function of reading proficiency in preadolescents. *Language Speech and Hearing Services in Schools, 32*, 90–100.

Perfetti, C. A., Beck, I., Bell, L., & Hughes, C. (1987). Phonemic knowledge and learning to read are reciprocal: A longitudinal study of first grade children. *Merrill-Palmer Quarterly, 33*, 283–319.

Pumfrey, P. D., & Reason, R. (1991). *Specific learning difficulties: Challenges and responses.* Berks, UK: NFER-Nelson.

Rasinski, T., & Padak, N. (2000). *Effective reading strategies: Teaching children who find reading difficult* (2nd. ed.). Upper Saddle River, NJ: Merrill, Prentice Hall.

Rassool, N. (1999). *Literacy for sustainable development in the age of information.* Toronto, Ontario, Canada: Multilingual Matters.

Ratcliff, A., & Little, M. (1996). A conversation based barrier task approach to teach sight-word vocabulary to a young augmentative communication system user. *Child Language Teaching and Therapy, 12*(2), 128–135.

Scanlon, D. M., & Vellutino, F. R. (1996). Prerequisite skills, early instruction, and success in first-grade reading: Selected results from a longitudinal study. *Mental Retardation and Developmental Research Reviews, 2,* 54–63.

Schloss, P. J., Alper, S., Young, H., Arnold-Reid, G., Aylward, M., & Dudenhoeffer, S. (1995). Acquisition of functional sight words in community-based recreational settings. *Journal of Special Education, 29,* 84–96.

Schlosser, R. (2003). *Efficacy of augmentative and alternative communication: Towards evidence-based practice.* New York: Academic Press.

Share, D. L. (1995). Phonological recoding and self-teaching: *Sine qua non* of reading acquisition. *Cognition, 55,* 151–218.

Smith, J., & Warwick, B. E. (1997). *How children learn to write.* London: Paul Chapman.

Smith, M. (1991). Assessment of interaction patterns and AAC use—A case study. *Journal of Clinical Speech & Language Studies, 1,* 76–102.

Smith, M. (1996). The medium or the message: A study of speaking children using communication boards. In S. von Tetzchner & M. H. Jensen (Eds.), *Augmentative and alternative communication: European perspectives* (pp. 119–136). London: Whurr.

Smith, M. (1998). *Pictures of language: The role of PCS in the language acquisition of children with severe congenital speech and physical impairments.* Unpublished doctoral disseration, Trinity College, Dublin, Ireland.

Smith, M. (2001). Literacy challenges for individuals with severe congenital speech impairments. *International Journal of Disability, Development and Education, 48,* 331–353.

Smith, M. (2003). Perspectives on augmentative and alternative communication and literacy. In S. von Tetzchner & M. Jensen (Eds.), *Perspectives on Theory and Practice in Augmentative and Alternative Communication: Proceedings of the Seventh ISAAC Biennial Research Symposium, Odense, Denmark, August 2002.* Toronto, Ontario: ISAAC, 170–182.

Smith, M., & Blischak, D. (1997). Literacy. In L. Lloyd, D. Fuller, & H. Arvidson (Eds.), *Augmentative and alternative communication: principles and practices* (pp. 414–444). London: Allyn & Bacon.

Smith, M., & Grove, N. (1999). The bimodal situation of children learning language using manual and graphic signs. In L. Lloyd (Ed.), *New directions in AAC: Research and practice* (pp. 9–30). London: Whurr.

Smith, M., & Grove, N. (2003). Asymmetry in input and output for individuals who use AAC. In J. Light, D. R. Beukelman, & J. Reichle (Eds.), *Communicative competence for individuals who use AAC: From research to effective practice* (pp. 163–195). Baltimore: Paul H. Brookes.

Snow, C., Burns, M. S., & Griffin, P. E. (1998). *Preventing reading difficulties in young children.* Washington, DC: National Academy Press.

Snow, C., & Tabors, P. (1996). Intergenerational transfer of literacy. In L. A. Benjamin & J. Lord (Eds.), *Family literacy: Directions in research and implications for practice.* Washington, DC: Office of Educational Research and Improvement, U.S. Department of Education.

Soto, G., & Toro-Zambrama, W. (1995). Investigation of Blissymbol use from a language research paradigm. *Augmentative and Alternative Communication, 11,* 118–130.

Stanovich, K. (1994). Constructivism in reading education. *The Journal of Special Education, 28*(3), 259–274.

Stanovich, K., West, R. F., Cunningham, A. E., Cipielewski, J., & Siddiqui, S. (1996). The role of inadequate print exposure as a determinant of reading comprehension problems. In C. Cornoldi & J. Oakhill (Eds.), *Reading comprehension disabilities*. (pp. 15–32). Hillsdale, NJ: Erlbaum.

Steelman, J. D., Pierce, P. L., & Koppenhaver, D. (1993). The role of computers in promoting literacy in children with severe speech and physical impairments. *Topics in Language Disorders, 13*(2), 76–88.

Sutton, A., & Gallagher, T. (1993). Verb class distinctions and AAC language encoding implications. *Journal of Speech and Hearing Research, 36*, 1216–1226.

Sutton, A., Gallagher, T., Morford, J., & Shahnaz, N. (2000). Relative clause sentence production using augmentative and alternative communication systems. *Applied Psycholinguistics, 21*, 473–486.

Sutton, A., Soto, G., & Blockberger, S. (2002). Grammatical issues in graphic symbol communication. *Augmentative and Alternative Communication, 18*(3), 192–204.

Tattershall, S. (2002). *Adolescents with language and learning needs: A shoulder to shoulder collaboration*. London: Singular Press.

Teale, W., & Sulzby, E. (1987). Literacy acquisition in early childhood: The roles of access and mediation in storybook telling. In D. A. Wagner (Ed.), *The future of literacy in a changing world* (pp. 111–130). New York: Pergamon Press.

Teale, W., & Sulzby, E. (1989). Emergent literacy: New perspectives on young children's reading and writing. In D. Strickland & L. M. Morrow (Eds.), *Emerging literacy: Young children learn to read and write* (pp. 1–15). Newark, DE: International Reading Association.

Templeton, S. (2002, February 19th). Spelling: Logical, learnable—and critical. *The ASHA Leader*, 4–5.

Templeton, S., & Morris, D. (2000). Spelling. In M. Kamil, P. Mosenthal, P. D. Pearson, & R. Barr (Eds.), *Handbook of reading research* (Vol. 3, pp. 525–543). Mawah, NJ: Erlbaum.

Udwin, O., & Yule, W. (1990). Augmentative and alternative communication systems taught to cerebral palsied children: A longitudinal study: I. The acquisition of signs and symbols, and syntactic aspects of their use over time. *British Journal of Disorders of Communication, 25*, 295–309.

Wallach, G. P., & Butler, K. (1994). On being observant and dynamic in school-based contexts and elsewhere. In G. P. Wallach & K. Butler (Eds.), *Language learning disabilities in school-age children and adolescents*. New York: Merrill, 174–178.

Wilkinson, L. C., & Silliman, E. (2000). Classroom language and literacy learning. In M. Kamil, P. Mosenthal, D. Pearson, & R. Barr (Eds.), *Handbook of reading research* (Vol. 3, pp. 337–360). London: Erlbaum.

Woll, B., & Barnett, S. (1998). Toward a sociolinguistic perspective on augmentative and alternative communication. *Augmentative and Alternative Communication, 14*, 200–211.

Yaden, D. B., Rowe, D., & MacGillivray, L. (2000). Emergent literacy: A matter (polyphony) of perspectives. In M. Kamil, P. Mosenthal, D. Pearson, & R. Barr (Eds.), *Handbook of reading research* (Vol. 3, pp. 425–454). London: Erlbaum.

Zutell, J. (1996). The directed spelling thinking activity (DSTA): Providing an effective balance in word study instruction. *The Reading Teacher, 50*(2), 98–108.

CHAPTER 8

Some Practicalities: SCRAWLing
a Path to Literacy

I. INTRODUCTION

In this chapter, the focus is on specific practical approaches to enhancing literacy learning opportunities for children and adults who use aided communication. As outlined in the previous chapter, the emphasis is on expanding literacy needs, minimizing barriers to learning, and maximizing opportunities to learn. How those goals are achieved varies according to the ages of those learning to read and write, but the nature of the goals remains relatively constant. Effective literacy instruction meshes reading and writing seamlessly, encourages meaningful active participation in relevant literacy activities, encourages the learner to use both analytic skills and holistic skills in synchrony, and recognizes the need for specific instruction in certain aspects of the process, most specifically in the analytical components implicated in processing print. An acronym is used here to link these intervention components together—*SCRAWL*:

Shared stories
Comprehension
Rapid Recognition
Analysis and Articulation
Writing
Language, Literacy and Literature

What is outlined here is not a program for literacy instruction, but rather a framework into which elements addressing many different facets of literacy intervention can be inserted. How these elements are addressed within specific activities will vary according to the age of the participants and their level of literacy skills, as well as their own literacy goals and the creativity of the educational partner. We know from the writings of those associated with successful literacy interventions with children and adults who use augmentative and alternative communication (AAC) that certain key elements characterize effective programs:

1. An emphasis on integrating all aspects of communication and encouraging independent communication (Nunes da Ponte, 2002; Pebly, 2002; Wershing & Hughes, 2002);

2. Harnessing of motivation and raising of expectations for literacy achievement (Fukushima, 2002; McNaughton, 2002; Wershing & Hughes, 2002) to support literacy interventions;

3. Intensive input over extended periods of time (Gandell & Filippelli, 2002; Hogan & Wolf, 2002; Pebly, 2002; Wershing & Hughes, 2002) in the context of functional, real, and meaningful activities;

4. Integration of reading, writing, spelling, and communication across activities and goals (Hogan & Wolf, 2002; Pebly, 2002; Wershing & Hughes, 2002);

5. Harnessing the supports of voice output and other technologies (Gandell & Filippelli, 2002; Given, 2002; Hogan & Wolf, 2002; Wershing & Hughes, 2002); and

6. A willingness to adapt, take risks, use trial-and-error approaches, and maintain a flexible and questioning attitude to intervention (Bialik & Seligman-Wine, 2002; Pebly, 2002; Wershing & Hughes, 2002).

II. KEY GOALS

A. EXPANDING LITERACY NEEDS

In our "information society" it is hard to imagine that it may be necessary to consider how best to expand and develop literacy needs for some individuals. However, two factors suggest that this might indeed be worth exploring:

(a) the available research indicates that for many individuals who use aided communication, literacy development may be seen as a lesser priority than it is for their typically developing peers (Light & Kelford-Smith, 1993); and (b) positive expectations for literacy development may be influential in determining the ultimate achievements in this domain (Given, 2002; Koppenhaver, Evans, & Yoder, 1991; Mirenda, 2003). A key to achieving a fully specified range of literacy needs is to ensure that active participation in appropriate literacy activities is expected and required of those using aided communication. For very young children, this participation may be in storybook reading in preschool, in joining in by contributing repeated lines within a story, by creating drawings, or by "writing" for display within the preschool or home environment. For older children in school, it may involve creating expectations that the child will select some reading materials independently, will actively participate and contribute during specific instructional times, will produce written work, and will pay attention to environmental signage and will be able to interpret it. Adolescents and adults may have developed accommodations for their limited literacy skills. For many of them literacy may be viewed as an unattainable skill by those in positions powerful enough to influence literacy outcomes. On the other hand, adolescents and adults are often able to constructively explore the existing literacy demands placed on them and to discuss other unidentified needs they view as important. The goal should be to gradually increase the immediate literacy needs (Foley & Staples, 2003), facilitating a change of mindset in those who perhaps may have an impact on the opportunities for acquiring literacy skills that are made available (Mirenda, 2003).

B. MAXIMIZING OPPORTUNITIES

Evidence to date suggests that the literacy learning opportunities provided to individuals who use aided communication may occur less often than those for their typically developing peers and may be less interactive in nature (Coleman, 1992; Koppenhaver et al., 1991; Koppenhaver & Yoder, 1992; Light, Binger, & Kelford Smith, 1994; Light & Kelford-Smith, 1993; Light & McNaughton, 1993). Maximizing learning opportunities requires analysis of the daily routine and exploration of where additional or existing opportunities can be directed specifically to the needs of the target individual. For young preschool children, this may mean encouraging parents to engage in rhyme play, to schedule and plan story reading on a daily basis, and to create "print-rich" environments, in which they also draw attention to print materials. Repeated readings of stories to build familiarity with the language and the story structure can be encouraged. Expansion of the story into conversations on related themes or reviews of events in the story or having children imagine alternative endings are activities that emphasize the link between oral and written language. Messy paint play, use of picture and letter stamps, and assisted drawing can all support the development of the concept of the active writer. Labeling of letters, highlighting initial letters in names, and naming components of books, such as pages, words, and front and back, set the scene for early print concepts that will be available as resources when the child is exposed to the more formal aspects of learning to read and write.

School-aged children in their early school years need continuing opportunities to experience literacy—through story reading, sound-based activities, and writing—as well as opportunities to develop core skills related to alphabetic mastery. These include knowing the names of letters of the alphabet and recognizing key words, such as their own names. At this stage literacy learning goals can be specified, and the opportunities that will be provided to meet these targets should be documented. This should be a shared collaborative process between educators, parents, and therapists.

Such careful planning and scheduling of learning opportunities become even more crucial after the first year of formal school, when the focus typically shifts to development of alphabetic skills. This step requires specific focused instruction targeted to a child's learning style and needs and must also incorporate an element of developing skills in analysis and synthesis in relation to speech and to print. Dedicated instructional time is required, and interruptions should only be tolerated when absolutely necessary. Opportunities to develop an increased pool of sight recognition words are important, both as part of planned instructional time, but also as part of a print-rich environment and a print-attentive orientation that should be fostered. At this stage, opportunities to practice both with support and independently are equally relevant. Each context requires slightly different planning and organization, and both must be addressed.

For adolescents and adults who have limited literacy skills, opportunities to experience success in meaningful literacy activities must be created. This could be achieved, for example, by setting up email groups to create a genuine and motivating context in which communication occurs via a written medium. There may be scope for embedding literacy opportunities into recreational activities. Television schedules can be used to plan an evening's viewing. Newspapers can be used to develop a performance league of teams for football or other sports. Where appropriate, opportunities can be created for horse-racing enthusiasts to track performance of different horses under different racing conditions and to fill in betting slips independently. Work-related literacy opportunities can be highlighted (Foley & Staples, 2003), from planning travel to work and selecting target signage along the way for sight word practice to following specific work instructions presented in written form. Opportunities to create extended pieces of text (e.g., biography, poetry, rap, narratives, and fiction) must also be provided. For some individuals, creating opportunities to relate events requires first of all that relevant experiences are provided so that they have a story to relate. Maximizing opportunities to engage in literacy learning activities may involve broadening the range of experiences in the first place—forcing a broad interpretation of literacy learning.

C. Minimizing Barriers to Learning

Creating literacy learning opportunities and expanding literacy learning demands on individuals who use aided communication will be of limited use in terms of development of literacy skills unless it is possible for these same individuals to actively participate in the opportunities that are provided. Barriers can be both intrinsic to the individual and extrinsic, or related to the environment. Likewise, modifications to overcome barriers should have a dual focus. Careful positioning of the individual to accommodate specific visual field defects, to optimize postural tone, and to establish a motor set that is favorable for learning can mitigate some intrinsic barriers. Specific seating supports may significantly affect what learners can see and pay attention to and their level of motor control for activities involving turning pages, pointing, coloring, or writing. Other barriers must be addressed through modification of materials. Magnification of print, alternative formats of presentation such as computer-based presentation, superimposition of graphic symbols onto printed text, or provision of auditory feedback are all modifications that may be considered.

For very young and preschool children, active participation in storybook reading is often limited by poor positioning and the challenges to parents or teachers of managing to position the child, hold the book, encourage active page turning, and orchestrate communicating using an aided system. Some of these barriers can be reduced through provision of supported seating. Other simple techniques can also make the juggling task much less difficult. Repeated lines within books can be recorded on single message devices that can be accessed easily and rapidly. Other "control" messages (e.g., "Read it again," "That was wrong!," and "Not so fast") can be recorded, so that the child has the opportunity to direct the experience of storybook reading. Communication displays that contain the relevant vocabulary can be developed and integrated into the book, either as a pop-up page or as a fold-down strip on each page of the book. The same symbols can also be provided separately, with Velcro on the back of each symbol. Velcro strips along the end of each page of the book can then be used in myriad ways to encourage retelling of the story, predicting what might happen next, or commenting on what has happened so far. Page fluffers (Musselwhite & King-DeBaun, 1997) can be used to separate pages so that it is possible for children with very limited hand function to turn pages independently.

Many of the same modifications can be used effectively with older school-aged children also. Most children in a school setting have adapted seating available to maximize their functional ability to engage in learning. Provision of appropriate technology support (discussed further in Chapter 9) and development of age-appropriate and relevant materials can combine to address motivational and access barriers. Of fundamental importance for all age groups is addressing the potential barriers created by the expectations for literacy learning of those in the environment. Mirenda (2003, p. 271) described Stanley, a young boy of 6 who has a diagnosis of autism. In describing his difficulties in learning to read and write, Mirenda suggested that, "because, even at the tender age of 6, Stanley is not expected to learn to read, write, spell, or become otherwise literate, he probably will not." Expectations for older students, adolescents, and adults may be even more entrenched and may also have been assumed by the individuals using aided communication, based on their experiences of failure. This most subtle but powerful of barriers must be a key focus if intervention is to succeed.

Literacy learning opportunities, needs, and barriers should be considered in relation to the learning context, the language context, and the print context. Some of the specific suggestions outlined by Smith and Blischak (1997, pp. 434–435, 437–438, 440) are reprinted here, as possible pointers, and the background to these suggestions is discussed later in Section IV.

III. EMERGENT LITERACY THEMES

Since the early 1980s, there has been a paradigm shift in perspectives on literacy development. The traditional concept of *reading readiness*, with its implications of the need for prerequisite skills before reading and writing instruction could be implemented, has been replaced by a focus on the early behaviors relating to print that are evident in even very young children as part of informal, daily experiences (Sulzby & Teale, 1991; Yaden, Rowe, & MacGillivray, 2000). Emergent literacy perspectives opened up a new viewing lens through which children's own understandings of the processes of reading and writing could be explored. New research programs were spawned not only to describe the early literacy experiences of children, but also to evaluate the impact of these early experiences on subsequent literacy success. Over the last two decades, considerable research efforts have been focused on this aspect of literacy development, both for typically developing children and also for those with particular educational difficulties. Detailed reviews of these findings can be found in Sulzby and Teale (1991) and Yaden *et al.* (2000). There has been considerable support for emergent literacy research within the field of AAC (Bloom & Bhargava, 2003a; Coleman, 1992; Erickson, 2003a, 2003b; Erickson, Koppenhaver, Yoder, & Nance,

Table 8.1

The Learning Context: Some Specific Suggestions for Intervention

Previous and present experience of life

Preschool age

- *Create a "print-rich" environment* by displaying literacy materials at an appropriate level, providing a range of books and writing/drawing equipment, alphabets, personal names and labels; encourage parents to watch programs such as *Sesame Street* with their child.
- *Encourage storybook reading*, using page fluffers, tabs, etc., so that the child can assist in turning pages; develop individualized photograph books for personal interest; use materials that reflect the child's experiences, or consider how new experiences might be provided—by a shopping trip, a visit to the park, or going to a birthday party—and refer back to the experience when reading.
- *Encourage multiple readings of books*, allowing time for discussion, retelling the story at other times during the day, predicting what will happen next, and "mis-reading" keys parts in a playful manner.
- *Provide a means of control*, including messages such as "My turn," "Stop," or "I want to turn the page" on communication displays.
- *Encourage active participation* by providing thematic communication displays.
- *Provide models of reading/writing*, such as reading notes, writing lists, or signing one's name.
- *Encourage drawing and scribbling*, using fingerpaints, sponges, or other adaptations.

School age

- *Consider how time is being used* and where necessary, adapt the daily schedule.
- *Fill in gaps in life experience* by providing the experience itself or through preparatory discussion before reading or writing about a topic.

Adolescent/Adult

- *Evaluate current life experiences* by analyzing a typical weekly schedule, preferred activities, and interests and selecting reading materials accordingly; encourage students to draw on their own experiences in writing, through use of a private journal.
- *Provide vicarious experience* through "wide reading," supplemented with discussion, audiovisual materials, etc.

Expectations of enjoyment and competence

Preschool age

- *Share information* about the value of early literacy experiences and caregiver involvement.
- *Provide "intergenerational" literacy instruction* as necessary.
- *Foster positive and appropriate expectations.*
- *Provide experiences of success*; use stories with repeated lines, such as "I'll huff and I'll puff . . ." from the Three Little Pigs with the repeated line programmed into a speech-generating device (SGD), so that the AAC user can participate actively and help "read" the story.

School age/adolescent/adult

- *Help students realize how familiar they are with print.*
- *Encourage "co-reading"* and small group reading/writing, balancing abilities within the group.
- *Select materials carefully*, ensuring plenty of success, if necessary devise materials on an individual basis.

Table 8.1   *(Continued)*

Focus on meaning

Preschool age

- *Encourage paraphrasing* of stories where possible; "mix up" story endings and discuss; use multiple readings so stories are familiar; before reading notes, introduce a question such as "I wonder what this is about" or "What does Daddy need today?"
- *Encourage acting out* of stories read.
- *Plan and discuss messages* that are to be written, for example, shopping lists, by checking cupboards for items needed, repeating item names as they are written down, and referring often to the list when shopping.

School age/adolescent/adult

- *Frame content of a text*, outlining the organizational structure, making students aware of how much they already know about the topic before they engage in reading/writing, and using discussion, quizzes, etc.; check how much they can predict about a story, accepting all predictions and rechecking after reading for accuracy of predictions.
- *Scan texts* before starting to read, encouraging students to pick out any unfamiliar vocabulary that may cause problems in comprehending the text.
- *Role play* major parts from a story, presenting an alternative viewpoint, for example, a court-room dramatization of a fairy tale such as "Hansel and Gretel."
- *Value content over form* in written output; encourage risk taking and extended text output while emphasizing content and ignoring grammatical or spelling errors and allowing time for editing and correction of specific errors *after* content has been completed and evaluated; minimize form demands, by focusing on one type of error only in editing.
- *Rewrite familiar stories from a different perspective*, for example, "Jack and the Beanstalk," from the point of view of the Giant.

Shared knowledge

Preschool age

- *Build around life experiences*, selecting materials accordingly.

School age/adolescent/adult

- *Brainstorm* a particular topic before the written task, encouraging students to build semantic maps of concepts related to the topic; use probe questioning to determine any areas of difficulty or when background knowledge needs to be developed; identify possible questions students may have about the topic.

Smith, M., & Blischak, D. (1997). Literacy. In L. Lloyd, D. Fuller & H. Arvidson (Eds.), *Augmentative and alternative communication: principles and practices* (pp. 434–435). London: Allyn & Bacon.

1997; King-DeBaun, 1990; Koppenhaver & Erickson, 2003; Koppenhaver & Yoder, 1992, 1993; Musselwhite & King-DeBaun, 1997; Nunes da Ponte, 2002; Pierce & McWilliam, 1993), reflecting perhaps the keen awareness within the field that the life experiences of individuals who use aided communication are in some respects quite different from those of their naturally speaking peers. For this reason, the implications of this research are considered briefly here. Some of the key findings from emergent literacy research include the following:

Table 8.2

The Language/Communication Context: Some Specific Suggestions for Intervention

Purpose of language

Preschool age/school age/adolescent/adult
- *Maximize opportunities* to engage in communicative interaction with a range of communication partners, ensuring that a range of communicative functions can be met.

Purpose of print

Preschool age
- *Describe and demonstrate purposes*; encourage caregivers to express a reason for using print: "Let's read a book, just for fun." "I need to find out Anna's phone number." "I have to remember what to buy."
- *Recap the purpose* after a task has been completed: "So that's what happened to the bad fox." "Now I can phone Anna." "Gerard's birthday card is ready now."
- *Label and indicate printed message* on AAC displays, whether the word is written with a graphic symbol or is presented on a screen.

School age/Adolescent/Adult
- *Brainstorm*; encouraging students to list where around them they see print—in a particular room, within their home, in their neighborhood; discuss what that print means; list possible reasons for reading and writing in their own daily lives; discuss who they see reading and writing, when they themselves reading or writing and why; when they would like to read or write; if appropriate list the reading/writing requirements of employment.
- *Provide the alphabet on communication displays*, ensuring that format (upper or lower case) is the same as that of instruction, adapting voice output communication aid overlays/screens as necessary.
- *Highlight orthography on a communication display*, through color emphasis and draw attention to the printed message output, whether presented in a visual display or printed as hard copy.
- *Encourage use of orthographic strategies* in communication to communicate messages otherwise unavailable through first-letter cueing; if necessary, elicit vocabulary through semantic strategies, then model first-letter cue strategies.

Language structures—syntax/morphology

Preschool age/school age/adolescent/adult
- *Be aware* of the expressive language level of the AAC user.
- *Model* a range of syntactic structures, using the learner's own communication display; rephrase and/or expand on their own output to encourage greater syntactic and morphological complexity.
- *Foster experience* with as broad a range of sentence types as possible.

Language structures—phonology/phonological awareness

Preschool age
- *Rhyming*: encourage caregivers to engage in nursery rhyme activities as they would with a child who was developing speech, pausing at predictable points, even if the child is unable to produce an intelligible vocalization; mix up rhymes, for example "Jack and Jill went up the . . . mountain!" and monitor responses; program rhymes into SGDs where possible, ideally when one activation yields the full rhyme.
- *Segment* words into onset and rime, in "silly talk," prolonging the initial phoneme, starting with continuants, such as /s/, /m/, etc., so that "sun" is produced as "ssssun."

Table 8.2 *(Continued)*

School age
- *Rhyme recognition*: hide objects or pictures of rhyming objects around the room, present a sample of the target rhyme (e.g., cat), students gesture, eye gaze, etc., to other objects (hat, mat, bat, etc.); present two spoken words, students indicate by gesture, manual sign, switch activation, or yes/no signal whether words rhyme; sort objects according to rhyme, for example, only things that rhyme with "mat" get put on a mat and those that rhyme with "sack" go in the sack, indicate by eye gaze or gesture where the object should go.
- *Odd one out*: produce the target rhyme, then list other words; students indicate by gesture, manual sign, or buzzer when adult gets one "wrong."
- *Rhyme production*: provide spoken word; students find a rhyming word on communication board or SGD with semantic clues given as necessary.
- *Segmentation—syllables*: students sort objects into groups on the basis of the number of syllables each word contains, indicating through pointing, eye gaze, etc.
- *Segmentation—onset-rime identification*: have a bag for "sound of the day"; only words beginning with that sound go into the bag; students indicate through yes/no response.
- *Segmentation—onset-rime alliteration*: choose one student's name and identify the initial phoneme(s); students then identify other items in room that share the same onset.
- *Segmentation—phoneme level*: activities are similar to those outlined above, moving from the onset phoneme as a singleton to initial consonant clusters, final phoneme, and medial phoneme in (C)CVC words; student response is based on identification, through gesture, eye gaze, yes/no response, or switch activation.
- *Segmentation—phoneme counting*: the student taps out the number of segments or selects objects (e.g., chips) to represent individual segments, through tapping, eyeblink, or alternative motor response.
- *Segmentation—phoneme deletion*: the adult produces a CVC(C) word (e.g., /mit/); the student deletes final consonant and produce "new" word on communication display.
- *Phoneme reversal*: the adult produces a word or nonsense word (e.g., fog); students reverse the initial and final consonants and find a "new" word (god) on the communication display.
- *Synthesis—onset-rime*: an adult/puppet uses "silly speech," producing a word segmented into onset rime (e.g., m-at); the student identifies the word via a communication display; this activity can be made into a story for which the student has to first signal when a word has been segmented and then provide the synthesized word.
- *Synthesis—phoneme level*: this activity is similar to the previous one, but the adult segments all phonemes of the target word.
- *Use unaided AAC methods*, such as fingerspelling to promote phoneme-grapheme corespondence, capitalizing on the visual similarity of graphic and manual alphabet letters (Koehler *et al.*, 1994).

Adolescent/Adult
- It may not be considered appropriate to focus on developing phonological awareness, because a developmental model of intervention may not be the model of choice. However, where indicated, activities similar to those suggested above may be adapted with age appropriate materials, such as rap songs or limericks.

Smith, M., & Blischak, D. (1997). Literacy. In L. Lloyd, D. Fuller & H. Arvidson (Eds.), *Augmentative and alternative communication: principles and practices* (p. 437). London: Allyn & Bacon.

Table 8.3

The Print Context: Some Specific Suggestions for Intervention Using Letter Sounds

Letter sounds

Preschool age

- *Name letters*: label letters of title of favorite books, draw attention to letter at beginning of own name, family member's names.
- *Communication display*: specify section of communication display for letters, adding letters as they are encountered in activities as above—first letter of own name, mommy, daddy.

School age

- *Incorporate letters onto communication displays*: demonstrate access to letters in high-tech devices; ensure format is compatible with that known to student (upper or lower case).
- *Encourage sound play*: using an SGD, activate the spell mode; encourage student to explore letter sounds, selecting sequence of letters and then activating the "speak" function.
- *Encourage invented spelling*: encourage students to explore spelling options, particularly with voice output.
- *Word or nonword*: provide a word ending/rime (e.g., "-an"); the student tries different onset letters with SGD and decides whether output is a word or nonword.
- *"Change a word"*: provide a CVC word, for example, *cat*, and then give a semantic clue to a related word that requires a one-letter change only (e.g., "you use it in baseball—*bat*"; "the opposite of good—*bad*").

Smith, M., & Blischak, D. (1997). Literacy. In L. Lloyd, D. Fuller, & H. Arvidson (Eds.), *Augmentative and alternative communication: principles and practices* (p. 437). London: Allyn & Bacon.

1. Storybook reading continues to be widely viewed as an extremely valuable context for early immersion in literacy (Phillips, Norris, & Mason, 1996), although as Yaden *et al.* (2000, p. 428) pointed out, the longer-term effects of this preschool storybook reading are still not universally agreed upon.

2. Children's experiences in these contexts are fluid and dynamic, related to constantly changing interaction styles of both adults and participating children.

3. Literacy-related dramatic play is important in building cognitive, linguistic, and metacognitive skills relevant to comprehending and producing texts.

4. For story reenactment, adult support is beneficial, but children may not need intensive adult help to engage in other types of valuable, story-related play (Yaden *et al.*, 2000).

5. Children's social experiences, the books they read, their observations of other authors, and their interactions with others about their writing influence their writing processes and strategies.

6. The home environment and the relevance and role assigned to literacy within this environment exert an important influence on children's subsequent construct of literacy.

7. Comprehensive emergent literacy programs can have profound and positive effects on children with widely diverse abilities and needs and widely varying experiences with print (Yaden *et al.*, 2000).

8. According to Yaden *et al.* (2000, p. 443), key features of successful programs include "(a) drawing children in as socially competent partners, (b) allowing them to experiment without undue duress, (c) providing them with a variety of adult- and peer-mediated dialogue about literature and ways to read and write, and (d) creating any number of opportunities for them to practice their unconventional, yet emerging skills."

Taken together, these findings suggest that, in very real and practical ways, we need to pay attention to the early print experiences of individuals at risk for nondevelopment of functional speech. Storybook reading should continue to be encouraged, with multiple rereadings of familiar stories, adapted so as to be maximally accessible. Attention needs to be paid to the interaction patterns within these contexts, with a focus on active participation and communication. It is also important to avoid an overly prescriptive approach to structuring interactions, given the evidence of the range of experiences available to typically developing children. Increasing of opportunities to engage in story-related play and story reenactment offers valuable support for the development of a range of skills. Props such as puppets, tokens from a story, costumes, and recorded lines on voice-output devices can all be developed to create a story package to support not only reading of the story, but also play and dramatization attempts. A library can become a place in which books and all other associated props are stored. Dress-up materials, puppets, toys, pictures, and photos can all be collected to support particular books that have been found to be interesting for children.

Writing or expressive opportunities should be meshed within the fabric of these communication opportunities, offering a model of reading and writing as accessible, relevant, important, valued, and fun. Emergent literacy interventions address only one stage of the journey to expert skills, but their focus is on a critically important stage in the journey to expertise, a stage that may determine whether the journey is one deemed sufficiently interesting and important to continue. The beauty of emergent literacy, as pointed out by Erickson, Koppenhaver, & Yoder (2002) is that it is not bound by age or developmental level. It is, as they stated, "nourished by experience and opportunity" (p. 5). For this reason, the growing body of information and intervention suggestions addressing emergent literacy in relation to individuals who use AAC is both welcome and timely.

IV. THE SCRAWL APPROACH

The acronym *SCRAWL* is used here as a simple reminder of the multiple components involved in successful literacy instruction. Although each component is discussed in sequence in the following sections, in practice these components overlap and intermesh and should not be conceived of as being independent of each other. Furthermore the components suggested here are not new or unique to individuals who use aided communication. They are drawn from many different sources, and surface in many guises in approaches as diverse as whole language approaches and phonics instruction.

A. S—SHARED STORIES

Authenticity, engagement, ownership, and motivation can all be harnessed by involving aided communicators in discussions about the stories they want to read and write. Shared stories can mean many things. They may refer to narratives of real events or to fictional stories that reflect real experiences that are familiar or "accessible." Stories can be shared in the sense that there is collaboration in choosing a particular story to reflect personal interests. Stories may be shared in the very real sense that the experience within the story was also a shared experience. For example, a trip to the shop to buy stamps may be a shared experience that is subsequently discussed and evolves into a shared story. On the other hand, the shared experience may be a holiday, a trip to a rock concert or a football game, a shared frustration over equipment or transport possibilities, or a visit to a farm with a group of peers. Shared stories do not necessarily have to be about long or exciting events—even routine experiences can become the basis for a shared story or can be adapted through the creation of a new ending or a twist in the tale. Apart from the obvious interest and motivation value, using stories as a starting point for developing reading and writing materials offers several advantages. It ensures that extended texts are the focus, rather than an emphasis on short, worksheet materials. Stories can be supported through props to encourage extending of a text or to support reading comprehension. Cinema tickets, receipts from a store, photos, a transport ticket, or any other such souvenir of an experience can be included as a visual and/or a tactile prop to prompt memory and reinforce the link between the narrative and the experience itself. Stories can be created through discussion, through the development of an oral narrative that serves as the basis for a written narrative, or coconstructed by the person using aided communication and his or her parent, therapist, or educator, as is typified in a language experience approach (Rasinski & Padak, 2000). Symbol support can be used, so that a story is created through pictures, symbols, and words. Photos relating to the story can act as a link for the full story or can supplement specific elements of a story. In this structure, oral and written language are interwoven, with oral or aided language acting as the basis for generating a story and then recorded in traditional orthography and used as the foundation for targeted reading and writing practice.

From the point of view of the learning context (Pumfrey & Reason, 1991), shared background knowledge is intrinsic to the process, because the stories build on real and relevant experiences. The nature of the process focuses attention on meaning rather than on skill, and expectations of enjoyment are typically high, given that the theme of the story is developed collaboratively and in partnership. Although the final written version of the story may differ in some ways from the original version developed through discussion and elaboration, typically the changes are not substantive, but rather focus on editing, reducing, or restructuring. The process of transitioning from an "oral" or aided communication product to a written story fosters awareness of the functions and forms of print and the similarities and differences between spoken and written language format. In addition, there is the potential for discussion and exploration of narrative structure (Bloom & Bhargava, 2003b), the grammar of stories, and many other aspects of the metalinguistic skills that must be harnessed for successful writing. Two examples of the use of shared stories, one with preschool children and the other with adults are presented in Figures 8.1 and 8.2.

B. C—COMPREHENSION

Meaningful reading and writing involve comprehension processes—skills in word recognition or phoneme-grapheme mapping are not functional, unless meaning can be constructed from the printed text. Comprehension of a text requires understanding at many levels. Linguistic comprehension is clearly involved, because the meaning is encoded in linguistic units. Individual words must be understood, as must smaller morphological units such as plural or verb tense agreement markers. Comprehension of syntactic units is also required—the ability to recognize and understand a whole range of syntactic structures such as questions, statements, and relative clauses and to interpret the relationships within the sentence expressed through these structures. The meaning of each word decoded must be compared with the overall meaning of the text to determine whether the word as decoded makes sense in the present context (Pressley, 2000). These are the elements that are processed through the meaning processor proposed by Seidenberg and McClelland (1989). For example, to comprehend the sentence, "When he leaves, she will not stay long," the reader must first decode the individual words, understand that "when" refers to a time dimension, and recognize that although it often functions as a question word in this position within a sentence, for this particular sentence it marks the start of a relative adverbial clause. The reader must also recognize from the syntactic structure that "leaves" in this sentence is a present tense verb, marked for agreement with the third person singular, and does not refer to the plural of things that grow on trees. The contrasting pronouns, "he" and "she" must be appropriately interpreted

Dear Zoo, by Rod Campbell, a Lift-the-Flap Book by Puffin

This book relates the story of writing to the zoo for a pet. The story followed a visit to the zoo by a preschool group of children, some of whom used AAC. It thus built on a shared experience. The experience was also shared in the sense that the story was read many times within the group, with discussing suitable and unsuitable pets, making lists of favorite pets, and drawing up lists of those who had pets.

I wrote to the zoo to send me a pet. They sent me an...(elephant)

He was too big! I sent him back.

So they sent me a...(giraffe)

He was too tall! I sent him back.

So they sent me a...(lion)

He was too fierce! I sent him back.

So they sent me a...(camel)

He was too grumpy! I sent him back.

So they sent me a...(snake)

He was too scary! I sent him back.

So they sent me a...(monkey)

He was too naughty! I sent him back.

So they sent me a...(frog)

He was too jumpy! I sent him back.

So they thought very hard, and sent me a...(puppy)

He was perfect! I kept him.

Figure 8.1. Shared stories—preschool children.

Story 2: Special Olympics is a story developed through discussion with adults who had all either attended an event at the Olympics or had watched it on television. This was a very significant event in Ireland at the time, and there were few homes in the country that were not involved in at least some peripheral way in the hosting of the Olympics.

Special **Olympics** were held in Ireland in June. It was sunny. The athletes came from around the world. The opening ceremony was in Dublin.

The President lit the flame at the ceremony. There were many different sports. The athletes wanted to win medals.

There were lots of volunteers to help the athletes. Everyone had good fun.

Figure 8.2.   Shared stories—a story by adults who use AAC.

to signal that two different persons are referred to within the sentence. The word "long" must be interpreted to refer to a time episode rather than to a dimension of the individual "she." The potential ambiguity of many of the individual linguistic units must be resolved through integration of information from the syntactic and morphological structure of the sentence. However, arriving at this point of comprehension is only one level of understanding.

The context processor (Seidenberg & McClelland, 1989) must be engaged for true comprehension, whereby the intent of the writer is interpreted by the reader through a system of integrating the decoded meanings with a system of knowledge. Tattershall (2002) distinguished between these two levels of meaning processing in terms of comprehending and comprehension. In her view, *comprehending* refers to the on-line processing of linguistic units and interpretation of syntactic and morphological relations, whereas *comprehension* refers to the process of the construction of a meaning that links the decoded linguistic structure to a system of knowledge and beliefs (Tattershall, 2002). For example, the earlier sentence, "When he leaves, she will not stay long," is open to many different interpretations, depending on the context constructed by the reader: a scene in a hospital in which an elderly man is ill, while his spouse sits by his bed; an office party at which there are suspicions about relationships between two employees; or a birthday party to which a father has brought his 3-year-old daughter. The context processor influences the interpretation constructed. Although only one

- Play with toy animals, sorting zoo animals and farm animals

- Pick a pet game: each child selects a favorite pet and explains his or her choice

- Exploration of attributes of animals

- Finding pictures of wild animals in magazines—compare to the pictures in the book

- List all the people who have pets, and list their pets

- Develop a photo chart of pets and their owners

- Develop a "fantasy pet" chart: each child selects the pet they want and finds the appropriate picture for a wall chart

- Write-a-letter activity: each child picks a person to "write" to within the group and posts the letter either into a post-box developed as part of the activity; alternatively, an activity is set up to go to the post office and post the letters there.

Figure 8.3.   Comprehension activity suggestions: *Dear Zoo.*

of the three possibilities outlined above might be deemed reasonable, given the preceding text, nonetheless the nuances of the specific interpretation constructed are unique to individual readers and colored by their unique past and present personal experiences.

By using shared stories as outlined earlier, information is provided for the context processor to guide text comprehension. Specific comprehension activities to support comprehension and to draw attention to related background knowledge and experience can also be developed. Some examples of these activities are provided in Figures 8.3 and 8.4. An abundance of further ideas for similar or related activities specifically adapted for individuals using aided communication can be found, for example, in the work of Bloom and Bhargava (2003a, 2003b), Johnson (1996), and Musselwhite and King-DeBaun (Musselwhite, 1993; Musselwhite & King-DeBaun, 1997).

At a meta level, it is important also that readers are aware of the need to search for meaning—and to monitor comprehension. According to Pressley (2000, p. 550), expert readers flexibly use a variety of processes as they read texts, including the following, among others:

- Making associations to ideas presented in a text based on prior knowledge

- Reviewing newspapers and television footage for stories related to the event

- Reviewing the types of sports involved

- Visiting the Web site for updates and news

- Picking a country with participants in the games and finding out further

  information about that country; mapping their progress through the games. This

  can be done in a league format also within the group, if considered appropriate.

Figure 8.4.   Comprehension activity suggestions: *Special Olympics.*

- Evaluating and revising hypotheses that occurred in reaction to earlier parts of the text, revising hypotheses if needed
- Revising prior knowledge that is inconsistent with ideas in the text, if the reader is convinced by the arguments in the text
- Figuring out the meanings of novel words in text, especially if they seem important to the overall meaning of the text

Use of these strategies is based on a clear understanding that comprehension is the essence of the process and that self-regulation of comprehension is an implicit part of dealing with a text. For older children, adolescents, and adults, specific attention may need to be drawn to this aspect of the comprehension process. A range of comprehension strategies can be targeted to processes that occur before reading, during reading, and after reading (Erickson, 2003a, 2003b). Some helpful suggestions adapted for individuals who use AAC can be found in Erickson (2003a) and in Foley and Staples (2003).

Under the heading of comprehension, attention must also be paid to the linguistic units and structures that are used to encode and capture the shared story. Facility with a range of language structures supports all aspects of text processing (Pumfrey & Reason, 1991; Snowling, 2000). This dimension of comprehension can be addressed through careful construction of the story and through the development of additional support activities to provide practice with specific linguistic structures, to target skills with particular syntactic or morphological units, or to develop insights into words and their structure. Examples of how sentences from a story may be selected for particular attention are suggested in Figures 8.5 and 8.6. The aim is to ensure that the requisite linguistic skills have been mastered at a functional level, or at the epilinguistic level (Gombert, 1992), so that they can be brought to awareness at the metalinguistic level. Providing sufficient opportunities to engage with the language structures in an oral language context may underpin the development of metaskills that can then be used

Word meanings

- Names of animals (elephant, giraffe, lion, camel, snake, monkey, frog, puppy)

- Attributes: big, tall, fierce, grumpy, scary, naughty, jumpy, perfect

- Finding other animals that fit these characteristics

- Adopt a characteristic—role-play activities

- Sorting activities: What things are scary? Big? Tall?

Morphology and syntax

- Irregular past tense: write-wrote, send-sent, think-thought

- Too + adjective (too big, too tall, etc.)

- Repeated lines for production: *So they sent me a . . . ; he was too . . . ; I sent him back.*

- Sentence assembly games using the above phrases

  - Unscrambling activities: e.g., *sent I back him,* etc.

  - Create a new sentence: e.g., *So they sent me a . . .(new car, computer, horse).*

  - Why won't it fit? Activities, involving clothes and toys that are too big, small, long, or short, with the target production phrase *I/it/he/she is too . . . .*

Figure 8.5. Comprehension activity suggestions: *Dear Zoo.*

as a resource, for example, in the more demanding context of constructing written texts (Frost, 2000). These kinds of activities also emphasize the links between spoken and written language, an approach to instruction that has a long history and a great deal of research support (Snow, Burns, & Griffin, 1998; Wilkinson & Silliman, 2000).

C. *R*—RAPID RECOGNITION

One feature of the development of efficient, fluent reading is the expansion of a store of words that can be easily and rapidly recognized without undue

Word meanings

- Athlete(s), volunteer(s), coach(es), ceremony.

Morphology and syntax

- Sentence assembly activities

- Unscrambling activities: e.g., athletes wanted The medals win to

- Rewrite the story in the future tense

- Fill in the blanks——delete key prepositions or function words that must be

  reinserted by the participants

Figure 8.6. Comprehension activity suggestions: *Special Olympics.*

effort being expended on component analysis (Rasinski & Padak, 2000; Share, 1995). Although expert readers have access to decoding skills to mediate word recognition as needed, most of their reading is achieved through a more direct route of recognition of orthographic patterns, often at the level of the whole word. Building a store of sight words that can be rapidly and accurately identified is important in developing reading efficiency and in building early reading success. There are many sources of possible targets for sight word vocabulary, including vocabulary items already on a communication display, personalized vocabulary lists identified through discussion with the individuals involved or with key communication partners, commercial resources such as reading primers, or lists of commonly occurring words. According to Cunningham (2000), 100 words account for almost half of all the words we read and write, and 10 words— "the," "of," "and," "a," "to," "in," "is," "you," "that," and "it"—account for almost one quarter of all the words we read and write. One commonly used list of frequently occurring English words is often referred to as the Dolch list. This list of approximately 200 words was developed by E. W. Dolch, a reading teacher. The revised list used here and presented in Appendix A was taken from the Web site http://www.interfacecontrol.com/gemini/sheppard/reading/dolch.html. A wide range of additional resources for Dolch words is available on the World Wide Web.

However target sight words are chosen, these words can be embedded into the shared story constructed or, alternatively, can be drawn from the text of a preexisting story for specific targeted practice. Attention can be drawn to the target words, for example, through color coding, the use of additional support flash cards for Lotto games, and the development of word walls (Cunningham, 2000; Rasinski & Padak, 2000; Zutell, 1996), where the target words are put on

---

Dear Zoo, by Rod Campbell, a Lift-the-Flap Book by Puffin

I wrote *to the* zoo *to* send *me a* pet. *They* sent *me an* ... (elephant).

He was too big! *I* sent *him* back.

So they sent *me a* ... (giraffe).

He was too tall! *I* sent *him* back.

Etc.

So they thought *very* hard, *and* sent *me a* ... (puppy).

He was perfect! *I* kept *him.*

Possible targets: I, me, a, an, and, he, him, to, the, they, was, very, big

---

Figure 8.7. Possible sight word targets, drawn from the Dolch Sight Word List.

display within a classroom or at home to support incidental learning outside of specific structured literacy time. In Figures 8.7 and 8.8 the words within these stories that are found on the Dolch list are highlighted and, as can be seen, represent more than one half of all the words in both stories. It can be useful to select a specific subset of these words (perhaps 10 words in total within each story) that will be the focus of targeted instruction, building up a bank of words that can be reliably and accurately identified. Further specific activities such as filling in the missing words, identifying the sight words from a range of distracters, and creating new sentences using the same sight words can be used to supplement this aspect of the reading process.

D. *A*—Analysis and Articulation

Concurrent with developing a bank of sight words, individuals must develop specific skills in word analysis to support both decoding and encoding of new words. There is now substantial evidence that skills in analyzing the sound structure of the target language (i.e., phonological awareness skills) are reliable predictors of early reading success, that intervention programs focused on increasing phonological awareness skills are effective for the majority of children considered at risk for having reading difficulties, and that the same programs have a

Special Olympics *were* held *in* Ireland *in* June. *It was* sunny. *The* athletes *came from around the* world. *The* opening ceremony *was in* Dublin.

The President lit *the* flame *at the* ceremony. *There were many* different sports. *The* athletes wanted *to* win medals.

There were lots *of* volunteers *to* help *the* athletes. Everyone *had good* fun.

Possible targets: it, in, the, was, were, came, at, there, were, of, had, good, around, many

Figure 8.8.   Possible sight word targets, drawn from the Dolch Sight Word List.

significant impact on the performance of children who have already been identified as having specific reading difficulties (Snow *et al.*, 1998). It would also seem that the most successful programs are intensive and explicit in their focus (Torgesen, Wagner, & Rashotte, 1997) and include specific targeted links to letter knowledge and print (Ball & Blachman, 1991; Blachman, 1991; Blachman, Ball, Black, & Tangel, 1994). Building of phonological awareness skills is not a panacea for all reading difficulties. First, a minority of children do not appear to benefit from this type of instruction (approximately 25% as estimated by Torgesen *et al.*, 1997), perhaps because of much more pervasive difficulties. Second, the evidence suggests that phonological awareness instruction primarily affects word recognition, rather than comprehension (Snow *et al.*, 1998), the ultimate goal in literacy instruction. Based on current research data, however, a focus on phonological awareness must be considered essential in any literacy instruction approach (Adams, 1990).

The discussion here focuses on activities to support phonological awareness at the syllable level and the phoneme level. Throughout this element of instruction, attention is drawn to the link between phonological shape and acoustic form—in other words, individuals are encouraged to think about sounds and to "hear" sounds as they analyze them. The goal is to draw attention to the individual's own internal phonological representations and to promote analysis of those representations. Tasks suggested here draw on the resources implicit in the stories created but can be expanded to include other materials and activities. There are many useful resources for developing phonological awareness activities (Bloom & Bhargava, 2003a, 2003b; Cunningham, 2000; Goldsworthy, 1996; Goldsworthy & Pieretti, 2004), and only a few are provided here as a starting point. Both phonological awareness and spelling skills appear to proceed from syllables, to units intermediate between syllables and phonemes, to phonemes

Figure 8.9. Sample of rhyming word activity—all words that rhyme with a set target work ("win" in the grid below) must be selected. Only correcting rhyming words ("tin," "win," "fin," "thin," "pin") will "send" to the display grid.

(Treiman & Bourassa, 2000). Target activities should therefore address the inter-syllabic, intrasyllabic, and phoneme level. As outlined in the discussion on assessment, it is important also to balance input and output tasks (Stackhouse & Wells, 1997) where possible and to build skills across both types of tasks.

At the syllabic level, activities such as counting syllables, segmenting words into syllables, deleting syllables, and sorting words by number of syllables can be used. Output tasks can involve finding words with a similar number of syllables and reconstructing words from syllables. Intrasyllabic activities draw attention to units within the syllable—the onset and rime. Rhyming tasks are the most common tasks used at this level. Examples of activities for both of these levels are presented in Figures 8.9 and 8.10.

At the phoneme level (a level that may coincide with onset-rime divisions) attention is drawn to the individual sound, and the related phoneme-grapheme correspondence. At this point, specific support for thinking about sound production may be useful. Typically developing children draw on their own articulatory skills as they sound out words and play with sounds. In so doing, they reinforce the articulatory information that is to be activated by a particular grapheme. For some individuals who are unable to directly access the articulatory experience to link to phonological representations, alternate strategies using explicit visual, tactile, and auditory cues to supplement or replace direct articulatory experience may be a valuable support (Lindamood & Lindamood, 1998). Therapeutic tools such as cued articulation (Passy, 1990) or Metaphon resources (Howell & Dean, 1994) can be harnessed to provide information on the place and manner of production and voiced-voiceless contrasts. Alternatively, clinicians

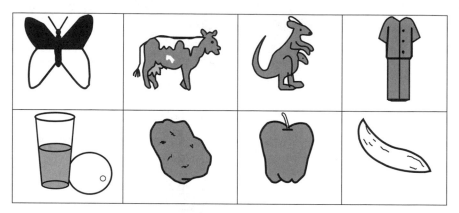

Figure 8.10. Sample of activity selecting words of three syllables.

can develop their own materials and support information. Phonological and orthographic information should guide decisions on the sequence of phoneme-grapheme correspondences to be targeted.

Some sounds are highly visible and are produced near the front of the mouth (e.g., /b/, /m/, and /f/). Typically these sounds emerge relatively early in speech development also (Ingram, 1989). Others are less easily seen and described, being produced at the back of the mouth (e.g., /k/ and /g/) or with no clear point of articulatory contact (/r/). Some sounds occur often (e.g., /s/), whereas others, although visible, are encountered only occasionally (e.g., /v/). The production of fricative or continuant sounds can be maintained and extended without compromising intelligibility (e.g., s-s-s-s), whereas other sounds such as plosives (e.g., /p/, /t/, and /k/) cannot be extended in articulation and so may be less salient. These considerations may all be taken into account when one plans a sequence of phonemes to be targeted in specific analytical activities.

Orthographic considerations may also be important. Typically phonemes that are represented by single letters are introduced before phonemes represented by a digraph, such as "sh" or "ch." Some sounds are represented consistently by the same letter (e.g., "m" or "t"), whereas others may be represented by a range of letters or letter combinations, depending on the position of the sound within the word, or other morphological information. For example, /k/ may be represented by "c," "k," or "ck." Similarly, the letter "c" may represent the sound /k/ or /s/, depending on its orthographic neighbors. Although adoption of either a letter-to-sound approach or a sound-to-letter approach may be effective in developing phoneme-grapheme skills, Groff (2001) outlined many reasons why sound-to-letter approaches offer a more logical and efficient way to develop both phonemic awareness *and* consistent sound-letter correspondence skills.

When one targets a group of phoneme-grapheme correspondences, maximal contrasts across the phonemes and the graphemes may be desirable, and both consonants and vowels should be included as potential learning targets. Vowels are difficult for most individuals learning to read and spell, because a limited set of vowel letters (a-e-i-o-u) must represent a wide range of vowel articulations. Short vowels, although less salient acoustically than their long counterparts, are generally introduced first when spelling is taught (Cunningham, 2000) and so may be important to include in the early stages of analyzing articulation information. Touch cues can be particularly helpful in drawing attention to different vowel articulations, because there is only limited visual information available to support differentiation between the short vowels. Once a target phoneme has been selected, based on some of the considerations mentioned earlier, cues must be constructed to support identification and generation of the target sound linked to the appropriate grapheme. Figure 8.11 provides some suggestions for such activities linked to the target phoneme /m/ and the grapheme "m," from the Special Olympics story.

The *A* of the SCRAWL acronym here refers to both analysis and articulation, and articulation itself is considered under two dimensions—highlighting and supplementing articulation information in relation to key target phonemes and also developing subvocal articulation or an "inner voice" (Cunningham, 1993; Erickson, 2003b) to support text comprehension. In drawing attention to the articulatory properties of sounds and print, apprentice readers and writers should also be encouraged to "listen" to the sounds as they are reading and to pay attention to their own inner voice. Wolff Heller, Fredrick, Tumlin, & Brineman (2002) described the strategies they used to encourage attention to internal speech in their nonverbal reading approach, designed for those with severe speech and physical impairments.

Figure 8.11.   Target sound "m"—suggested activities.

E. W—Writing

Effective literacy instruction programs interweave spoken and written language skills and integrate reading and writing activities together to develop the complementary skills implicit in these activities as a bootstrapping mechanism. In early literacy development, written language serves as a pacemaker for the development of phonological awareness skills, particularly at the phonemic level (Ehri, 2000; Groff, 2001). As outlined previously, writing is a more complex activity than reading. Children read what they write as they write it and reformulate or modify their planning of what they will write next on the basis of what they have read of their own writing. It is important therefore to interweave writing activities throughout an instructional program for individuals who use aided communication. Three types of activities are considered under writing here: spelling activities, sentence construction activities, and creative writing. As before, only a few suggestions are offered for specific tasks, because there are many other resources that can be consulted (Bloom & Bhargava, 2003a, 2003b; Cunningham, 2000; Rasinski & Padak, 2000; Smith & Warwick, 1997).

1. Spelling Activities

a. What to Teach

Templeton and Morris (2000) argued strongly that spelling instruction must focus on more than mere orthographic sequences and should emphasize spelling instruction as word study—a means of looking at words from a variety of perspectives that serve reading, writing, and vocabulary development. A variety of strategies can be used to explore and examine words, such as word sorting or categorization activities, word-building activities, and analogical reasoning with semantic and orthographic categories (Moats, 1995; Templeton, 2002; Templeton & Morris, 2000). Nonetheless, spelling or orthographic patterns must be selected in some principled way to support and develop spelling skills and to present a level of instruction that matches the learning needs of apprentice readers and writers. There are many resources that can be used in determining how best to sequence spelling targets, while considering the phonological and morphological information to be gleaned and highlighted (Bear, Invernizzi, Templeton, & Johnston, 2000; Cunningham, 2000; Moats, 1995; Snowball & Bolton, 1999). Templeton (2002) summarized key developmental transitions in spelling, as outlined in Figure 8.12, and these guidelines can also be used to decide on targets.

b. How to Teach It

How best to teach spelling remains somewhat controversial. Traditional approaches emphasized rote learning by working through word families, with a

Beginning literacy	Beginning single consonants
Alphabetic spelling	Consonant digraphs
	Consonant blends
	Short-vowel patterns
Transitional literacy	Common long-vowel patterns
Within-word-pattern spelling	r- and l-influenced vowels
	Three-letter consonant blends
	Complex consonants:
	Final sound of /k/
	Final /ch/: *ch, tch*
	/j/: *dge, ge*
Intermediate literacy	Inflectional suffixes: *-ed, -ing*
Syllables and affixes spelling	Plural endings
	Changing final *y* to *l*
	Syllable patterns
	VCCV: *bas ket*
	VCV open: *hu man*
	VCV closed: *cab in*
	Less frequent vowel patterns
	Two-syllable homographs:
	PREsent/preSENT
	REcord/reCORD
	Vowel patterns in accented and unaccented syllables
	Base words + common prefixes and suffixes

Figure 8.12. Spelling features as a function of development level (From Templeton, 2000, p. 12).

Advanced literacy	Spelling/meaning connection:

Derivational-relations spelling	*Sign-signal; music-musician, ignite-ignition; reside-resident; mental-mentality*
	
	Greek and Latin elements
	
	   -therm- -spect- -photo- -dic-
	
	Assimilated/absorbed prefixes:
	
	   in + mobile = immobile
	
	   ad + tract = attract

Figure 8.12. *(Continued)*

preset spelling test at the end of each week of instruction. Clearly, there is some element of rote learning that is necessary for most individuals learning to spell. However, the emphasis here is on spelling as both an orthographic task and a linguistic task, and so the key skills to be developed are skills in identifying word patterns and the use of analogy. Close attention to visual, orthographic, and morphological clues should be encouraged. Berninger *et al.* (1999) argued that from the outset, developing readers and writers should be encouraged to focus not only on single-letter spelling units but also on spelling units larger than the single letter to support subword analysis that may yield benefits for both reading and spelling. One tried and tested teaching technique, which has been demonstrated to be effective with individuals who use augmentative communication (Blischak & Schlosser, 2003; Koppenhaver & Yoder, 1989; McNaughton & Tawney, 1993), is a strategy that involves a sequence of looking at a target spelling word, attempting to pronounce it while looking, removing the printed stimulus and attempting to retain the visual image, checking the printed stimulus again, covering it, and attempting to write down the word. Accuracy of spelling is then checked against the target stimulus. There are many variations on this general technique. Students can be encouraged while they are trying to "spell" the word in their head (e.g., c-a-t), and spellings can be repeated a number of times (although ideally not more than three times, or tedium can be a problem).

McNaughton and Tawney (1993) contrasted the effectiveness of two instructional techniques (copy-write-compare [CWC] and student-directed cueing [SDC]) in teaching two adult users of AAC to spell. The first technique, CWC, involves copying a correct model of a target word twice, and then spelling the word independently. The student's attempt is then checked for accuracy with the target word, but attention is not drawn to studying any differences that might occur between the realized spelling and the correct spelling. In SDC, students are encouraged to first attempt to spell a target word before being shown the correct model. The instructor imitates the student's spelling before writing the correct spelling. The student then compares both spellings and highlights any differences between both spellings. In their study, McNaughton and Tawney reported that although both strategies were effective in improving spelling accuracy, the use of SDC resulted in superior retention of spelling patterns for both participants and was also their preferred method of instruction. This study suggests that careful planning of spelling instruction can yield important gains in skills. Encouraging students to access their existing knowledge and to apply analysis to their own and target spellings, while exploring differences and similarities, are all elements that support building an effective instructional approach. As the authors themselves pointed out, choosing spelling patterns or "word families" as the primary focus for analysis could have further optimized success for the participants.

Zutell (1996) described a range of instructional techniques that are integrated into what he termed a *directed spelling thinking activity (DSTA)*, in which learners are encouraged to analyze, categorize, and sort words according to spelling patterns, drawing on both the orthographic and morphological information within words. DSTA is grounded within a word-study approach, rather than a rote memorization approach to building spelling skills.

Within the SCRAWL approach a target word pattern (or patterns) can be drawn from some element in the story to become the focus of spelling practice or alternatively can be derived from analysis of spelling attempts of targets selected by the educator, based on developmental or assessment information. For example, in the Special Olympics theme, the target pattern "-in" is linked to the word "win," as a natural focus within the theme. Practice can then be provided in spelling possible words that end in this rime. A related activity focuses on going through the consonants of the alphabet and placing each consonant before the rime "-in," the task being to determine which of the words produced are real words. Access to voice output is especially helpful in this activity. Suggestions for many other similar or related activities can be found in texts relating to literacy instruction (e.g., Cunningham, 2000).

Finally, the role of invented spelling should not be overlooked (Ehri, 2000). Indeed, invented spelling may be even more important for those with extremely limited speech production abilities, in terms of providing insights into emerging phonemic and morphological awareness skills. Again, access to voice output may be of crucial importance in supporting exploration of spelling possibilities and in encouraging inventiveness and sound play and may yield longer-term benefits for overall literacy competence (Basil & Reyes, 2003; Blischak & Schlosser, 2003; Foley & Pollatsek, 1999; McGinnis & Beukelman, 1989; McNaughton, 1993).

2. Sentence Construction Activities

Writing must involve creating units of print that are larger than single words and that relate in some meaningful way to the interests of apprentice readers and writers. Many different writing activities can be developed. One bridge between writing of single words and "real" creative writing is to use the story that is the focus of a theme to focus on sentence construction. Either all or some of the sentences within the original story can be presented as single words or as phrases to be reconstructed by the individual learners (for an example, see Figure 8.13). Alternatively, complete sentences can be presented to be reordered into the appropriate sequence for the story (Figure 8.14). The advantage of such an approach is that the material is familiar, has been specifically selected to address motivation and interests, as well as learning goals (e.g.,

Special Olympics	here	in Iceland
	were	in Ireland
	wore	in Australia
		in France

Figure 8.13. Sample of sentence construction tasks from the Special Olympics theme.

Everyone had good fun.
The opening ceremony was in Dublin.
The President lit the flame at the ceremony.
There were many different sports.
The athletes wanted to win medals.
The athletes came from around the world.
There were lots of volunteers to help the athletes.
It was sunny.
Special Olympics were held in Ireland in June.

Figure 8.14. Sample of sentence construction task from the Special Olympics theme: place sentences in order. (Note: For this theme, the sequence of sentences has less significance than it would in a narrative piece.)

Special Olympics were held __ Ireland __ June. It __ sunny. The athletes ___ from

around the world. The opening ceremony was __ Dublin.

The President lit the ___ at the ceremony. There were many different sports. The athletes

wanted to ___ medals.

There were lots of volunteers to help __ athletes. Everyone __ good fun.

is in came cage was were wos it flame won win the them has had

---

Figure 8.15.   Sample of a cloze activity from the Special Olympics theme.

target sight words or spelling patterns), and by having been the focus of most of the rest of the work, should be within an appropriate learning zone.

The same materials can be used to develop maze and cloze activities. These activities involve provision of texts in which words are missing, and possible targets must either be supplied by the reader–writer or selected from a set of possible options. Such activities focus attention on the importance of context in supporting reading comprehension but can also be used to offer additional practice in word recognition and spelling tasks. Individualization of the materials to be used can offer a very effective way of tracking and supporting the development of both reading and writing skills. An example of a cloze activity task is provided in Figure 8.15, again drawn from the Special Olympics theme.

3. Creative Writing

As Rasinski and Padak (2000, p. 193) pointed out, children learn about the writing cycle (what writers do) and the writing process (the thinking that may occur at all stages of the cycle) through their own writing. These insights increase their shared understanding of the author's perspective and aims (the learning context referred to by Pumfrey and Reason, 1991). Apprentice readers and writers learn about writing through writing, and through their writing they also gain insights into reading. Encouraging creative writing is therefore an important element in any literacy instruction program. Creative writing can be fictional or factual. It can be personal (such as a personal diary), interpersonal (such as a letter or email), or public (such as a magazine feature). Each learning session should incorporate some time devoted to creative writing. Deciding what to write can take some time, but this time can provide useful opportunities for formulating thoughts using a communication board or speech generating device, setting out plans and topics, making editorial decisions, and identifying props that may be needed to support the production of a finished piece of text. Differing levels of support may be necessary. For some individuals, concrete props may be important to stimulate ideas and discussion. For others, pictures of key elements or events may be required. Some writers may benefit from an activity in which an opening sentence is provided, and each student or writer contributes one more sentence to build up a story. Cue words may be sufficient for more able students, whereas others may only need guided prompting at key points to develop a plan or to stay on track. The key is to identify the level of support needed for creative writing attempts and then gradually aim to reduce the level of support while the same level of output is maintained.

F. *L*—LANGUAGE, LITERACY, AND LITERATURE

The final element of the SCRAWL approach involves linking many of the threads that have been previously mentioned, particularly in relation to language skills and literature. Almost all language work can be incorporated within this element of the approach. Reading and writing instruction offer rich opportunities for exploration of the morphological makeup of words. Prefixes such as "re-," "im-," and "dis-" not only contain a stable spelling pattern across words but also provide important semantic clues to word meaning and word class. Similarly, suffixes such as "-er," "-less," and "-ment" offer opportunities to explore how words come to mean different things and how spelling provides clues to relationships between words. Compound words and word families likewise offer potential intellectual puzzles that can be used to engage interest and motivation in exploring words from a metalinguistic perspective, while issues such as spelling are addressed at the same time. Cunningham (2000, pp. 166–167) provided a list of 50 words that she termed the *Nifty Thrifty Fifty*. This list contains the prefixes, suffixes, and spelling changes most prevalent in multisyllabic words students might encounter that are embedded in words likely to be known by most fourth grade readers. There are endless possibilities for how this list might be used for spelling, word study, and word games.

Although for many individuals who use aided communication achievement of literacy may remain a struggle, one outcome of instruction should be an interest in written language. It is unrealistic to expect that all readers and writers will develop a lifelong love of literature. However, all apprentice readers and writers deserve the opportunity to develop such a love. Careful selection of materials, active discussion, collaboration, and a spirit of exploration in approaches to reading and writing should maximize the chances of developing such an interest and passion. There are many resources to prompt ideas about appropriate reading materials. Some suggestions are provided in Appendix B, but these represent only a tiny sample.

V. SUPPORTING SELF-TEACHING

As discussed earlier, one powerful theory of how children learn to read and write is that, given a critical level of skills in phonemic awareness and a stable set of words that can be recognized visually, as well as ample opportunities to read materials at an appropriate level of difficulty, apprentice readers and writers effectively teach themselves to read (Share, 1995). Through regular practice, associations between orthographic patterns and phonological forms are strengthened and developed into a spreading network of connections that serve as the basis for further word learning. Good readers read more than their peers who are struggling, and in so doing, they provide themselves with the critical ingredient to maintain their progress—practice. The challenge for all struggling readers, but particularly for those with physical and communication impairments, is to find ways to support and foster similar independent reading opportunities and so to set in motion a chain of events to serve as a catalyst for self-teaching to emerge. The extent of the challenge should not be underestimated. Typically developing children actively seek their own reading materials. They can find materials that are of interest to them, whether the back of a cereal box, a set of instructions on the side of a toy box, or a particular book. They quickly reject materials that are either too difficult or, occasionally, too easy, although anecdotal experience suggests that many readers enjoy an occasional break with a book that is well below their own levels of reading competence.

Technology may provide some answers or at least some support in simulating these experiences for individuals who have limited physical mobility, who are unable to independently select reading materials, and who may lack communication skills or vocabulary to indicate their desired reading choices. For some individuals who use aided communication, the very act of making a choice in any domain may be difficult. Although there are no easy solutions to this challenge, one critical component for success is awareness that regular and frequent independent reading opportunities, with materials that are well within competence levels, are essential to support the development of fluency.

VI. WORKING WITH ADULTS

There are important considerations when one works with older adolescents and adults. Malone and Arnove (1998, p. 44) summarized them as follows:

1. Adults possess a wide range of experience and knowledge related to a variety of topics and are aware of their own problems and their own educational goals.

2. They do not learn the same way that children do and do not want to be taught in the same way that children are taught.

3. They have additional demands on their time and do not want to be involved in activities that they feel are a waste of time.

4. They may be uninterested in individualized learning and yet be overwhelmed and embarrassed in competitive situations or, conversely, may enjoy competition and still learn best on their own.

These authors suggested a focus on encouraging prospective adult learners to identify their own educational goals (the *why* of the intervention), to share planning of the intended learning outcomes (the *what* of the program), and to help build from that point an instructional method (the *how*) that can be jointly reviewed by all involved (Malone & Arnove, 1998).

As mentioned previously, finding materials that are appropriate for and of interest to adult learners is challenging, yet remains a crucial step in the process. There may be a temptation to focus on functional or needs-driven materials and in some instances this focus may be appropriate. Tax forms, bank statements, and the like may be of high importance to some individuals at certain points and are certainly a valid source of instructional materials. However, it is unlikely that they will be sufficient by themselves to maintain interest in literacy learning in the long run. Some adults who use aided communication may be very motivated by materials that relate directly to their medical condition or their disability or to the experiences of others who use aided communication. Others may be more interested in materials that relate to recreation—information on sports, television, fashion, or music. It is important therefore to offer a range of materials, incorporating both extended text experience (whether in reading or writing) and shorter texts, such as greeting cards, calendar information, and signage directions. Some materials may be commercially available, and require a greater or lesser degree of adaptation to be accessible. Aided communicators themselves can also generate materials. Malone & Arnove (1998, p. 52) outlined the following sequence: adult learners discuss a particular topic and then collaboratively compose their own story, poem, etc., about the topic. The group dictates its composition to the teacher, who writes it on a board to use as the focus for a reading lesson. If the group decides it is worth preserving, the composition is made into a booklet or poster, so that the learners are involved in rewriting and editing their previously produced work. It is easy to see how this approach could be adapted to aided communication contexts—and indeed this is one element of the shared stories component described earlier.

A second element crucial to success in working with adults is the identification of contexts and functions of print that are relevant, motivating, and authentic in their lives. Many adults have already experienced failure in their attempts to read and write. A commitment to consistent and sustained programs of intervention that respect their goals and needs is fundamental to good practice. As pointed out by Foley and Staples (2003), skill development may be slow and uneven, particularly for those with additional disabilities. However, as these authors also pointed out "language learning (both spoken and written) can continue across the life span if supported across environments, including sheltered workshop and supported employment settings" (p. 342). One possible support in working with adults is a network of existing adult education opportunities, many specifically focused on development of adult literacy. Linking in with such programs can support community integration spawn new skill development opportunities for all involved, and yield many longer-term benefits. With some additional support and opportunities for training and professional development, many adult literacy instructors are both enthusiastic and highly skilled. A further advantage in availing of this network is that it acknowledges the role of the adult using AAC within the community, as an equal participant, entitled to inclusion in the educational opportunities available to others.

VII. SUMMARY

In this chapter we have focused on some practical approaches to literacy intervention for individuals with severe speech and physical impairments. One framework for instruction, interweaving communication, word analysis, visual word recognition skills, and writing, has been outlined. The emphasis throughout has been on expanding literacy needs, maximizing opportunities for engaging in literacy learning across the lifespan, and minimizing barriers to participation in such opportunities. For those with severe physical difficulties, many solutions to minimize barriers can be found in the technological developments that have emerged over the last decades. In the next chapter, the focus shifts to some of these developments and how they might be used to address the many barriers faced by children and adults who use aided communication.

REFERENCES

Adams, M. J. (1990). *Beginning to read: Thinking and learning about print.* Cambridge, MA: MIT Press, A Bradford Book.

Ball, E. W., & Blachman, B. A. (1991). Does phoneme awareness training in kindergarten make a difference in early word recognition and developmental spelling? *Reading Research Quarterly, 26,* 49–66.

Basil, C., & Reyes, S. (2003). Acquisition of literacy skills by children with severe disability. *Child Language Teaching and Therapy, 19*(1), 27–48.

Bear, D., Invernizzi, M., Templeton, S., & Johnston, F. (2000). *Words their way: Word study for phonics, vocabulary, and spelling instruction* (2nd ed.). Upper Saddle River, NJ: Prentice Hall.

Berninger, V., Abbott, R., Zook, D., Ogier, S., Lemos-Britten, Z., & Brooksher, R. (1999). Early intervention for reading disabilities: Teaching the alphabet principle in a connectionist framework. *Journal of Learning Disabilities, 32*(6), 491–503.

Bialik, P., & Seligman-Wine, J. (2002). "I see, I hear, I speak: So what's the problem?" In K. Erickson, D. Koppenhaver, & D. E. Yoder (Eds.), *Waves of words: Augmented communicators read and write* (pp. 133–141). Toronto, Ontario, Canada: ISAAC Press.

Blachman, B. A. (1991). Early intervention for children's reading problems: Clinical applications of the research in phonological awareness. *Topics in Language Disorders, 12*(1), 51–65.

Blachman, B. A., Ball, E. W., Black, R., & Tangel, D. (1994). Kindergarten teachers develop phoneme awareness in low-income, inner-city classrooms: Does it make a difference? *Reading and Writing: An Interdisciplinary Journal, 6*, 1–17.

Blischak, D., & Schlosser, R. (2003). Use of technology to support independent spelling by students with autism. *Topics in Language Disorders, 23*(4), 293–304.

Bloom, Y., & Bhargava, D. (2003a). *Let's read together. Part 1: Using commercially available books to promote literacy. AAC ideas for children with communication difficulties.* Beecroft, New South Wales, Australia: Innovative Communication Programming.

Bloom, Y., & Bhargava, D. (2003b). *Let's read Together. Part II: Creating personalised material to promote literacy. AAC ideas for children and adults with communication difficulties.* Beecroft, New South Wales, Australia: Innovative Communication Programming.

Coleman, P. P. (1992). *Literacy lost: A qualitative analysis of the early literacy experiences of preschool children with severe speech and physical impairments*, University of North Carolina, Chapel Hill.

Cunningham, J. W. (1993). Whole-to-part reading diagnosis. *Reading and Writing Quarterly, 9*, 31–49.

Cunningham, P. M. (2000). *Phonics they use: Words for reading and writing* (3rd ed.). New York: Longman.

Ehri, L. C. (2000). Learning to read and learning to spell: Two sides of a coin. *Topics in Language Disorders, 20*(3), 19–36.

Erickson, K. (2003a). Reading comprehension in AAC. *The ASHA Leader, 8*(12), 6–9.

Erickson, K. (2003b). *Evaluation techniques: The particular problem of how to assess output skills of individuals with complex communication needs and limited literacy skills.* Paper presented at the ISAAC Biennial Research Symposium, Odense, Denmark.

Erickson, K., Koppenhaver, D., & Yoder, D. E. (2002). *Waves of words: Augmented communicators read and write.* Toronto, Ontario, Canada: ISAAC Press.

Erickson, K., Koppenhaver, D., Yoder, D. E., & Nance, J. (1997). Integrated communication and literacy instruction for a child with multiple disabilities. *Focus on Autism and Other Developmental Disabilities, 12*(3), 142–151.

Foley, B. E., & Pollatsek, A. (1999). Phonological processing and reading abilities in adolescents and adults with severe congenital speech impairments. *Augmentative and Alternative Communication, 15*, 156–173.

Foley, B. E., & Staples, A. (2003). Developing augmentative and alternative communication and literacy interventions in a supported employment setting. *Topics in Language Disorders, 23*(4), 325–343.

Frost, J. (2000). From "Epi" through "Meta" to Mastery. The balance of meaning and skill in early reading instruction. *Scandinavian Journal of Educational Research, 44*(2), 125–144.

Fukushima, I. S. (2002). Finding the will, finding the way: Lessons from two augmented communicators. In K. Erickson, D. Koppenhaver, & D. E. Yoder (Eds.), *Waves of words: Augmented communicators read and write* (pp. 91–100). Toronto, Ontario, Canada: ISAAC Press.

Gandell, T., & Filippelli, F. (2002). Face-to-face, computer-to-computer: Telecommunications in adult literacy. In K. Erickson & D. Koppenhaver, & D. E. Yoder (Eds.), *Waves of words: Augmented communicators read and write* (pp. 105–114). Toronto, Ontario, Canada: ISAAC Press.

Given, F. (2002). From sentence construction to thesis writing. In K. Erickson & D. Koppenhaver, & D. E. Yoder (Eds.), *Waves of words: Augmented communicators read and write* (pp. 121–127). Toronto, Ontario, Canada: ISAAC Press.

Goldsworthy, C. (1996). *Developmental reading disabilities: A language based treatment approach.* London: Singular Press.

Goldsworthy, C., & Pieretti, R. (2004). *Sourcebook of phonological awareness activities.* London: Singular Press.

Gombert, J. E. (1992). *Metalinguistic development.* Hemel Hempstead, Herts. UK: Harvester Wheatsheaf.

Groff, P. (2001). Teaching phonics: Letter-to-phoneme, phoneme-to-letter, or both? *Reading and Writing Quarterly, 17,* 291–306.

Hogan, N., & Wolf, L. (2002). "i Amam a writer": Literacy, strategic thinking and metacognitive awareness. In K. Erickson, D. Koppenhaver, & D. E. Yoder (Eds.), *Waves of words: Augmented communicators read and write* (pp. 21–40). Toronto, Ontario, Canada: ISAAC Press.

Howell, J., & Dean, E. (1994). *Intervention in phonological impairment.* London: Whurr.

Ingram, D. (1989). *First language acquisition.* Cambridge, UK: Cambridge University Press.

Johnson, A. M. (1996). *More social skills stories.* Solana Beach, CA: Mayer-Johnson.

King-DeBaun, P. (1990). *Storytime: Stories, symbols and emergent literacy activities for young special needs children.* Acworth, GA: Pati King-DeBaun.

Koehler, L. J. S., Lloyd, L. L., & Swanson, L. A. (1994). Visual similarity between manual and printed alphabet letters. *Augmentative and Alternative Communication, 10,* 87–94.

Koppenhaver, D., & Erickson, K. (2003). Natural emergent literacy supports for preschoolers with autism and severe communication impairments. *Topics in Language Disorders, 23*(4), 283–292.

Koppenhaver, D., Evans, D., & Yoder, D. E. (1991). Childhood reading and writing experiences of literate adults with severe speech and motor impairments. *Augmentative and Alternative Communication, 7*(1), 20–33.

Koppenhaver, D., & Yoder, D. E. (1989). Study of a spelling strategy for physically disabled augmentative communication users. *Communication Outlook, 10*(3), 10–12.

Koppenhaver, D., & Yoder, D. E. (1992). Literacy learning of children with severe speech and physical impairments in school settings. *Seminars in Speech and Language, 12,* 4–15.

Koppenhaver, D., & Yoder, D. E. (1993). Classroom literacy instruction for children with severe speech and physical impairments (SSPI): What is and what might be. *Topics in Language Disorders, 13*(2), 1–15.

Light, J., Binger, C., & Kelford Smith, A. (1994). Story reading interactions between preschoolers who use AAC and their mothers. *Augmentative and Alternative Communication, 10,* 255–268.

Light, J., & Kelford-Smith, A. (1993). The home literacy experiences of preschoolers who use augmentative communication systems and of their nondisabled peers. *Augmentative and Alternative Communication, 9,* 10–25.

Light, J., & McNaughton, D. (1993). Literacy and augmentative and alternative communication: The expectations and priorities of parents and teachers. *Topics in Language Disorders, 13*(2), 33–46.

Lindamood, C. H., & Lindamood, P. (1998). *The Lindamood phoneme sequencing program for reading, spelling and speech.* Austin, TX: Pro-Ed.

Malone, S., & Arnove, R. (1998). *Planning learner-centred adult literacy programmes.* Paris: UNESCO, International Institute for Educational Planning.

McGinnis, J. S., & Beukelman, D. R. (1989). Vocabulary requirements for writing activities for the academically mainstreamed student with disabilities. *Augmentative and Alternative Communication, 5,* 183–191.

McNaughton, D., & Tawney, J. (1993). Comparison of two spelling instruction techniques for adults who use augmentative and alternative communication. *Augmentative and Alternative Communication, 9,* 72–82.

McNaughton, S. (1993). Graphic representational systems and literacy learning. *Topics in Language Disorders, 13*(2), 58–75.

McNaughton, S. (2002). What to look for on the literacy voyage. In K. Erickson, D. Koppenhaver, & D. E. Yoder (Eds.), *Waves of words: Augmented communicators read and write* (pp. 63–73). Toronto, Ontario, Canada: ISAAC Press.

Mirenda, P. (2003). "He's not really a reader . . .". Perspectives on supporting literacy development in individuals with autism. *Topics in Language Disorders, 23*(4), 271–282.

Moats, L. C. (1995). *Spelling development, disability, and instruction.* Baltimore: York Press.

Musselwhite, C. (1993). *RAPS: Reading activities project for older students.* Phoenix, AZ: Southwest Human Development.

Musselwhite, C., & King-DeBaun, P. (1997). *Emergent literacy success.* Birmingham, AL: Creative Communicating.

Nunes da Ponte, M. M. (2002). When I grow up, I want to help my mother at the shop. In K. Erickson, D. Koppenhaver, & D. E. Yoder (Eds.), *Waves of words: Augmented communicators read and write* (pp. 7–15). Toronto, Ontario, Canada: ISAAC Press.

Passy, J. (1990). *Cued articulation.* Hawthorn, Victoria: Australian Council for Educational Research.

Pebly, M. (2002). The education of a young man. . .and an educational system. In K. Erickson, D. Koppenhaver, & D. E. Yoder (Eds.), *Waves of words: Augmented communicators read and write* (pp. 79–86). Toronto, Ontario, Canada: ISAAC Press.

Phillips, L., Norris, S., & Mason, J. (1996). Longitudinal effects of early literacy concepts on reading achievement: A kindergarten intervention and five-year follow-up. *Journal of Literacy Research, 28,* 173–195.

Pierce, P. L., & McWilliam, P. J. (1993). Emerging literacy and children with severe speech and physical impairments: Issues and possible intervention strategies. *Topics in Language Disorders, 13*(2), 47–57.

Pressley, M. (2000). What should comprehension instruction be the instruction of? In M. Kamil, P. Mosenthal, D. Pearson, & R. Barr (Eds.), *Handbook of reading research* (pp. 545–562). London: Erlbaum.

Pumfrey, P. D., & Reason, R. (1991). *Specific learning difficulties: Challenges and responses.* Berks, UK: NFER-Nelson.

Rasinski, T., & Padak, N. (2000). *Effective reading strategies: Teaching children who find reading difficult* (2nd. ed.). Upper Saddle River, NJ: Merrill, Prentice Hall.

Seidenberg, M., & McClelland, J. L. (1989). A distributed, developmental model of word recognition and naming. *Psychological Review, 96,* 523–568.

Share, D. L. (1995). Phonological recoding and self-teaching: *Sine qua non* of reading acquisition. *Cognition, 55,* 151–218.

Smith, M., & Blischak, D. (1997). Literacy. In L. Lloyd, D. Fuller & H. Arvidson (Eds.), *Augmentative and alternative communication: principles and practices* (pp. 414–444). London: Allyn & Bacon.

Smith, J., & Warwick, B. E. (1997). *How children learn to write.* London: Paul Chapman Publishing.

Snow, C., Burns, M. S., & Griffin, P. E. (1998). *Preventing reading difficulties in young children.* Washington, DC: National Academy Press.

Snowball, D., & Bolton, F. (1999). *Spelling K-8, planning and teaching.* York, ME: Stenhouse.

Snowling, M. (2000). Language and literacy skills: Who is at risk and why? In D. V. M. Bishop & L. B. Leonard (Eds.), *Speech and language impairments in children* (pp. 245–260). Hove, East Sussex, UK: Psychology Press.

Stackhouse, J., & Wells, B. (1997). *Children's speech and literacy difficulties: A psycholinguistic framework.* London: Whurr.

Sulzby, E., & Teale, W. (1991). Emergent literacy. In R. Barr, M. Kamil, P. Mosenthal, & D. Pearson (Eds.), *Handbook of reading research* (Vol. 2, pp. 727–757). New York: Longman.

Tattershall, S. (2002). *Adolescents with language and learning needs: A shoulder to shoulder collaboration.* London: Singular Press.

Templeton, S. (2002, February 19th). Spelling: Logical, learnable—and critical. *The ASHA Leader,* 4–5, 12.

Templeton, S., & Morris, D. (2000). Spelling. In M. Kamil, P. Mosenthal, P. D. Pearson, & R. Barr (Eds.), *Handbook of reading research* (Vol. 3, pp. 525–543). Mawah, NJ: Erlbaum.

Torgesen, J. K., Wagner, D. A., Rashotte, C. A., & Hecht, S. S. (1997). Prevention and remediation of severe reading disabilities: keeping the end in mind. *Scientific studies of reading: Components of effective reading intervention*, *1*(1), 217–234.

Treiman, R., & Bourassa, D. (2000). The development of spelling skill. *Topics in Language Disorders*, *20*(3), 1–18.

Wershing, A., & Hughes, C. (2002). "Just give me words." In K. Erickson, D. Koppenhaver, & D. E. Yoder (Eds.), *Waves of words: Augmented communicators read and write* (pp. 45–56). Toronto, Ontario, Canada: ISAAC Press.

Wilkinson, L. C., & Silliman, E. (2000). Classroom language and literacy learning. In M. Kamil, P. Mosenthal, D. Pearson, & R. Barr (Eds.), *Handbook of reading research* (Vol. 3, pp. 337–360). London: Erlbaum.

Wolff Heller, K., Fredrick, L., Tumlin, J., & Brineman, D. (2002). Teaching decoding for generalisation using the Nonverbal Reading Approach. *Journal of Developmental & Physical Disabilities*, *14*(1), 19–35.

Yaden, D. B., Rowe, D., & MacGillivray, L. (2000). Emergent literacy: A matter (polyphony) of perspectives. In M. Kamil, P. Mosenthal, D. Pearson, & R. Barr (Eds.), *Handbook of reading research* (Vol. 3, pp. 425–454). London: Erlbaum.

Zutell, J. (1996). The Directed Spelling Thinking Activity (DSTA): Providing an effective balance in word study instruction. *The Reading Teacher*, *50*(2), 98–108.

CHAPTER 9

The Role of Technology

I. INTRODUCTION

Over the past few decades, the steady advance of technology in all aspects of life, including education, has been unrelenting and often breathtakingly rapid. In some respects, people with physical impairments have been major beneficiaries of these technological advances (Quist & Lloyd, 1997). Tasks that could not be performed independently have been made possible through the advent of sophisticated environmental control systems, switch-controlled powered mobility solutions, and switch-accessible communication devices. In *Waves of Words*, many of the individuals who use augmentative and alternative communication (AAC) and who have written about their successful literacy learning experience, refer to the positive outcomes deriving from a creative and persistent search for technological solutions to their difficulties (Gandell & Filippelli, 2002; Given, 2002; Hogan & Wolf, 2002; Wershing & Hughes, 2002).

However, the same technologies that have transformed apparently insurmountable tasks into relatively mundane routines have also pervaded all aspects

Literacy and Augmentative and Alternative Communication

of daily life. The "solutions" offered by technology come at a price (Quist & Lloyd, 1997). In many instances, the ability to read and write fluently is no longer adequate to cope with common tasks, such as managing money transactions, making travel arrangements, or looking up contact information. Other critical skills include computer and mouse use, navigation of on-screen menus, and the ability to sift through information rapidly to retrieve relevant elements. We all use an increasing variety of technological strategies to search, retrieve, and store information. The forms of the technologies change with extraordinary frequency, and the power and potential of technology seem equally volatile. In some respects, information has become increasingly accessible through the application of technology. On the other hand, the skills needed to access the information are also constantly changing and developing. As a consequence, what is meant by the term *being literate* has changed subtly, to include an element of computer literacy, text message literacy, and cellular phone literacy.

Leu (2000) proposed three views on the relationship between technology and literacy. The first is that technology changes literacy—what it means to be literate changes in response to the demands of technology. In the second view, literacy and technology are perceived to transact. Technology offers new opportunities for literacy experiences. As these opportunities are exploited, new potential literacy opportunities are identified, and technology is adapted and developed to meet what Leu described as new literacy envisionments. In the third view, the focus is on the rapid and continuous change in the forms and functions of literacy, both responding to but also driving rapidly changing technologies— literacy as *technological deixis* (Leu, 2000). In this last view, what is meant by "literacy" can only be interpreted in the context of the existing technologies, just as the meaning of the word "today" can only be interpreted with reference to the moment in time in which it is uttered.

It is as yet unclear how technology will continue to affect our understanding of literacy or what it means to be literate. In Leu's view, however, what is clear is that "the literacy of yesterday is not the literacy of today, and it will not be the literacy of tomorrow" (p. 744). What is also clear is that technology is now an integral part of the educational process, bringing with it dividends in terms of increased motivation, interest, enjoyment of schoolwork, task involvement persistence, time on task, and retention in school (Kamil, Intrator, & Kim, 2000). Harnessing these positive attributes to yield maximum benefits for those engaging in the process of learning to read and write is a challenge that is constantly changing. It would seem that computer-assisted instruction (CAI), that is, the application of computer-based tools to support learning, is here to stay.

In this chapter, the focus is on the potential uses of technology to support the development of literacy—recognizing that the concept of "literacy" is now irrevocably fluid and that for very many individuals it must include at least a passing nod to technological literacy. The goal within the chapter is not to provide a comprehensive overview of current technologies. Changes and developments occur so rapidly that such an endeavor would be doomed to failure. The focus here is on some general principles and uses of technology, with occasional reference to particular hardware or software applications. Organizations such as Closing the Gap, RESNA (Rehabilitation Engineering Society of North America), CAMA (Communication Aid Manufacturer's Association), ISAAC (International Society for Augmentative and Alternative Communication), and AAATE (Association for the Advancement of Assistive Technology in Europe) and education software catalogues and exhibits can be invaluable for those who need to keep abreast of developments of relevance to those who use AAC. As mentioned earlier, determining the appropriate use of technology requires careful assessment of individual short-term and long-term needs, including opportunities afforded to their typically developing peers and barriers experienced by the AAC user.

Smith and Blischak (1997) suggested that technology to support literacy—that is, computer hardware and software, as well as dedicated communication devices—can be divided into three broad categories. These include technology that provides opportunities for (a) early literacy experiences, (b) skill development, and (c) text composition, editing, and printing.

II. TOOLS TO SUPPORT EARLY LITERACY

For young children, technology can be used to promote emerging literacy and to support active participation in reading and writing experiences, as well as opportunities for interactive learning with peers (Steelman, Pierce, & Koppenhaver, 1993). Typically developing preschool children engage in emergent literacy experiences such as independent book handling, rhyming and alliterative songs and poems, alphabet learning, and writing/drawing activities. Providing similar opportunities for their peers who have motor difficulties may involve the use of both light and high technology such as switches, loop tapes, computers, synthetic speech output, enlarged keyboards, "touch" screens, and specialized software. Key goals are to maximize opportunities for early literacy experiences, to broaden the range of literacy experiences, and to promote independent access to these opportunities, including independence of choice to encourage self-directed literacy experiences.

For all children and adults, appropriate positioning and a comprehensive assessment of access possibilities are fundamental to the effective use of technology. It is imperative that a team consider the positioning and access solutions that will maximize availability for learning and the potential for active participation.

A. HARDWARE

The *hardware* used by young children can range from light technology, including communication boards and single-message voice output devices, to more sophisticated high-technology options, such as modified keyboards, touch screens, and computers. For some individuals, simple adaptations or modifications are sufficient to enable access. For example, the use of page tabs, page separators, and/or thickened pages may enable a child with limited upper limb dexterity to independently turn pages in a book. For other children, more sophisticated solutions may be needed, such as the use of switch-operated page turners or presentation of books in an alternative computer-based format. For example, favorite books can be scanned into a computer and reformatted into a PowerPoint™ presentation that can be independently accessed by means of a single switch to move through slides.

Independence of choice in literacy experiences can be supported through the provision of simple communication charts that include the names of possible book selections, modified to reflect changing preferences and possibilities. Similarly, simple messages to indicate a general desire to read a story are important. These messages (e.g., "I want a story now" or "Can I read now?") can easily be programmed into single-message speech generating devices, such as a BIG-mack™ or a Step-by-Step. In addition, they can be included in a graphic communication chart as single-symbol messages or programmed within an individual's general communication device. Providing access to speech output for these messages can be a powerful motivator. Devices that use digitized speech are particularly useful, because they can be easily and quickly programmed with any voice. Peers and siblings can be pulled into service, allowing age-appropriate voices to be used.

During storybook reading, typically developing children often comment and ask questions, later reenacting the story alone or with another child. One study (Yaden, Smolkin, & Conlon, 1989) cited by Snow, Burns, and Griffin (1998, p. 139) traced the storybook interactions of two preschooler children during parent-child reading activities and found that the preschoolers asked more than a thousand questions about print and books during these interactions. Unfortunately, these levels of active participation and these spontaneous uses of language are particularly difficult to provide for those who use AAC. However, technology can offer some possible solutions.

In general, two predictable types of communication can be anticipated in storybook reading. One type of predictable language is relatively generic and relates to the interaction surrounding storybook reading—the language needed to control and direct the reading experience. Messages such as "Let's change book," "Read it again," "Go back," "I want a turn," "What was that?," and other similar examples all offer some degree of power. These phrases allow children to direct their experiences as well as offering them the opportunity to participate actively in the interaction surrounding storybook reading. The second type of predictable language is book-specific, reflecting the specific focus or vocabulary of the book. This second type of language or communication varies in its overall strength of predictability, depending on the type of book. Some books contain highly predictable repeated lines, for example, "I'll huff and I'll puff and I'll blow your house down." These repeated lines could be programmed as single utterances into a speech generating device. In other early child storybooks, the predictable feature may be based on rhyme (e.g., "Come inside Mr. Bird said the mouse, I'll show you what there is in a People . . . house"). In this last case, a range of single words can be preprogrammed into speech generating devices or displayed on graphic communication displays. In yet other books, although overall vocabulary can be identified and programmed for voice output or displayed on a communication board, there is less predictability about how that vocabulary may be used. A useful strategy is to include both control utterances and book-specific vocabulary, so that a child is offered opportunities to communicate about both the process of story reading and the content of individual stories.

Voice output devices can also be used for messages and vocabulary to support a broad variety of play and imaginative experiences, as a follow-up to reading a story. Reenactment of stories that have been read has been found to support literacy development (Snow *et al.*, 1998) as well as the development of narrative-related spoken language skills.

B. SOFTWARE

Software, or computer programs, for young children can be used to support skill development, to increase access to storybook experiences, or to facilitate early writing experiences. Skill development solutions are discussed in more detail in Section III, and so the discussion here focuses on storybook and early writing experiences. Snow *et al.* (1998) have cautioned that software can promote learning only to the extent that it engages students' attention—"yet software that engages students' attention may or may not promote learning . . . to date a great deal of educational software design is a commercial art rather than an instructional science; it needs to be both." Selection of appropriate software requires consideration of the educational goals, the strengths and needs of the individual, and the match between these features and the potential of any individual program. Steelman *et al.* (1993) outlined several features that can be used to guide software selection, regardless of the age group in focus. In their view, software should

1. Be easy to use
2. Come with clear documentation
3. Be flexible, allowing for individual modification
4. Be interactive, so that the format can be altered in response to student input
5. Support the classroom curriculum
6. Be interesting to students
7. Be appropriate to student age and abilities
8. Support easy record keeping to track progress
9. Be multimedia based (e.g., should use graphics and synthetic speech)

These features should apply to software that is relevant across all stages of literacy development, from early emergent literacy experience to sophisticated word processing and publishing packages.

1. Talking Storybooks

Talking storybooks are hypermedia texts with digitized pronunciations of words and larger textual units (see Table 9.1 for some examples). Many talking storybooks also include animation and other features such as highlighting of text as it is read and "hidden activities" within a page. They can be used across a range of different skill levels, from beginning apprentice readers to those who are moving toward fluency in reading. Early readers may pay little attention to the text features and focus primarily on the images or activities embedded within the story and the spoken narrative and oral language. More advanced readers may split their focus across the spoken and written information, while attending also to the visual images.

Talking storybooks have a broad appeal, and many have been designed to improve comprehension and reduce decoding difficulties. Their effectiveness in this respect has not yet been fully explored, because much of the research has focused largely on age groups (8 years and older) in whom comprehension and

Table 9.1

Examples of Talking Storybooks

Talking books
Storytime software (www.creativecommunicating.com)
Living Books Series™/Broderbund/Softkey (The Learning Company)
Little Critter™ (Mercer Mayer)
IBM's Stories
Clicker Books™ (Crick Software)
Oxford Reading Tree™ Talking Stories

decoding difficulties might not be expected to dominate (Leu, 2000). However, with cognizance of this limitation, the existing research suggests that multimedia tools such as talking storybooks have real potential for supporting reading development. Both comprehension and decoding ability may increase when children can access digitized speech support, although it is not clear how these two factors relate to each other (Leu, 2000). Kamil *et al.* (2000) suggested that the dynamic images in hypermedia or multimedia texts may be excellent for mental model building and therefore offer important support for story comprehension. Drawing on Paivio's (1986) dual coding theory, they also proposed that the dual stimuli presented in talking storybooks (dynamic visual images and auditory feedback through speech synthesis) may lay down two complementary memory traces, and these dual traces may be an important support for learning. However, although there is a growing body of evidence to testify to the effectiveness of using multimedia tools to support both comprehension and the development of decoding skills, the mechanisms underpinning this effectiveness are still poorly understood.

2. Supporting Early Writing

Technology may also be invaluable in providing opportunities for early drawing and writing experiences for AAC users—a challenging, yet critical, aspect of literacy development. Low-technology adaptations such as splints may allow a child to hold a crayon or paintbrush independently. The use of fingerpaints, rubber stamps, felt or magnetic boards, or other unconventional drawing/writing materials (e.g., shaving cream) offers an alternative means of making writing and drawing accessible. Children who have severe physical difficulties may be limited to experiencing writing in a more indirect manner, by using switch-activated or touch screen software to draw, select graphic symbols (e.g., cartoon figures or orthography), and compose lists of simple word/picture stories using talking word processing software. Like early reading experiences, drawing and writing activities may be used as part of an interactive group project (e.g., writing a language experience story after a cooking activity) or for independent exploration (King-DeBaun, 1990).

III. TOOLS TO SUPPORT SKILL DEVELOPMENT

A. Young Children

Young children entering the alphabetic stage of reading and writing must acquire a range of different skills, some of which are needed to use technology and others that are related more directly to literacy acts. Some of these skills are

Table 9.2

A Summary of Some of the Skills Relevant for Young Children

1. Technology access skills:
    i. The ability to orient to an item of technology
    ii. Consistent motor responses, either for direct selection or for switch use
    ii. For those using indirect selection, understanding of scanning and the ability to reliably and consistently generate a motor response to make a selection
2. Print-related skills
    i. Visual skills of scanning a visual array, scanning from left to right; discrimination of perceptually similar letter and word shapes
    ii. Recognition of letters and the ability to locate letters within an array
    iii. Recognition of simple words
3. Phonological awareness skills
    i. The ability to recognize and generate phonological forms related either by rhyming units or by letter onset
    ii. Consistent phoneme–grapheme correspondence and the ability to identify and generate items by initial phoneme
    iii. The ability to analyze the sounds within words, and to manipulate sounds within words to generate new or similar words
4. Reading skills
    i. An understanding of the range, forms, and functions of print
    ii. The ability to participate actively in storybook reading and to relate to elements within the story
    iii. The development of an early sight-word lexicon
    iv. Early decoding skills—the ability to identify sounds in simple words and use context to guide informed guesses about the word
5. Writing skills
    i. The ability to generate individual letters
    ii. Early spelling—the ability to select and sequence letters based on phonological analysis of target words
    iii. The ability to generate linguistic structures as the context of written materials
    iv. An understanding of the range, form, and functions of print as a communicative medium

summarized in Table 9.2 and include those related to (a) technology access, (b) visual skills, (c) print-related skills, (d) reading skills, and (e) writing skills. These skill areas are reviewed briefly together in this section, and a few suggestions for possible software applications are outlined in Table 9.3. As stated earlier, these suggestions are limited and are likely to be outdated within a very short time.

Before the potential of technology can be harnessed to support development of literacy or other knowledge domains, there are skills related to technology use that must be acquired (see the earlier discussion). These skills may include attention to a visual display, skill in use of a switch to access a computer or a voice output device, the ability to use scanning to make selections, visual skills of scanning and processing information on-screen, and computer functions such as deleting selections or accessing voice output feedback. Often with young

Table 9.3

Software Applications to Support Skill Development in Young Children

Access skills, switch use, visual skills, and scanning

Inclusive Technology
Abrakadabra
Build It
Happy Duck
Hey Presto!
Ooops!
Spider series
Step by Step
Switch It! Series
Touch!
Touch Balloons

Don Johnston
Switch Basics
SimTech Software
UkanDu™ Switches, Too!

Early reading skills

Edmark
Let's Go Read!™
Bailey's Book House
Stanley's Sticker Stories

Edmark-Iona

Muppets—Beginning to Read
Muppets—Read, Listen & Learn

Don Johnston
A Day at Play™
BuildAbility™
Earobics™
Out & About™
Start-to-Finish™

Inclusive Technology
From Word to Word
Learn More About Words
Making Sense with Words

Crick

Clicker Books
All My Words

Early Writing Skills

SEMERC
Face Paint 2
Smart Alex
Doodle Plus (simple art)

Table 9.3 *(Continued)*

Widgit
FirstKeys 2
Inter_Comm™
Making Tracks to Literacy
Writing with Symbols 2000™

Inclusive Technology
Inclusive Writer™

Crick

All My Words™
Clicker 4™
Clicker 4™ Resources
ClozePro™

Don Johnston
WordMaker™
Simon Spells™

Suggestions here are drawn from a range of resources and catalogs with particular help from Ann Jackson, Central Remedial Clinic, Dublin, Ireland.

children, it is not clear what the preferred mode of access will be. Direct selection is the most efficient and fastest form of input and so is likely to be the preferred solution, if motor skills permit (Quist & Lloyd, 1997). Considerable practice may be needed before it becomes clear whether the child's motor skills are sufficiently reliable and consistent to support direct access and also whether this is a realistic solution from the point of view of physical fatigue. For indirect access, with the use of a single or multiple switches and determination of the most appropriate scanning options, substantial amounts of practice and trial time may be needed for clear indicators of the optimal choice for each child. Although these skills may not be perceived as being direct literacy skills, they nonetheless are key *gate skills* if technology is to be functionally useful as a support for literacy development.

Other skills relate more directly to the process of reading and writing. Reading requires careful attention to visual information and recognition of visual patterns, both at the level of single letters and single words. (Of course, functional reading also requires a range of other linguistic and cognitive skills.) Writing involves skills in the production or selection of letters and words and the generation of linguistic content onto which these selections are mapped. Keyboard skills, including the ability to consistently locate letters within an array, are also important.

There are many software programs that support skill development in each of these areas. If a new skill is to be developed, it can be helpful to select activities that focus specifically on that task and that do not require attention across a range of other skills areas also. For example, if a child is learning to follow a scanning system on a computer screen, the content of what is being scanned should be well within his or her competence. Trying to establish both letter recognition and scanning control simultaneously within the one activity may represent a task overload for the child and may also make it impossible for the interventionist to establish where any difficulty lies. However, it is equally important that the availability of particular software options to support skill development does not obscure the overriding principle that skill development is only one small component in learning to read and write and that at all times every effort must be made to create meaningful, interactive, and authentic (Rasinski & Padak, 2000) literacy learning experiences.

B. OLDER CHILDREN

Children at the upper ends of the primary education range or moving into early second-level education (i.e., aged 8 to 13 years) may still be at the very early stages of literacy development or alternatively may be consolidating literacy skills and building fluency in their reading and writing. It is likely that both skill development and the process of reading and writing will continue to require attention for this age group. Many of the suggestions outlined earlier for younger children remain appropriate. However, for skill development, alternative software may be needed to reflect their older age. Some suggestions are made in Table 9.4.

When the focus is on consolidation of reading and writing and developing fluency, frequent and regular practice and opportunities for self-directed literacy activities are crucial. At this stage, the integration of reading and writing is particularly important, and a key focus must be on encouraging students to write. Reluctant writers can be offered many supports. One strategy can be to experiment with fonts to find the font that is best suited to individual students. Increasing the font size means that less effort is required to fill a page (Jackson, 2002), and this can be motivating for students. By using a package such as Clicker 4™, elements of the target text or story can be provided for the student, so that the task is sequencing the elements in the correct order, expanding on individual elements or events within a story, or filling in gaps in a story line. Further suggestions to promote writing skills, particularly for reluctant students, are included in Table 9.5.

Table 9.4

Some Software Suggestions for Older Children

Reading

PowerPoint™

Crick
Clicker 4™

Sherston
Oxford Reading Tree™—Stages 3–5

Don Johnston
Start-to-Finish™

Writing

Microsoft Word™

Words+
EZ Keys™

Crick
Clicker 4™
ClozePro™
Penfriend™
PredictAbility™
Wordbar™

Don Johnston
Co:Writer™ 4000
Write:OutLoud™

Widgit
Writing with Symbols 2000™

Sensory Software
The Grid™

The Learning Company
Storybook Weaver™ Deluxe 2004

Publishing and Planning

Don Johnston
Draft Builder™

Inspiration Software
Communicate: In Print™
Inspiration™
Kidspiration™

Table 9.5

Suggestions to Promote Writing Skills Using Computers

- Give student a title and short paragraph to stimulate ideas.
- Use an interesting picture from ClipArt or Google Images scanned into a program.
- Use a series of very short sentences for students to expand.
- Present a paragraph of concise text for a student to expand, while retaining the overall meaning. Reverse the process.
- Specifically address the text demands of different formats, such as essay writing or answering questions.
- Develop strategies for organizing written pieces:
  - Write down ideas (Inspiration™ may be particularly helpful at this stage).
  - Expand into sentences.
  - Punctuate.
  - Check spelling (speech synthesis may be particularly helpful, as well as built-in spellcheckers in the program).
  - Proofread (speech synthesis may be particularly helpful, as well as built-in spell-checkers in the program).
  - Save or print.
- Teach as many features of the word processing program as are needed to support high-quality text.
- Use speech feedback if quality is acceptable.

Adapted from Jackson, A. (2002, March 1). *Software for pupils with special educational needs.* Paper presented at the ISAAC Ireland: Technology and AAC Conference, Dublin, Ireland.

C. Adults

As with older students, one of the main requirements for adults is the need to find materials that are appropriate for their age and experience. The range of software for adults with limited literacy skills is less extensive than that for children, and interventionists may need to be creative and innovative in finding solutions that can be integrated into existing software options. To provide experience with texts, a wide range of books are available as audio recordings on CD or tape. Alternatively, favorite texts such as poems, short stories, or news events can be recorded onto tape or minidisk for independent playback. These texts can then be used for both reading and writing practice, at single word, sentence, paragraph, or chapter levels, using packages such as Clicker 4™, Co:Writer™ 4000™, Grid™, EZKeys™, Microsoft PowerPoint™, and Microsoft Word™. The National Adult Literacy Association in Ireland, in association with well-established fiction authors such as Roddy Doyle, Marian Keyes, and Dermot Bolger, have developed a series of high-quality books specifically for adults learning to read and write. The content and focus of each of the books are appropriate for adults. However, the language used is simple and carefully graded in terms of levels of difficulty. Work currently in progress with adults who use AAC (Smith, 2004) suggests that the books are of high interest value and quickly harness motivation. Because the authors are well known and are likely to be read by age peers, there is a degree of prestige associated with using their work. Vocabulary demands are relatively low, with a large proportion of high-use words occurring, supporting the development of a sight word vocabulary. The books are interesting to read and are also interesting to write about. Selected segments from the texts can be used for specific practice in sentence construction, cloze tasks, paraphrasing, summarizing, and predicting or for related free discussion. These activities can be embedded into software packages as outlined earlier. It is likely that similar initiatives have been undertaken in other regions. Adult literacy services can be invaluable sources of support and information for resources and materials.

IV. TEXT PREPARATION AND PRODUCTION

Before the advent of computers, providing direct access to writing for those with significant physical involvement was extremely difficult. We can look back in wonder at the efforts and achievements of individuals such as Christy Brown, who labored initially to draw letters with chalk held between his toes and subsequently typed using a head-stick (Brown, 1954). Technology has not provided perfect solutions or made writing either easy or independently accessible for all individuals (Nolan, 1987). Nonetheless, word processing capabilities, in combination with developments in access technologies have greatly increased the opportunities and possibilities for text generation, even for those with extremely limited motor control. Two topics are covered briefly in this section: (a) the use of technology in rate enhancement and (b) text prediction facilities.

A. RATE ENHANCEMENT

Rate enhancement techniques are designed to eliminate or save keystrokes in generating novel messages in conversation and in text composition and, hence, reduce demands on the user's time and physical energy. Some of the more common techniques include (a) semantic encoding (Baker, 1982), (b) abbreviation expansion, and (c) text prediction (e.g., Newell, Arnott, Booth, & Beattie, 1992).

Semantic encoding involves associating multiple meanings with graphic symbols called icons (Quist & Lloyd, 1997). A restricted range of multiple meaning icons can be combined in a wide range of combinations to uniquely associate with prestored vocabulary or communicative messages. Complete utterances can be accessed using a unique two-icon sequence, or novel utterances can be constructed word-by-word, with each word accessed through its own unique icon sequence. Whereas *hospital* might require a total of 16 keystrokes for an individual typing each letter using a single-switch scanning system, the same item could be retrieved in four or even two keystrokes by the same individual using semantic encoding, which represents a significant rate enhancement.

Abbreviation expansion uses typical or idiosyncratic abbreviations to code full words (Quist & Lloyd, 1997). Abbreviations have become extremely commonplace, and in fact normative, with the growth in popularity of text messaging. Software can be configured to recognize an individual's abbreviations and to automatically send the expanded version to a display or to speech synthesis. So, for example, the abbreviation "h-s-p-l" may expand to "hospital," again representing a significant saving in time and energy for the individual selecting letters individually.

B. Text Prediction

Text prediction (also known as lexical prediction or word prediction) and word completion have come to be used synonymously in discussions of rate enhancement. However, as has been pointed out (Klund & Novak, 2001), this confusion masks organizational differences in how words are predicted. In word completion, once an initial letter has been typed, the software offers a list of words that could potentially be the target, based on the letters typed. As more letters are added, the list is modified and refined to offer plausible options. For example, if the letter "d" is typed, a list might include "daddy," "dark," "dinner," and "dog." With the selection of "i," the list is modified automatically to "dig," "dinner," "disk," and "dish" and with the selection of "v," again only appropriate words are offered (e.g., "divide," "division," and "divisive"). Thus, the word "division" could be retrieved through a three-step process. Word prediction, as defined by Klund and Novak (2001), is based on similar principles and a list of words is again offered after an initial selection has been made. However, in word prediction, the words offered as possible targets can be based on spelling, frequency of word usage, word recency, association, and grammar. For example, after selection of the word "the," the options offered may include only nouns, or only nouns that have occurred recently, or a list based on a combination of initial letter, recency, and grammatical status.

The use of word prediction can yield significant keystroke savings (Higginbotham, 1992; Klund & Novak, 2001; Newell *et al.*, 1992). However, it is important to bear in mind that keystroke savings are only one measure of efficiency of text generation (Klund & Novak, 2001; Smith & Blischak, 1997). Those using word prediction must visually search a list of words and decide whether the list contains the desired word. This also involves perceptual demands, shifting gaze and focus from one section of a screen to another and back again. Non-target words within the list may distract the writer and disrupt the flow of thought. There are increased cognitive demands, both in terms of memory requirements and the demands of guiding the overall activity, and these increased demands may work against acceleration for some individuals (Levine, Gauger, Bowers, & Khan, 1986; Venkatagiri, 1993). Klund and Novak (2001) concluded that even though there may be demonstrable keystroke savings with the use of word prediction, there is not always an improvement in overall text generation or rate, because of the other associated increased demands. However, consistent practice with word prediction may go a long way to developing strategies to cope with the additional processing and cognitive demands. The reduced number of keystrokes required may reduce physical fatigue levels and thereby make it possible for individuals to work for longer in greater comfort. This potential for increased practice time may not only yield benefits in familiarity with the word prediction software, but also may have spillover benefits to all aspects of writing skills, including spelling (MacArthur, 1998b, 2000) and grammatical skills (Morris, Newell, Booth, Ricketts, & Arnott, 1992).

In summary, the evidence to date suggests that text prediction can be a powerful support for literacy engagement and for many aspects of literacy skill development. However, the effects may be unique to each individual user and may reflect their own individual characteristics and skill mix, as well as "the costs versus benefits of using word prediction, and the characteristics of the word prediction system itself" (Klund & Novak, 2001). Further information is needed about the efficacy of using text prediction in increasing length or quality of writing, as well as a deeper understanding of the learning styles and specific challenges that are best addressed through these programs (MacArthur, 1998a). Some of the studies reported, including those by MacArthur, used text prediction systems that also incorporated voice output or speech synthesis. In the next section, we look more specifically at the role of voice output in supporting literacy development.

V. THE ROLE OF VOICE OUTPUT

There is an intuitive appeal to the concept that provision of speech output should support all aspects of literacy development. Provision of voice output may increase motivation to generate expressive output generally and hence lay the foundation of support for expressive language skills. More specifically, provision of voice output yields direct access to speech signals that can serve as a source for phonological analysis. Preliminary evidence indeed suggests that access to voice output may have positive effects on literacy development, not only for those with congenital speech and physical impairments (Foley & Pollatsek, 1999) but also for those with learning disabilities (Basil & Reyes, 2003; MacArthur, 1998a, 1998b, 2000) and with autism (Blischak & Schlosser, 2003). However, not all those who have access to voice output seem to reap these positive benefits, (Smith, 2001), suggesting that the role(s) played by voice output are complex and possibly influenced by levels of literacy skills.

Several studies have explored the impact of voice output in supporting the development of spelling. It is easy to see why having access to voice output might support analysis of spelling attempts, provide direct feedback on accuracy of attempts, and allow independent review of attempted modifications of spellings. In addition, it is not hard to imagine that spelling errors might become a source of great amusement, and hence motivating, again encouraging active exploration of letter-sound relationships. A small number of studies (Koke & Neilson, 1987; McNaughton & Tawney, 1993) have indicated positive effects on overall learning, when access to synthetic speech is provided. Again, however, results from research are equivocal. Schlosser and Blischak (cited in Blischak & Schlosser, 2003) explored the impact of voice output on the spelling learning of four students with autism. They contrasted progress in spelling learning across three conditions: (a) speech feedback only; (b) print feedback only; and (c) speech and print feedback. All four students reached the criterion in each of the three conditions. For three of the students, the most rapid progress was noted with conditions for which print was available as a source of feedback (i.e., condition b or c). For the other student, feedback conditions that incorporated speech (conditions a and c) yielded more rapid progress. Blischak and Schlosser concluded that, notwithstanding an overall advantage for learning in contexts in which there is access to multiple sources of information, individual differences in cognitive style and stage of literacy development may be influential in determining the "value" of speech feedback in supporting spelling.

In summary, the evidence to date highlights the potential importance of voice output in supporting many aspects of literacy development. However, the mechanisms underpinning the effects of voice output are as yet poorly understood. Individual differences remain central to effective intervention planning.

VI. THE WORLD WIDE WEB

One of the revolutions of the last decade has been the explosion in access to the World Wide Web. In a very short time, the Web has changed the way we communicate with each other, search for, store, and send information and materials, plan and arrange our holidays, buy our groceries and books, browse for clothes, monitor our finances, and educate our students. The continuing spread of the scope of the Internet has extraordinary potential for individuals whose mobility, access to independent shopping and planning, and communication with others are otherwise limited. As chronicled in personal accounts of adults who use AAC (Gandell & Filippelli, 2002; Wershing & Hughes, 2002), the potential of the Internet to harness motivation and to provide a forum for genuine exploration and communication is exciting. On the other hand, the challenges of optimizing the learning environment represented by the Internet are also significant. The wide range of additional skills required to effectively use the Internet extends far beyond mere reading and writing ability.

For many individuals, being able to use the Internet is a primary motivator driving interest in developing and refining literacy skills. The opportunities afforded by email for communication with a wide range of individuals are almost limitless. Messages can be prepared in advance and then sent in "real time," creating a relatively even playing field for all those able to compose a message, regardless of their physical abilities. Increasingly, research is focusing on applications to allow symbol-based messages to be easily translated to text-based format, regardless of the symbol format, thus breaking down former barriers and operational difficulties. The challenge for educators is to find mechanisms and strategies by which access to the vast potential of the Internet can be made available to those using AAC. As pointed out by Leu (2000), no new technology is entirely value free. The degree to which a new technology or application is integrated into existing educational practices is determined in part by the values and practices of the teacher and the organization into which it is placed. Teachers adopt technologies that fit existing practices (Leu, 2000). In many respects we are at the start of the Internet road for those who use AAC. It is likely to be an exciting journey, one probably vulnerable to errors and false starts on all sides but nonetheless worth pursuing.

VII. WHAT KIND OF LITERACY?

This chapter started with a consideration of the impact of technology on our understanding of literacy itself. We return briefly to this topic here and consider some of the remaining challenges and questions. The question "What kind of literacy?" echoes the themes discussed in the first section. The pervasive influence of technology on all aspects of our education and of our daily lives means that we may need to redefine our educational goals and our outcomes to reflect this change. Technology may simultaneously be used to support literacy development through computer-assisted learning and at the same time to create new literacy challenges, implicit in the use of the technology itself.

The rapid pace of change in technology creates problems on many fronts—not the least of which is the challenge for all those working with people who use AAC to stay abreast of relevant developments. A second problem is that

Table 9.6

Educational Strategies for Integrating Technology

- Ensure that the software and peripherals (access devices) meet the needs and abilities of the student. Ensure that positioning and seating requirements have been addressed through team involvement.
- The positioning of equipment needs careful monitoring. Computer components need to be at the correct height and in an appropriate position for use by the student. Devices need to be securely anchored at all times. Communication devices need to be accessible for use at all times.
- Care should be taken that students using special equipment are not isolated from peers and regular classroom activities for long periods of time.
- Physical fatigue levels should be carefully monitored.
- Systematic training is essential for successful use of all technology.
- Plan a realistic timetable for computer use for students—for both individual and group work. Regular short periods are usually most effective.
- Make new activities as "single-task" as possible.
- Group computer activities involving students of mixed abilities can be useful for language development and to encourage social skills.
- Make sure that programs with speech or sound and print output can be accommodated within the educational environment.
- Choose software on the basis of specific educational/therapeutic value, rather than on popular appeal and marketing. Base choice on needs and not on what is available.
- Use supplementary resources and materials (worksheets, pictures, and paper materials) with many programs. Many effective programs are content-free and text, pictures, and words lists must be inserted and tailored to the individual student.
- Use computer programs to supplement other methods of teaching and learning.
- "High-tech" solutions are not always recommended or needed.
- Regular review of use of the computer and software with students is essential.

Adapted from Jackson, A. (2002, March 1). *Software for pupils with special educational needs.* Paper presented at the ISAAC Ireland: Technology and AAC Conference, Dublin, Ireland.

technology often changes faster than we can effectively evaluate its utility for literacy and learning (Leu, 2000). Despite all the advances, some relatively basic problems remain. Reading at a computer screen is less comfortable than reading from a printed page, as well as being slower and less efficient, at least for those who have developed skills in both formats (Kamil *et al.*, 2000). The questions of the cost effectiveness of computers for teaching literacy and the aspects of reading and writing that benefit most from CAI are only now being explored in detail (Kamil *et al.*, 2000; Leu, 2000).

Of central importance in the discussion of technology and its role in literacy and literacy learning is the role of instruction and education. Technology is a tool, albeit a tool with potentially immense power. However, it is not a replacement for instruction (Williams, 2002). Some suggestions for integrating technology as an educational tool are outlined in Table 9.6. As pointed out by Jackson (2002), technology is unlikely to solve all of a student's problems or indeed those of the educationalist! The final impact of computer-assisted learning or assistive technology is likely to reflect the nature of instruction and feedback that accompanies use of the technology at least as much as the efficacy of the technology itself.

VIII. SUMMARY AND CONCLUSIONS

In this chapter, consideration has been given to the many roles technology can play in supporting the development of literacy in children and adults who use AAC. An over-riding theme has been the need to use technology as a tool to support increased active participation in literacy experiences across individuals of all age levels. Although advances in technology proceed at an extraordinarily rapid pace, it is important that our attention remains focused also on advancing our understanding of the processes of learning to read and write. Only this dual focus will allow us to harness the power of technological developments to meet functional literacy outcomes that include technological literacy for those who use AAC.

REFERENCES

Baker, B. (1982). Minspeak™: A semantic compaction system that makes self-expression easier for communicatively disabled individuals. *Byte, 7,* 186–202.

Basil, C., & Reyes, S. (2003). Acquisition of literacy skills by children with severe disability. *Child Language Teaching and Therapy, 19*(1), 27–48.

Blischak, D., & Schlosser, R. (2003). Use of technology to support independent spelling by students with autism. *Topics in Language Disorders, 23*(4), 293–304.

Brown, C. (1954). *My left foot.* London: Secker and Warburg.

Foley, B. E., & Pollatsek, A. (1999). Phonological processing and reading abilities in adolescents and adults with severe congenital speech impairments. *Augmentative and Alternative Communication, 15,* 156–173.

Gandell, T., & Filippelli, F. (2002). Face-to-face, computer-to-computer: Telecommunications in adult literacy. In K. Erickson, D. Koppenhaver, & D. E. Yoder (Eds.), *Waves of words: Augmented communicators read and write* (pp. 105–114). Toronto, Ontario, Canada: ISAAC Press.

Given, F. (2002). From sentence construction to thesis writing. In K. Erickson, D. Koppenhaver, & D. E. Yoder (Eds.), *Waves of words: Augmented communicators read and write* (pp. 121–127). Toronto, Ontario, Canada: ISAAC Press.

Higginbotham, D. J. (1992). Evaluation of keystroke savings across five assistive communication technologies. *Augmentative and Alternative Communication, 8*(4), 258–272.

Hogan, N., & Wolf, L. (2002). "i Amam a writer": Literacy, strategic thinking and metacognitive awareness. In K. Erickson, D. Koppenhaver, & D. E. Yoder (Eds.), *Waves of words: Augmented communicators read and write* (pp. 21–40). Toronto, Ontario, Canada: ISAAC Press.

Jackson, A. (2002, March 1). *Software for pupils with special educational needs.* Paper presented at the ISAAC Ireland: Technology and AAC Conference, Dublin, Ireland.

Kamil, M., Intrator, S., & Kim, H. (2000). The effects of other technologies on literacy and literacy learning. In M. Kamil, P. Mosenthal, D. Pearson, & R. Barr (Eds.), *Handbook of reading research* (Vol. 3, pp. 771–788). London: Erlbaum.

King-DeBaun, P. (1990). *Storytime: Stories, symbols and emergent literacy activities for young special needs children.* Acworth, GA: Pati King-DeBaun.

Klund, J., & Novak, M. (2001, May). *If word prediction can help, which program do you choose?* Retrieved January 15, 2004, from http://trace.wisc.edu/docs/wordprediction2001/.

Koke, S., & Neilson, J. (1987). *The effects of auditory feedback on the spelling of nonspeaking physically disabled individuals.* University of Toronto, Toronto, CA.

Leu, D. (2000). Literacy and technology: Deictic consequences for literacy education in an information age. In M. Kamil, P. Mosenthal, D. Pearson, & R. Barr (Eds.), *Handbook of reading research* (Vol. 3, pp. 743–770). London: Erlbaum.

Levine, S. P., Gauger, J. R., Bowers, L. D., & Khan, K. J. (1986). A comparison of mouthstick and Mores code text inputs. *Augmentative and Alternative Communication, 2,* 51–55.

MacArthur, C. A. (1998a). From illegible to understandable: How word recognition and speech synthesis can help. *Teaching Exceptional Children, 30*(3), 66–73.

MacArthur, C. A. (1998b). Word processing with speech synthesis and word prediction: Effects on the dialogue journal writing of students with learning disabilities. *Learning Disability Quarterly, 21,* 151–166.

MacArthur, C. A. (2000). New tools for writing: Assistive technology for students with writing difficulties. *Topics in Language Disorders, 20*(4), 85–100.

McNaughton, D., & Tawney, J. (1993). Comparison of two spelling instruction techniques for adults who use augmentative and alternative communication. *Augmentative and Alternative Communication, 9,* 72–82.

Morris, C., Newell, A., Booth, L., Ricketts, I., & Arnott, J. (1992). Syntax PAL: A system to improve the written syntax of language-impaired users. *Assistive Technology, 4*(2), 51–59.

Newell, A., Arnott, J., Booth, L., & Beattie, W. (1992). Effect of the "PAL" word prediction system on the quality and quantity of text generation. *Augmentative and Alternative Communication, 8*(4), 304–311.

Nolan, C. (1987). *Under the eye of the clock: The life story of Christopher Nolan.* New York: St Martins' Press.

Paivio, A. (1986). *Mental representations: A dual coding approach.* Oxford, UK: Oxford University Press.

Quist, R., & Lloyd, L. L. (1997). Principles and uses of technology. In L. L. Lloyd, D. Fuller, & H. Arvidson (Eds.), *Augmentative and alternative communication: A handbook of principles and practices* (pp. 107–126). Boston: Allyn & Bacon.

Rasinski, T., & Padak, N. (2000). *Effective reading strategies: Teaching children who find reading difficult* (2nd. ed.). Upper Saddle River, NJ: Merrill, Prentice Hall.

Smith, M. (2001). Literacy challenges for individuals with severe congenital speech impairments. *International Journal of Disability, Development and Education, 48,* 331–353.

Smith, M., & Blischak, D. (1997). Literacy. In L. Lloyd, D. Fuller, & H. Arvidson (Eds.), *Augmentative and alternative communication: Principles and practices* (pp. 414–444). London: Allyn & Bacon.

Snow, C., Burns, M. S., & Griffin, P. E. (1998). *Preventing reading difficulties in young children.* Washington, DC: National Academy Press.

Steelman, J. D., Pierce, P. L., & Koppenhaver, D. (1993). The role of computers in promoting literacy in children with severe speech and physical impairments. *Topics in Language Disorders, 13*(2), 76–88.

Venkatagiri, H. S. (1993). Efficiency of lexical prediction as a communication acceleration technique. *Augmentative and Alternative Communication, 9,* 161–167.

Wershing, A., & Hughes, C. (2002). "Just give me words." In K. Erickson, D. Koppenhaver, & D. E. Yoder (Eds.), *Waves of words: Augmented communicators read and write* (pp. 45–56). Toronto, Ontario, Canada: ISAAC Press.

Smith, M. (2004). A literacy intervention program for adults who use augmentative and alternative communication. Manuscript in preparation.

Williams, S. (2002). How speech-feedback and word-prediction software can help students write. *Teaching Exceptional Children, 34*(3), 72–78.

Yaden, D. B., Smolkin, L. B., & Conlon, A. (1989). Preschoolers' questions about pictures, print convention, and story text during reading aloud at home. *Reading Research Quarterly, 24*(2), 188–214.

CHAPTER 10

Planning the Way Forward

I. Introduction
II. Looking Back
III. Looking Forward
    A. Building Practice
    B. Setting an Agenda for Research
IV. Summary and Conclusions

I. INTRODUCTION

The final chapter in any book is traditionally one in which the reader is encouraged to reflect on the journey traveled and to consider where the next journey might lead. In earlier chapters in this book (Chapters 1 to 3), consideration was given to the nature of the processes of reading and writing and how young children engage with these processes. Through their engagement with the task of learning to read and write, children's construct of language and perhaps even of the processes underlying their language systems undergo revision and modification. The journey from apprentice to expert reader-writer extends over many years. It could be argued that it is a journey that is never complete—that the richness of literature awaiting the reader and writer means that it *can* never be fully complete.

Learning to read and write has significance not only for the individual but also for society. In its written form, language becomes available for inspection, for argumentation, for dispute, and for arbitration. The journey toward expertise in reading and writing is fraught with challenges for individuals who use augmentative and alternative communication (AAC). Over the last decade and a half, we have come some way in understanding the extent of those challenges, as outlined in Chapter 4. We are, however, still at the early stages in understanding the nature of the challenges and the best strategies to use to overcome these challenges. In Chapters 5 through 9, some suggestions were made about principles and practices underpinning the journey toward literacy with individuals who use AAC. A key step in this process must be effective assessment. This process requires input from a range of team members and must allow consideration of both the intrinsic resources an AAC user brings to the learning process and also the external influences on that learning process: instructional focus and effectiveness; environmental support for literacy development; and expectations for success.

This final chapter starts with a review of some of our early understandings of how severe physical and speech difficulties might affect the acquisition of literacy skills. The potential for future developments is then considered briefly. Finally, development within any field of activity is best guided by well-designed research. Possible areas for research focus are considered in the final section.

II. LOOKING BACK

We can look back in awe at the achievements of the many individuals who use AAC and who overcame almost insurmountable barriers in their quest for literacy. Until almost the 1980s, there was a common perception that physical impairments inevitably were associated with cognitive impairments. This perceived association in turn led to a conclusion that any chance of progress in learning to read and write was precluded, so that many individuals were not afforded even the opportunity to attempt to learn. A second prevailing myth in many quarters was that an inability to speak intelligibly was, as a necessary consequence, associated with an inability to learn to read. This misunderstanding frustrated the attempts of many pioneers in the field of AAC. The challenges of overcoming physical access barriers were matched only by the challenges presented by beliefs about the extent to which individuals with significant physical and speech impairments could benefit from attempts to overcome access issues. There were, of course, some notable exceptions to the view of literacy as being unattainable for those with limited speech (Butler, 1979; Fourcin, 1975; Nolan, 1987), but the individuals pioneering these views were truly exceptional.

Some of the early innovative attempts to harness the power of written language for expressive communication are still in use today and continue to provide both a means of expression and a source of learning for individuals with significant disabilities. Connolly (personal communication, January 21, 2003) recounted a recent visit to a residential center for adults with physical disabilities that led to a chance encounter with Janice, a lady with cerebral palsy. Janice is a very effective and active communicator, pointing out letters on a ceramic tablet, to communicate long messages. She has used this system of communication over many decades, without any suggestions that technological innovations might have the potential to increase her communication speed or sophistication. Christopher Nolan (Nolan, 1987) laboriously typed out sentences using a headstick, with head support provided by his mother. Rick Creech likewise has talked eloquently of his early experiences (Creech, 1992) as he picked the letters and words to weave into messages and stories to share with us all.

In 1990, David Koppenhaver and David Yoder addressed the ISAAC Biennial Conference (Koppenhaver & Yoder, 1990) on the issue of literacy and individuals who use AAC. They argued that the time had come for the community of AAC users and those working with them to wake up to the need to seriously consider and address the attainment of literacy skills for all individuals who use AAC. Since that time, there has been much progress across many domains. The myth that people who use AAC cannot learn to read has been laid to rest. The myth that speech production difficulties alone can explain the presence of a reading difficulty has likewise been disproved. Our understanding of what it means to be literate has evolved to an understanding that there is no single definition and that the state of being literate can be very different for different individuals. Likewise, we now recognize that there is no one path to literacy attainment and that the concept of a dichotomy between what was traditionally known as *preliterate* and *literate* is unhelpful and inaccurate.

Changes in these conceptions not only reflect evolving thinking within the field of AAC but also reflect the changes in conceptions of reading and writing, fields in which there has been so much rich and heated debate over the last decades. Some of these controversies were outlined in the first section of this book (Chapters 1 to 3). Central to many of the changes in thinking has been an increasing recognition of the complexity of the nature of written language and its relationships to spoken language. Several strands of change within these evolutions stand out. One is the theme of emergent literacy, exemplified by the work of Clay (1975, 1985, 1991). Emergent literacy research acknowledged that the path to becoming literate started long before formal schooling and formal introduction to letters and written words. This insight opened doors to new conceptions of how children are enculturated into literacy and how the construction of literacy is a process that can start in very early language experiences. In turn, this insight led to creative and innovative interventions with individuals who had many different kinds of disabilities, including those who use AAC (Light & Kent-Walsh, 2003; Pierce & McWilliam, 1993).

A second major strand of change has been the focus on the role assigned to speech processing and speech production in the processes of decoding and encoding written language. Although reading difficulties in speaking children in the past were often ascribed to visual problems, there has been increasing recognition over the past few decades that the vast majority of reading difficulties are related to underlying phonological or language processing difficulties. Visual difficulties may certainly contribute to the overall extent of the struggle but are rarely the sole and unique cause of reading difficulties (Rayner, 1999). This recognition has led to an increased focus on how children process spoken language, how they analyze and represent speech, and how they build a sufficiently robust system that allows them to extend into written language. The role of exposure to written language in this construction task has also been clarified to some extent. There is an emerging consensus that a reciprocal relationship between the analytic skills children apply to written language and their development of increasing sophistication in metalinguistic skills exists (e.g., Blachman, 2000; Gombert, 1992).

A third strand of change has been a reconception of how children learn to read and write. This reconception has included what might be construed as two diametrically opposed tenets. The first is the importance of structured teaching in supporting children learning the alphabetic code. Although children benefit enormously from their early literacy experiences, these early experiences are rarely sufficient in themselves to support the leap to understanding the precise connection between the specific print symbols on a page and the sounds they represent. The second aspect of this reconception is exemplified in the self-teaching hypothesis (Share, 1995): the view that given a critical mass of skills across a range of areas, children effectively teach themselves to read, through their active engagement with solving problems of sound-print relationships. Critical to the concept of self-teaching is a high frequency of engagement with the task. It is this high frequency of encountering orthographic patterns in meaningful contexts that provides the basis for representational redescriptions (Karmiloff-Smith, 1992) of orthographic patterns, setting up the necessary processing connections. Thus, children seem to need just enough instruction in decoding skills to be able to benefit from self-teaching opportunities and sufficient self-teaching opportunities to be able to keep the process on track.

A fourth major strand of change has been the advent of technology, which has revolutionized many aspects of our lives, including our experiences with written language and the context of education. The impact of this revolution was discussed in Chapter 9. As stated there, for individuals with disabilities, technology has opened up possibilities that a few years ago would have seemed unattainable.

Taken together, these four strands—(1) emergent literacy, (2) reconstruing spoken language–written language relationships, (3) the role of instruction and self-teaching, and (4) technological innovations—have offered new insights into the challenges facing individuals who use AAC as they approach the task of learning. They have also provided some possible pathways to advance our practice in encouraging and supporting AAC users in the transition from apprentice to expert readers and writers.

III. LOOKING FORWARD

A. BUILDING PRACTICE

Much progress has been made over the last decade and a half. The plan for the future is still unfolding. Part of the future plan is implicit in "A Literacy

Bill of Rights" referred to in Chapter 1. That future plan must include striving for access to meaningful literacy learning and literacy engagement opportunities for all individuals who use AAC (Rights 1 through 4 and 7, as outlined by Erickson, Koppenhaver, & Yoder, 2002, p. iii). The future plan must also address the issue of lifelong learning for individuals who use AAC and the question of access to knowledgeable instructors and facilitators as guides along the journey to literacy. There are as yet remarkably few programs for developing literacy skills that are available to support educators and clinicians working with individuals who use AAC. This lag is understandable in some respects, given the relative youth of the field of AAC. However, this youth should not become an excuse that prevents future growth. The needs of individuals who use AAC in this respect are now well recognized—a clear focus for the future must be on establishing, as a right, access to interventions that are maximally supportive of literacy development.

Many individuals are now involved in delivering and developing literacy skills with a wide range of individuals, yet much of this potential font of knowledge remains inaccessible to the majority of those working within the field. There is a clear and urgent need for documentation and dissemination of findings in relation to literacy intervention.

B. Setting an Agenda for Research

There is a clear need within our field to establish an evidence-based research foundation on which future literacy interventions can be developed. At this stage, there are a number of questions that stand out, some of which are suggested here. One question relates to *the role of speech production* in developing and stabilizing phonological representations that can serve as a basis for the development of literacy skills (Smith, 2003). There are clear indications of the kinds of skills that serve the needs of typically developing speaking children. However, we do not as yet have sufficient evidence to support the view that the same skills develop in the same way or serve the same purposes for children who have little experience of producing intelligible speech. Likewise, we do not yet know whether there may be important differences related to the spoken language background of individuals who use AAC. It would seem possible that the patterns evident in speaking populations might be mirrored in populations of individuals who use AAC—that is, that the payoff for developing phonological awareness skills might be greater when the relationship between the spoken and written language is relatively shallow and transparent. However, we do not know whether this is the case.

A related question concerns *the nature of the symbols* used by an AAC user. As was outlined in Chapter 4, it has been proposed that the nature of graphic symbols may influence the processing approach adopted by individuals using those symbols (McNaughton, 1998; McNaughton & Lindsay, 1995). McNaughton and Lindsay (1995) argued that symbols constructed of sublexical units support an analytic approach to processing. In their view, these are precisely the skills that are needed for effective processing of print, in which the visual unit of the word must be processed analytically, at least within alphabetic scripts. By contrast, picture-based symbols that do not have the potential for sublexical analysis focus processing at the level of the gestalt, the whole-word level in terms of reading. There is an attractive logic to this hypothesis. If proven accurate, it has important implications for intervention with AAC users, particularly in choice of symbol systems. Picture-based symbols may bias new readers toward whole-word strategies; component-based symbols such as Blissymbols may build important skills in analysis of sublexical units. There is therefore an urgent need to develop a research base to explore these questions and thus to guide the decisions of clinicians and educators. Are there important differences between graphic symbol systems? How important are these differences? Are there key features of symbols that support literacy development? What are the cognitive and linguistic demands of those features? Finding a research methodology that could yield answers to some of these complex questions is extremely challenging. It seems likely that it will be necessary to recruit naturally speaking children as participants to find answers for at least some of the questions. The transferability of findings from research with naturally speaking children to children who use AAC is questionable (Bedrosian, 1995). However, this should not be an excuse for rejecting the inclusion of typically developing participants at all stages of the research process.

A third possible question for research over the coming years is *the impact of texting and email* on written communication in general and in particular with reference to aided communicators. Initial research has already begun in these areas with natural speakers—the next step must be to explore the potential contribution these new media can make to the literacy expectations and skills of people using AAC and even perhaps the changing construct of literacy itself.

The fourth question proposed here relates to *the research process*, in particular the research context and the dissemination of research findings. Two related challenges arise here. One is the need to ensure that at all stages in the research process individuals who use AAC have the opportunities and support needed to become actively involved: in developing the questions of interest; in collecting the data; and in interpreting the results. By harnessing the insights and experiences of individuals who use AAC, we stand to travel farther and faster along the road toward understanding the processes involved in learning to read and write with use of an atypical communication system. There is also a need to ensure that the research efforts in relation to literacy acquisition and AAC do not diverge from general efforts in mainstream literacy research. Research information should flow both ways. Clearly, there is a need to contextualize research findings deriving from the field of AAC with research findings from other groups. It is also important that the unique experiences of individuals who have congenital motor speech difficulties be disseminated to update our broader interpretation of the relationships between speech, language, and written language.

IV. SUMMARY AND CONCLUSIONS

Since the early writings about the development of reading and writing skills in individuals who have cerebral palsy and significant speech difficulties, we have come far in our understanding of the potential and the challenges facing this group of individuals in acquiring effective literacy skills. Some of the early questions, such as those relating to the impact of dysarthria on the development of spelling (Bishop, 1985; Dahlgren–Sandberg, 2001), are as yet unresolved. At least within the AAC community, the most fundamental change has been in the expectations of what might be possible and what should be considered as a right. Many questions remain unanswered, but we are finally beginning to formulate the questions and to seek the answers. The United Nations Decade of Literacy focuses on *Literacy for All*. This focus includes individuals who use AAC. The challenge for all those involved in working with people who use AAC is to constantly challenge expectations, to demonstrate through practice the real potential for achievement, and to share those experiences and insights with the wider community. There is an old Irish saying, "Níl neart go cur le chéile," which, roughly translated means, "strength comes from working together." The field of AAC is rich and diverse. Through harnessing the energy and insights from people who use AAC and from their families, educators, clinicians, and researchers, we can better understand the roads to travel in the journey to literacy, in all its forms, for all.

REFERENCES

Bedrosian, J. (1995). Limitations in the use of nondisabled subjects in AAC research. *Augmentative and Alternative Communication, 13*, 179–185.

Bishop, D. V. M. (1985). Spelling ability in congenital dysarthria: Evidence against articulatory coding in translating between phonemes and graphemes. *Cognitive Neuropsychology, 2*(3), 229–251.

Blachman, B. A. (2000). Phonological awareness. In M. Kamil, P. Mosenthal, P. D. Pearson, & R. Barr (Eds.), *Handbook of reading research* (Vol. 3, pp. 483–502). London: Erlbaum.

Butler, D. (1979). *Cushla and her books*. Boston: Horn Book.

Clay, M. M. (1975). *What did I write?* Auckland, New Zealand: Heineman.

Clay, M. M. (1985). *The early detection of reading difficulties*. Portsmouth, NH: Heinemann.

Clay, M. M. (1991). *Becoming literate*. Portsmouth, NH: Heinemann Education Books.

Creech, R. C. (1992). *Reflections from a unicorn*. Greenville, NC: R.C. Publishing.

Dahlgren-Sandberg, A. (2001). Reading and spelling, phonological awareness and short-term memory in children with severe speech production impairments—A longitudinal study. *Augmentative and Alternative Communication, 17*, 11–26.

Erickson, K., Koppenhaver, D., & Yoder, D. E. (2002). *Waves of words: Augmented communicators read and write*. Toronto, Ontario, Canada: ISAAC Press.

Fourcin, A. J. (1975). Language development in the absence of expressive speech. In E. Lenneberg & E. Lenneberg (Eds.), *Foundations of language development* (Vol. 2). New York: Academic Press.

Gombert, J. E. (1992). *Metalinguistic development*. Hemel Hempstead, Herts, UK: Harvester Wheatsheaf.

Karmiloff-Smith, A. (1992). *Beyond modularity: A developmental perspective on cognitive science*. Cambridge, MA: MIT Press, A Bradford Book.

Koppenhaver, D., & Yoder, D. E. (1990, August). *The literacy literature: Individuals with speech and physical impairments*. Paper presented at the Fourth Biennial ISAAC Conference, Stockholm, Sweden.

Light, J., & Kent-Walsh, J. (2003, May 27). Fostering emergent literacy for children who require AAC. *The ASHA Leader, 8*, 4–5, 28.

McNaughton, S. (1998). *Reading acquisition of adults with severe congenital speech and physical impairments: Theoretical infrastructure, empirical investigation, education implication*. Unpublished doctoral dissertation, University of Toronto, Toronto, Ontario, Canada.

McNaughton, S., & Lindsay, P. (1995). Approaching literacy with AAC graphics. *Augmentative and Alternative Communication, 11*, 212–228.

Nolan, C. (1987). *Under the eye of the clock: The life story of Christopher Nolan*. New York: St Martins' Press.

Pierce, P. L., & McWilliam, P. J. (1993). Emerging literacy and children with severe speech and physical impairments: Issues and possible intervention strategies. *Topics in Language Disorders, 13*(2), 47–57.

Rayner, K. (1999). What have we learned about eye movements during reading? In R. Klein & P. McMullen (Eds.), *Converging methods for understanding reading and dyslexia* (pp. 23–56). London: MIT Press.

Share, D. L. (1995). Phonological recoding and self-teaching: *Sine qua non* of reading acquisition. *Cognition, 55*, 151–218.

Smith, M. (2003). *Perspectives on augmentative and alternative communication and literacy*. Paper presented at the ISAAC Biennial Research Symposium, Odense, Denmark.

APPENDIX A

Dolch Word List

Set 1	Set 2	Set 3	Set 4	Set 5
a	all	after	always	about
and	am	again	around	better
away	are	an	because	bring
big	at	any	been	carry
blue	ate	as	before	clean
can	be	ask	best	cut
come	black	by	both	done
down	brown	could	buy	draw
find	but	every	call	drink
for	came	fly	cold	eight
funny	did	from	does	fall
go	do	give	don't	far
help	eat	going	fast	full
here	four	had	first	got
I	get	has	five	from
in	good	her	found	hold
is	have	him	gave	hot
it	he	his	goes	hurt
little	into	how	green	if
look	like	jump	its	keep
make	must	just	make	kind
me	new	know	many	laugh
my	no	let	off	light
not	now	live	or	long
one	on	may	pull	much
play	our	of	read	myself
red	out	old	right	never
run	please	once	sing	only
said	pretty	open	sit	own
see	ran	over	sleep	pick
the	ride	put	tell	seven
three	saw	round	their	shall
to	say	some	these	show
two	she	stop	those	six
up	so	take	upon	small
we	soon	thank	us	start
where	that	them	use	ten
yellow	there	then	very	today

Set 1	Set 2	Set 3	Set 4	Set 5
you	they	think	wash	
	this	walk	which	
	too	warm	why	
	under	were	work	
	want	when	would	
	was		write	
	well		your	
	went			
	what			
	white			
	who			
	will			
	with			
	yes			

APPENDIX B

Useful Books

BOOKS WITH REPEATED LINES

Fitzpatrick, M. (2002). *I'm a tiger too.* Dublin, Ireland: Wolfhound Press.
Hest, A. (2001). *Kiss good night, Sam.* London: Walker Books.
Martin, B. (1967). *Brown bear, brown bear, what do you see?* New York: Henry Holt.
Rosen, M. (1989). *We're going on a bear hunt.* London: Walker Books.
Waddell, M. (1991). *Farmer duck.* London: Walker Books.
Waddell, M. (1992). *The pig in the pond.* London: Walker Books.
Waddell, M. (1992). *Owl babies.* London: Walker Books.
Waddell, M. (1998). *Yum, yum, yummy.* London: Walker Books.
Williams, L. (1986). *The little old lady who was not afraid of anything.* New York: Harper Collins.
Zemach, M. (1983). *The little red hen.* New York: Farrar, Straus & Giroux.

BOOKS WITH ALLITERATION

Base, G. (1997). *Jabberwocky.* New York: Larry N. Abrams.
Berenstain, S., & Berenstain, J. (1971). *The Berenstain's B book.* New York: Random House.
Boon, E. (1985). *Belinda's balloon.* William Heinemann.

BOOKS WITH RHYME

Cox, P. (2002). *Shark in the park.* London: Usborne Publishing.
Donaldson, J. (1999). *The gruffalo.* London: Macmillan Children's Books.
Donaldson, J. (2001). *Room on the broom.* London: Macmillan Children's Books.
Geisel, T. S., & Geisel, A. S. (1960). *Green eggs and ham by Dr Seuss.* New York: Beginner Books, A Division of Random House.
Jeram, A. (1995). *Contrary Mary.* London: Walker Books.
LeSieg, T. (1972). *In a people house.* New York: Random House.
West, C. (1996). *"I don't care!" said the bear.* London: Walker Books.
Yolen, J. (2000). *How do dinosaurs say good night?* New York: Scholastic.

BOOKS WITH LANGUAGE PLAYS

Child, L. (2002). *Who's afraid of the big bad book?* London: Hodder Children's Books.
Dallas-Conté, J. (2001). *Cock-a-moo-moo!* London: Macmillan Children's Books.
Root, P. (2000). *Foggy Friday.* London: Walker Books.
Scieszka, J. (1992). *The stinky cheese man and other fairly stupid tales.* New York: Penguin Books.
Trivizas, E. (1993). *The three little wolves and the big bad pig.* London: William Heinemann.

FOR ADULTS

Banville, V. (1999). *Sad song.* Dublin, Ireland: New Island Books.
Bolger, D. (1999). *In High Germany.* Dublin, Ireland: New Island Books.
Doyle, R. (1999). *Not just for Christmas.* Dublin, Ireland: New Island Books.
Kelly, C. (2002). *Letter from Chicago.* Dublin, Ireland: New Island Books.
Keyes, M. (2000). *No dress rehearsal.* Dublin, Ireland: New Island Books.
Nestor, T. (2002). *Driving with Daisy.* Dublin, Ireland: New Island Books.
Purcell, D. (1999). *Jesus and Billy are off to Barcelona.* Dublin, Ireland: New Island Books.
Purcell, D. (2002). *Has anyone here seen Larry?* Dublin, Ireland: New Island Books.
Scanlan, P. (1996). *Second chance.* Dublin, Ireland: New Island Books.
Scanlan, P. (2002). *Ripples.* Dublin, Ireland: New Island Books.
Schulman, A. (2000). *Pipe dreams.* Dublin, Ireland: New Island Books.
Sheridan, P. (2000). *Old money, new money.* Dublin, Ireland: New Island Books.

INDEX OF NAMES

SUBJECT INDEX